To

Brother

Sermons

One for Every Sunday of the Year*

Geoffrey F. Proud

Vicar, Orient Free Methodists

*Plus some great sermons from the past.

Copyright © 2017 by G.F. Proud.

Library of Congress Control Number: 2017903838
ISBN: Hardcover   978-1-5245-9105-2
             Softcover   978-1-5245-9104-5
             eBook   978-1-5245-9106-9

All rights reserved. No part of this book may be reproduced or transmitted in any form or by any means, electronic or mechanical, including photocopying, recording, or by any information storage and retrieval system, without permission in writing from the copyright owner.

Any people depicted in stock imagery provided by Thinkstock are models, and such images are being used for illustrative purposes only.
Certain stock imagery © Thinkstock.

Print information available on the last page.

Design. Text- Sylfaen 11 pt / Heads - Ariel 24 pt reg. (unless otherwise noted) Cover. Photos of ambos in basilicas and cathedrals of Europe taken by the author.

Rev. date: 05/15/2017

To order additional copies of this book, contact:
Xlibris
1-888-795-4274
www.Xlibris.com
Orders@Xlibris.com
753991

Dedication

To the four Marthas*

Martha Regina, Sr. Martha Mary, Martha Jane, and Martha Mary.

grandmother, aunt, mother, sister

So faith comes from what is preached, and what is preached comes from the word of Christ.
— St. Paul, Romans 10:17
(The Jerusalem Bible)

Introduction

Most of these sermons originated during the years 2010 to 2015, when I was a lay preacher in the Orient Methodist Church. I trained with the Methodists for that certification. I describe that experience in a previous book: *My Life as a Methodist.* This period gave me the opportunity to recover my preaching aptitudes that lay dormant during the years I spent as an advertising and public relations editor. Moreover, the prep for each Sunday's sermon was an intense study of scripture, together with the writings of the Fathers of the Church. The great Methodist (I consider him a "Doctor of the Church.") pastor and theologian, Thomas Oden, provided easily accessible writings of the Fathers in a handy book, *Ancient Christian Devotional.* It offers passages of commentary by the Fathers for each scripture assigned for reading at Sunday service. As I have often remarked, and I say it again here, this little book, plus Google and Wikipedia, have allowed me to sound quite erudite in the pulpit. Materials which in the past would have required hours of searching in stacks of resources were now at my finger-tips. Need a quote from St. Augustine on marriage? Google it. Virtually all the writings, his sermons etc., of Augustine are available online. Same for the great preachers John Chrysostom and John Wesley. These men produced sermons numbering in the thousands -- and we have them! My output in miniscule in comparison.

However, as weeks go by, sermons tend to pile up, and I happened to find hundreds of my sermons from my earlier years, all neatly typed but with handwritten notations, in boxes in our garage here in Orient where I had tucked them away. They're not that bad. Sound theologically, and I recognize familiar elements of my style as I write today. A few are included in this book.

It is not natural for sermons to be written down and collected in books. A sermon as an art form -- and I consider it such -- is vocal, the spoken word, delivered live. It is also, by its nature, ephemeral. Only those in the audience, the congregants, would have heard and felt the essence of the sermon. Reading a sermon from the page of a book is not the same -- to say the least. Nevertheless, preachers were pleased to leave us their written sermons, and *Deo gratias* for that! For many of them, their sermons were found to be the source of their theological thought, their distinct interpretation and commentary on gospel revelation. In past ages, sermons were an important element of the society's literature. There are thousands of sermons by Massachusetts Colony preachers preserved today in libraries in Boston. Not so much today.

Surely the style of preaching sermons has changed over the centuries -- evolved? In the Appendix of this book I have included sermons of four great and prolific preachers, each from a separate and distinct period. The variations in style will be evident; the first two are translations: from Greek and Latin respectfully. As for sermon length of these exhibits, I have had to edit and condense.

Sermons are the spoken word. As a gesture, and in an attempt to preserve their essential nature, I did produce videos of a few of my sermons, which can be viewed on YouTube: Google "Geoff Proud sermons." Take a look. Production values are modest, but you will get the idea . . . and perhaps, the message.

Geoff Proud

Orient NY, January 8, 2017

Contents

Part I Sunday Sermons 13

Advent and Christmas 15

'Nothing Lasts Forever' 16
The Stars of Advent 19
Holiness in the A.D. World 23
Fresh Grace 26
'The Last Gospel' 29
Journey of the Magi 33
We Are All Refugees 36

Ordinary Time to Lent 41

No Need for 'Converts' 42
Lamb of God Sunday 46
Jesus the Prophet 50
Learn to Preach from the Master 54
Questions about the Three Temptations of Christ 57
A Most Unusual Day 60
Jesus Prayed 64
'No More Mr. Nice Guy' 68
Jesus Heals the Man Born Blind or A Gospel Reality Show 71
Unity Through Diversity 74
Deals 78
Existential Jesus 82

Holy Week and Easter 87

'Words Have Meaning.' 88
The Main Mystery 92
"Today you will be with me in paradise." 96

[Sixth Word] "It is finished." 100
"Father, into your hands I commend my spirit." 103
An Easter Sermon: Love Exposed 106
Proof Positive 110
Jesus, We Hardly Knew Ye 114
Dispelling an Urban Myth 118
Faith 101 122
The Man Born Blind 126
Trinity Sunday or How We Know God 129

Pentecost and Ordinary Time 133

A Big Day [Pentecost Sunday] 134
The Kingdom Option 138
'Faith comes through hearing.' 141
Jesus and His Friends: A Family of Faith 145
The Good Samaritan Story 149
Social Jesus 152
'It's a jungle out there.' 156
Matthew's Mission 159
The Feast Day of Peter and Paul 162
A One-on-One with Jesus 165
A hard rain is gonna' fall. 170
Desire of the Everlasting Hills 173
Getting to Know Peter 177
490 - Do the Math 181
The Blue Haze: Divine Mercy 184
Mark's Gospel: Voice of the Lion 189
The Lord Plays Favorites. 193
Back to Basics 197
Philemon 200
'If I Were a Rich Man' 203
Jesus as the "Boss" 206
Slogans and Mottos 210
'Corragio' *213*
Jesus in a Somber Mood 217

Part II   Sermons from the Past 221
New York 222
Boston 247
Buffalo 253
Other Pulpits 258

Appendix   Four Great Preachers 271
John Chrysostom (347-407) 267
Augustine of Hippo (354-430) 269
John Wesley (1703 – 1791) 271
Ralph Waldo Emerson (1803-1882) 273

Acknowledgements 281

Part I

Sunday Sermons

Advent 15
Lent 41
Easter 87
Pentecost . . . 133

Advent and Christmas

'Nothing Lasts Forever'
The Stars of Advent
Holiness in the A.D. World
Fresh Grace
'The Last Gospel'
Journey of the Magi
We are All Refugees

'Nothing Lasts Forever'

TEXT Mark 13: 24-37

Where was Jesus when he delivered this discourse? We need to set the scene. That will help us understand it. It is called by the bible scholars the *Eschatological Discourse of Jesus*. And it is famous, mostly because it is dark and ominous and so challenging for study and interpretation. All the great Church Fathers of the early centuries, and all the academic theologians who came after them, have tried their hand at explaining it and clarifying its meaning for us. It is found in the three (they call them the *Synoptic*) gospel narratives -- Matthew, Mark, and Luke. John does not cover it. Jesus had just come down to Jerusalem . . . for the last time. It was the beginning of the final week of his life. The crowds were with him. He addressed them in an area of the temple; and it is at this time, when his disciples raised a question, he foretold the destruction of the temple: "Not a stone [to be] left upon a stone" – as we heard in a previous reading of the scriptures. It happened. About 40 years later the Romans flattened Jerusalem and the temple. You could say Jesus was in a somber mood. *Eschatological,* the term for these words, means in Greek, "the last things."

You may wonder why the liturgy planners have inserted this passage here for our reading in Advent. There are a couple of reasons. First, this scripture is about the coming of the Lord – as is Advent – although the coming he speaks of is the Second Coming, the *Parousia* (this time the Greek word means presence or arrival). It is the presence of the Lord at the world's end. That's something that is at the core of our faith. We declare it every time we recite the creed at Sunday service: ". . . he shall come again to judge the quick and the dead." We believe. It's a little scary to think of, and I think the Lord's disciples, to whom he was speaking at the time, were a bit taken back by it – as we are. But it is our faith. And in fact, it is quite logical, since what is evident in our experience is that nothing lasts forever. Not the flowers in your garden, not living creatures, not man's accomplishments. "Sic transit glory mundi," we say. So pass away the glories of the world. In my business, whenever we lost a client, my partner would console me with the reminder that "nothing last forever." And that's true. So it is also true of this world we live in. When the world's end will come -- as Jesus says, only the Father, God, knows. So, awareness of things eschatological and the Parousia, or the Lord's Second Coming, is an important theme of Advent. And Christians in their heart of hearts, in their deepest devotions and faith, long for the Lord's coming. In the meanwhile, we carry on with our business faithfully. Not to worry, as Paul tells the Ephesians: . . . *you are not lacking in any spiritual gift as you wait for the revealing of our Lord Jesus Christ. He will strengthen you to the end, so that you may be blameless on the day of our Lord Jesus Christ.*

What is perhaps more appealing to think about in the season of Advent is the other theme of coming. The celebration of Christmas commemorates the coming of Jesus, God's Son, into the world as a man, God in flesh and blood. And, as we know and believe, as our savior and redeemer. This scenario is easy to accept in our faith. Augustine calls attention to the contrast between the first coming in Bethlehem and the second coming, the Parousia. God did not enter into history in an overpowering manner, Augustine argues, but rather as an infant whose presence is irresistible. This mystery makes Christmas for us: the infant, the mother Mary, the manger scene, the Angel's proclamation. And one contemporary theologian reminds us that God coming into the world at Christmas, an historical event, is not confined to the restraints of human time and history; but by the Incarnation mystery, God's presence now pervades our lives. We have come up to the next level. It is this that we begin to grasp as we approach Christmas through these days of Advent: what the Old Testament prophet Isaiah could only have hoped for and begged God for: *O, that you would tear open the heavens and come down.*

This next level -- by that I mean, the Christian era, A.D. -- is much more peaceful and serene than in the day of Isaiah. Before Christ, B.C., the world was either in a state of confusion, not knowing the meaning if its existence, reeling around amid deities of their own making but who could never satisfy them; or there were the blessed beneficiaries of the revelation of the true God, the Israelites, waiting and longing for his appearance to settle them and make them secure in this rugged world.

Now, because of the coming of God into history, we are deep-down content, knowing our purpose and learning about love, and getting to experience it, as it came with the full revelation of the Incarnation. God is love. So evident in the manger scene, and in all that flows from it . . . in poetry and music, and in art. With this excitement, we spread out our anticipation of Christmas into these four weeks of Advent, and we watch it build to that crescendo of the midnight carols of the angels. Subdued we are today, praying to be worthy of the Christmas encounter. And our liturgies prepare us and help us. Start with the poetry and theology of Charles Wesley in his hymns for this season.

> Late in time behold Him come,
> Offspring of the Virgin's womb,
> Veiled in flesh the Godhead see,
> Hail the'Incarnate Deity.
> Come desire of nations come,
> Fix in us thy humble home.

We have our Advent wreath and candles to guide us and inspire us as we go along. The Advent wreath comes from the 16th century -- but I only recall it becoming popular in the past 50 years or so. You? Advent itself, as a period of devotions in preparation for Christmas, goes back to the 8th century. The advent wreath ceremony incorporates the *theme of light* that runs throughout our religious history, with a significance that conveys a deep theological truth:

(1) Hanukah (the word means dedication) is the "Festival of Light," celebrating with candle light the rededication of the temple of Jerusalem in the time of Judas Maccabeus, the Israelite warrior. (2) The light of the star leads the Magi to the Christ child in the nativity. (3) At the transfiguration of Christ where he is identified with God the Father on the mount before the apostles, *his face was shining like the sun and his clothes became white as light.* (4) But of course, Jesus says of himself, *I am the light of the world.* And to us he says *let your light shine before men.*

All of these light images serve to signify to us the truth which is Jesus and which is our faith: *I am the way, the truth, and the light.* "May the light that shines forth from these candles light our way to Christmas," – as the Advent wreath prayer says. And attending to other theme of Advent, the Parousia, may we always be prepared: *Be on your guard, stay awake; because you never know when the time will come.*

One more thing. There **is** something that lasts forever. It is Paradise, the eternal life promise of Jesus to the Faithful -- to be with him in Paradise. This too is our faith, when we say in the creed . . . "the forgiveness of sin and life everlasting. Amen."

Thanks be to God.

The Stars of Advent

TEXT John 1: 6-8,19-28

Who are the stars of Advent? I mean the most prominent persons in the scriptures leading up to Christmas. I'm going to name two of them and say some things about them this morning. Could you guess? One, of course, is John the Baptist, who appears for the second week in a row in the gospel readings. The other is Mary, the mother of Jesus, who makes her appearance today where we read that poem, "The Song of Mary." This is just a preview of Mary. She will be featured sensationally in the readings of the coming weeks. In fact, during the weeks of Advent, Mary's mysteries are celebrated in the daily liturgies: the Immaculate Conception, last Thursday (That's a topic for another time.), and Our Lady of Guadeloupe [Mexico] tomorrow. By that title, she is the patroness of the Americas.

But first let's talk about John the Baptist. He has been revered by Christians for centuries as one of the greatest men of the Bible . . . in art and in literature, as well as in theological study. He is a blood relative of Jesus, (distant?), said in Christian tradition to be a cousin, second cousin of Jesus. His mother, Elizabeth, was the cousin of Mary. That we know.

John was truly a charismatic person. He pursued his personal spirituality as an aesthetic, an early monastic type. He fasted, he lived a hermit's existence outside the city. The son of a priest, Joachim, he was schooled in the holy scriptures. He could quote the prophets, and he in fact would emulate the prophets. His preaching warned people to repent of sin and turn around their lives, for which he performed the ancient rite of baptism on his followers. He urged charity in his preaching: *If you have two coats, give one to someone who doesn't have any. If you have food, share it with someone else.* His own virtue qualified him for the extraordinary role he would have in God's plan of salvation. Coming out of that great long tradition of the prophets among the Israelites, he was to be the final prophet who points directly to the Messiah; he, in fact, touches him. He baptizes Jesus. This was the commencement of Jesus' public life as teacher, appointed to declare the fullness of God's revelation. To be, himself, that Revelation in person. From this point on, Jesus would become greater and John lesser . . . his job done.

In today's reading, we see John making it clear to some of the religious leaders who questioned him that he was not the Messiah they were waiting for. He defers to Jesus, to whom he says he feels unworthy even to buckle his shoes. *You will see,* he tells them, *the Spirit come down and stay on someone; and then you will know that he is the one who will baptize with the Holy Spirit. I saw this happen* (he refers to his baptism of Jesus when the Spirit said "this is my son in whom I am well-pleased") *and I tell you he is the Son of God.*

On the very next day, John sees Jesus, and it is then that he makes that familiar declaration that has become a part of our communion liturgy prayers: *Behold the lamb of God who takes away the sin of the world. He is the one I told you about.*

These words of John the Baptizer were not taken respectfully by his audience, because it was not long after that that John was jailed for his preaching. And then we read in Matthew's chapter 14 that the news of John's death is reported to Jesus (Matt 14: 13): *When Jesus heard the news about John, he left there in a boat and went to a lonely place by himself.* The Lord no doubt needed to grieve. John was a friend, a cousin, and he was gone now, leaving him on his own to deliver the Messianic message to a community of powerful persons who were not very receptive. But John's mission was complete. He had performed fearlessly and accomplished God's work.

Let us turn now to the other star of the season, Mary, the mother of Jesus. We go back to the Lord's birth . . . actually, before that, and what we hear today in our service is the *Magnificat,* called "The Song of Mary." It is her excitement and expression of joy at her acceptance of God's assignment for her. *My soul magnifies the Lord.* She sees her role as a reflection of the greatness of God the creator. It is a stirring and eloquent song. And frankly, I had to wonder how it might have come from a young woman of modest background, as we usually think of the virgin Mary. It is filled with allusions to the sacred scriptures, and takes on the tone of any one of the psalms. Mary would have known the sacred scriptures, as she was a child of the religious milieu, which was the people of Israel. Nearly all the theological commentators and Christian era Fathers of the church ascribe the song to her. I think that as it is presented in this form by the gospel writer Luke, it confirms her role in God's plan of salvation for mankind. (More about that plan later.)

Next we see Mary after the birth of Jesus, observing religious law and presenting the boy at the Temple in Jerusalem. Later, she also attended with him the wedding in Cana; and she was there during his passion and death. Finally, she was with the apostles after the resurrection in the upper room, when the Spirit descended upon them all with the strengths and graces of Pentecost. Little is known from the gospels of the later years of Mary's life. Tradition says that the apostle John cared for her. In Turkey (and also in several other places in that region of the world) there is what is said to be the House of Mary; and it is visited regularly by pilgrims and tourists. Christian theology holds that Mary was *assumed* bodily into heaven, and this image is portrayed profusely in classic Christian art. There never was a grave for Mary, and the church honors her in celebrating her Assumption into heaven each year on August 15. During the reform period, a few centuries ago, devotion to the Blessed Mother waned a bit in some churches. But it is coming back. In 1995, the World Methodist Council issued this statement, "Mary, Mother of the Lord, Sign of Grace, Faith and Holiness: A Shared Understanding." We'll take it forward from there.

The whole idea of sketching out the careers of these two "stars of the season" was to point out how God's plan of salvation is truly a plan, in which certain persons were selected each to have a role. John and Mary are unquestionably the super stars. But they had to respond to God's call and accept their assignments and then live them out. In John's case, it led to an execution, death for the cause; but he had seen the Messiah. In Mary's, a long life with joys and sorrows.

Are we not also called upon to have a role in God's plan of salvation? As our life proceeds, that role becomes clearer. We express acceptance little by little and over and over again in our prayers, confident of God's grace to carry out our role... whatever it may be. And for some it could be "plan B." The words of St. Paul in today's second reading should buoy us up: *Rejoice always, pray without ceasing, give thanks in all circumstances; for this is the will of God in Christ Jesus for you.* Add to that the message I always like to fall back on: an extract from the writings of that great preacher and Father of the Eastern Church, whose hundreds of sermons in the Greek language have been left to us, John Chrysostom: "Even if we are unable to unravel the details of our personal and collective history, we know that God's plan is always inspired by his love."

You will hear me quote this line from Chrysostom, whose prolific preaching makes him the John Wesley of the 4TH Century, many times; so, you may as well write it down right now.

Thanks be to God.

Holiness in the A.D. World

TEXT Luke 2: 1-20

Have you noted that our liturgy tends to schedule services in anticipation of great feasts? On Christmas, for example, we start the night before Christmas Day; and at Easter we celebrate the vigil at midnight or earlier. It happens also to be a new custom in some places to have the Sunday services the day before, on Saturday. Is it that we're anxious, that we can't wait? I think I may be able to draw a theme out of this practice for a Christmas sermon. But first, let's set the scene and go back to the era before the coming of Christ; they call it B.C., "before Christ." The known civilizations then were confused about the world and its origin. But they developed religious practices in their attempt to understand the meaning of their experiences. When Paul encountered some people in Athens, the place where many of the world's greatest philosophers have come from, he was impressed by their religious display. He walked through the city and saw many statues and altars dedicated to gods -- one to the god of the sun, another to the god of the ocean, another for the earth, and so forth. For people in pre-biblical times, there were many gods -- as far as they could figure out.

At the invitation of the people Paul met in Athens, he addressed them on the Areopagus, the rock hill near the Acropolis where the Greek leaders conducted intellectual and political business. "I see you are very religious," Paul began. You could take that as sarcasm, but in fact Paul was very respectful and serious. He asked them about one of the altars he had seen with the inscription: "To the Unknown God." "But you do not know him," he said. And he went on in a sermon that is today inscribed in the Greek language on a plaque at the foot of the Areopagus. In 269 words, Paul's sermon is the whole theology of our salvation, starting with creation: *This God made the world and everything in . . . and we are his children . . . and God has given proof of this to all of us by raising Jesus from the dead.*

The Areopagus

Paul's Sermon

A few hundred miles south of Greece on the Mediterranean, that theology began, when *the God the world did not know*, the "unknown god," revealed himself to the nomadic tribes who were the Israelites. The Israelites then were a people unlike all the other nations surrounding them: their faith was in one God. The first rule of that God was, "I am the Lord your God, and you shall not have strange gods before me." The Israelites paid dearly for that faith. They were tempted and attacked by the surrounding nations. But they raised up leaders who not only held them together and preserved their faith in the one God, but also promised for them a savior who would save them from their enemies . . . and who would also be the answer to all the questions the Greek philosophers had asked Paul – about life and death and beyond. The surprise was that this savior the prophets proclaimed came not as a warrior, but born as an infant.

I tell this back story in order to give context to the scriptures that we read as we approach Christmas . . . with all the allusions and historical references that are in the prophets and in narratives the evangelists present us about the birth of Christ. *Listen to us, O shepherd of Israel,* says the psalmist – as we heard in the readings last Sunday; *hear us and reveal yourself to us, show us your strength, come and save us.* I love the image in this verse of the psalm: *Look down on us . . . save this grapevine that you planted, this young vine you made grow so strong.*

And then there is the great prophet Isaiah, whose words define this season and its meaning: *The people who walked in darkness have seen a great light; they lived in the land of shadows, but now light is shining on them.* And Isaiah's poetry describes the greatness of the world redeemed by the savior, the Anno Domino, the A.D. world:

The desert will rejoice, and flowers will bloom in the waste land. The desert will be as beautiful as the Lebanon mountains . . . everyone will see the Lord's splendor . . . . Be strong and don't be discouraged. God is coming to your rescue.

The beauty of the A.D. world is expressed now in our liturgy, over and over again in the carols we sing, in the images in the crèche, in the Madonna and child, and all the great Christmas art that has come down to us.

And we know now the depth of meaning of the coming of the "unknown" God to us. The beauty of it was his coming as a child, born a man like us, irresistible as we ponder his image in the manger scene.

So easy to love, to become attached to, and follow at his invitation. For the infant grew to be a great teacher who outlined a way of life for men to live, that was grounded in love and which leads to eternal life after death – his promise over and over again. *I have come that you may have life and have it more abundantly. . . . I am the way and the truth and the life.* Jesus was more than the philosophers Paul met could ever have imagined, and he told them that. For Jesus is not only a redeemer sent by the one God, but he is the Son of God.

Now we go back to the anticipation idea. The way of Jesus in the A.D. world is holiness, to "be imitators," as Paul says, "of me as I am of Christ." That is the holiness of the Christian life we have signed up for. We are reminded of it each Christmas. We are re-initiated into it when we reflect on the Christ child and the meaning of his coming. Now some people tend to put off the life of holiness, perhaps, to a more critical time in their lives. But would it not be best instead to anticipate that later time, to get started earlier, just as we start our feast day liturgies earlier. John Wesley did not put off living the Christian life of holiness, but he committed himself to it as a young man, forming the Holiness Club with his brother and friends in their first year of college at Oxford. Let him be our model as we resolve at this Christmas to, without delay, anticipate and make our lives holy in following the way of Jesus.

> *O holy night! The stars are brightly shining,*
> *It is the night of our dear Saviour's birth.*
> *Long lay the world in sin and error pining,*
> *'Til He appear'd and the soul felt its worth.*
> *A thrill of hope the weary world rejoices,*
> *For yonder breaks a new and glorious morn.*

Thanks be to God.

Fresh Grace

TEXT Luke: 2: 15-20

I found in my file a sermon I had written for Christmas 2010, last year; but I never used it. That should work, I thought; I'll just touch it up a bit. Nope. It wouldn't work. It's hard to explain why. I was pleased with it when I wrote it. The reason is it's not fresh; and that became clear to me when I re-read it. But it gave me an idea for this year's Christmas message. The title: "Fresh Grace."

There is the possibility that year after year when we go through the Christmas liturgies, they will become "same ol' same ol'." That can happen. The story is the same; the music is always the same, and has been, for the most part, for the past hundreds of years. Us preachers try to nuance the message each year, but it's a challenge. We don't much succeed. Or do we?

Let me tell you: there is something about Christmas and its liturgy that does not lose its appeal and power . . . what I call *fresh grace*. To talk about grace, we may need a briefing on that subject. We bandy the word about with respect, but without much deep focus on its meaning. We have an expression – "There but for the *grace* of God . . ." We say in a prayer, the angel Gabriel's greeting to Mary, that we heard in last Sunday's scripture: "Hail full of *grace.*" *Grace* is a heavy word in theology. It is a central topic in theological study. There have been controversies upon controversies about grace in Christian church history. You might even dare to say a war was fought over grace . . . indirectly, that is. The 30-years war in Europe.

The reformers in the late middle ages sought a clearer understanding of the meaning and function of God's grace, and for a time the issue of grace was unsettled. That's all over now. After 400 or more years, in 1999, the two parties -- Lutherans of the Lutheran World Federation and the Vatican representing Catholics -- announced an historic settlement which stated, "[We] are now able to articulate a common understanding of our justification by God's grace through faith in Christ." Six years later in 2006, the World Methodist Council signed on to that settlement.

Grace is God's favor shown to us, to mankind, mainly through his Son, Jesus, whose life and sacrificial death were the sign. It is a favor that has an inherent dynamism. It is by God's favor -- or grace -- that we hold on to our faith. *No one can come to me unless he is drawn to me by the Father who sent me.* (John 6: 44). We learn much about grace and its power from St. Paul, who ascribes his dramatic conversion to God's grace: Writes Paul, *He set me apart before I was born, and called me through his grace, and was pleased to reveal his Son to me, in order that I might preach him among the Gentiles.* (Gal 1:15) Elsewhere in Paul's letters, the theology of grace is established. To the Corinthians he writes in the opening paragraph of his letter: *I never stop thanking God for the grace given you in Christ.*

(That phrase happens to the used for the title of the Methodist-Catholic Dialogue report of 2006.)

When Paul wrote to Timothy, his associate and a bishop, his greeting is *Dear child of mine, wishing you grace, mercy and peace from God the Father and from Christ Jesus our Lord.* Grace is what we ask the Lord for in our prayers . . . when we say in the short aspiration-like prayer: "Incline your ear to us O God; O Lord make haste to help us." And in the longer prayers of the service: "Open our hearts O Lord, and enlighten us by the grace of the Holy Spirit that we may seek what is pleasing to your will, and so order our doing after your commandments, that we may be found worthy to enter into your unending joy." Grace is what the psalmist pleads for in the famous *De Profundis* psalm:

> *Out of the depths I cry to you, O Lord; Lord, hear my voice!*
> *Let your ears be attentive to my voice in supplication:*

Grace is what we ask for when we pray the Lord's Prayer, when we say ". . . lead us not into temptation, but deliver us from evil."

There is a strain of Christian theology, particularly developed by Presbyterians: the "Covenant of Grace." It connects the various covenants between God and the people of the Old Testament: God's promise to Abraham, then to Moses, and to Noah in a chain leading to the coming of the Messiah. In this interaction with Abraham, Moses, and Noah, God testified that He would accomplish the restoration of fallen man, as he promised in the Garden of Eden. Christmas, the birth of the Savior, is the beginning of the fulfillment of that Covenant of

Grace. It is confirmed in scripture in the canticle of Zacharias at the presentation in the temple of his son John (the Baptist). *Blessed be the Lord God of Israel, for he has visited his peopled, he has come to their rescue . . . he remembers his holy covenant.* The same is echoed in the *Magnificat* of Mary, when she learned that she would bear the Savior. *He [God] has helped his servant Israel, in remembrance of his mercy, as he spoke to our fathers, to Abraham and to his posterity forever.*

As such, the feast of Christmas, marking this fulfillment of the Covenant of Grace, is a rich deposit of God's favor toward us his world, a treasure of grace we may draw from as we celebrate this mystery of the Incarnation. The spiritual writers tell us that in the Christian liturgy, when we celebrate an event of the past, we become contemporaries of its graces. In a liturgical event as great as this one today, the service where we are "gathered in his name," he is with us with his favor, fresh grace. All the more so, when we gather in numbers and we embellish the day and the hours of prayer in song and a ceremony of lights and flowers. The grace that is that Covenant of Grace abounds here now, fresh and powerful. It is in the words of the psalmist "plenteous."

For some, it has a cumulative effect, growth in spirituality, advancing to another level of personal holiness. For others, it is the kick-start to a better way of thinking about our lives, and an opening to Christian serenity and joy. Grace penetrates the season. It could be in what people call the "Christmas spirit," or the feeling that they seem to catch as the day approaches. People tend to be kinder, pleasanter, friendlier. I don't vouch for that interpretation entirely, but it is a good metaphor for grace, which can support all of those virtues and can truly lift our spirits and give us a new outlook. As God's favor, it will be available as long as we care to wallow in it, through our prayers and devotions and faithfulness to the Lord's word. It will carry on into the new year. And I believe also that it binds us together in a special way as stated in this Charles Wesley hymn:

> Jesus, united by thy grace
> and each to each endeared,
> with confidence we seek thy face
> and know our prayer is heard.

Thanks be to God.

'The Last Gospel'

TEXT John 1:1-18

Anyone here remember "The Last Gospel"? I doubt it. That's a kind of trick question. You would have to remember what the liturgy, the Mass, was like in Latin, before it was conducted in the vernacular, English. That goes back to the early 1960s and the Second Vatican Council. That's over 60 years ago.

Now before you all yawn and turn off, imagine this scene: yours truly, age 13, in black cassock and white surplice, an altar-boy standing at the foot of the altar (when there were steps up to the altar) near the end of the Mass when the priest, after the very last prayer and after the blessing of the congregation, went over to the right side of the altar, the "Gospel side," and began, back turned to us, reading (Latin) from a card. He was reading "the Last Gospel." So distinguished because earlier in the service an assigned gospel passage of the day was read. (The first gospel.) Now do you remember? . . . those of you who go back a few years? "The Last Gospel." It is now consigned to the nostalgia file. (*Traditional Latin Mass of the Roman Rite.*)

All of this is by way of introducing a key gospel passage of this holy season. The Last Gospel, what was read at the end of the old Latin Mass, was the [ironically] *first* 14 verses of the *first* chapter of the gospel of the evangelist John. In the middle ages, it had been used as a private meditation of the priest; and late in the 16th century, it was prescribed as a regular part of the Mass. It remained so for 370 years, until the liturgical reforms of 1960 at Vatican Council II.

In the beginning was the Word, and the Word was with God, and the Word was God. He was in the beginning with God. All things came into being through him, and without him nothing came into being.

The passage is still read in the liturgy of Christmas today -- as an alternative scripture gospel in the third service of the day. This was St. John's way of introducing his account of the life of Jesus. It differs from the first chapter verses of the gospels of evangelists Matthew, Mark, and Luke, who gave us the Bethlehem narrative -- in particular Luke, that precious sentimental description of the birth of Jesus in the stable with Mary, his mother, and his step-father, Joseph, and all the other persons of that marvelous story . . . angels, shepherds, magi; yes, and even farm animals. You can easily picture the scene of the birth of God's son, the Lord Jesus.

What a contrast to the first chapter of the gospel of John, which is abstract, and lofty, and fixed in the metaphor of light! *What has come into being in him was life, and the life was the light of all people. The light shines in the darkness, and the darkness did not overcome it.*

This so-called Last Gospel has been red meat for the great theologians from the very earliest life of the Church. It conveys the deepest mystery of the Incarnation. It sets the tone for the imagery which the Lord himself will use over and over again in his preaching to explain his message and who he is. *I am the light of the world. Whoever follows me will never walk in darkness, but will have the light of life.*

Understanding these images ("the Word was God" and "in him was life, and the life was the light of all") was easy for philosophers and theologians. In the centuries before Christ, Greek philosophers, pagans, used the term "logos" – Greek for "word" -- to describe the intermediate agency by which god created material things and communicated with them. *Logos* (translated *word*) was understood in a much broader sense than our "word." It was not only the outward expression, but also the internal thought and source of that expression, the intelligence, the rationale behind the expression, and its creative power as well. So it was that these great thinkers looked upon the created universe as essentially rational and organized. Its rational principle was the *logos,* the word. And in the Greek worldview before the Christian era, the *logos* (word) was the bridge between the transcendent god and the material universe.

In the Hebrew literature as well: in psalm 33, we read there was that same notion: "By the word of the Lord the heavens were made; and all the host of them by the breath of his mouth." And in another psalm (107): "He sent his word and healed them." And in many other places in the Old Testament. So, Christians who read John's gospel understood fully his meaning when he wrote, *In the beginning was the Word and the Word was with God and the Word was God.* "The Word is God" expressed in or as all his creative power: Jesus.

As we learn further along in this classic chapter one of John, the evangelist declares something that not the Greek Philosophers nor even the Hebrew psalmists could have ever have imagined -- ". . . and the Word became Flesh." This, succinctly put, is the statement of the mystery of the Incarnation that we celebrate at the Christ Mass, Christmas.

An early Christian philosopher, Justin Martyr (or St. Justin, who died in the year 165), who lived within the century after the evangelist John, and who interpreted the gospels in defense of the Church in its earliest period, laid the ground work for our theological understanding of Jesus as Logos, the Word of God, the creative mind and power of God. "Through the Word, God made everything," wrote the philosopher saint and martyr, Justin. Thomas Aquinas, arguably the greatest of the medieval Christian philosophers, saw this revelation of the first chapter of John's gospel, the Logos, as a way to understand the Oneness of God-and- Man in Christ.

If you are straining now at these lofty abstract discussions, fear not, God has not left us with only these revelations of his presence in the world. We have Bethlehem. It is so plain and simple: A virgin, named Mary, a young woman, gives birth to a child in an obscure locale in the nation of Israel (although that nation was at the time occupied by the Roman army). Her spouse was with her. And it all was explained to them by God's messengers:

This is the child the prophets have been announcing to you, whom you have been expecting for hundreds of years, whom you have been longing for in the words and prayers of your prophets. His name will be Jesus, and he will be the savior.

There was a small, but brief commotion at the event when angels appeared in the sky . . . as the other evangelists tell us. Shepherds from nearby came around. But after a short while, the family was on its way back to their home where the child, yes, the Messiah, the Savior, would grow up . . . until the time of his public teaching career. This story we can easily grasp, nothing lofty or abstract about it. This we can see and feel and depict in all our artistry, as we have done ever since, in paintings, in music, in poetry and pageants. It is a story that fills our churches on an evening like tonight. We are here because we love it. It is irresistible. It is beautiful. How easy it is, always in this story here, to remember how God entered human existence, how he appeared. It was in a natural way, no philosophical discussion needed. As devout believers, we need only bow and pray and sing praises.

And yet, the other aspect of the Lord's birth is important to remember as well, and focus on in our Christmas devotions. For it also is presented in the gospel of the day:

In the beginning was the Word, and the Word was with God, and the Word was God. He was in the beginning with God. All things came into being through him, and without him nothing came into being.

He is the Logos. Christians are people of the Logos; the faith we live is rooted in the Word, the Logos. We live a faith, the source of which comes from creative reason. It is ordered and rational. It is the basis of our moral strength. It is a reality that transcends the wonderful Bethlehem scene. But no less a holy mystery. Incarnation. God the Christ is Logos -- meaning Reason, Word, and so it is through the way of reason that man encounters God.

Were Thomas Aquinas to come here today and give a lecture on the Incarnation, based on the first chapter of John's gospel, I doubt he would draw a crowd. But we have Bethlehem. Embrace Bethlehem, and also embrace the Word, and know that your faith is a faith drawn from and sustained by the mind's most powerful human capacity, the light of reason. Because he, as he declared, is "the Light of the world." We believe because we understand . . . and we understand because we believe.

Thanks be to God.

Journey of the Magi

TEXT Matthew 2: 1-23
[before the reading of the T.S. Eliot poem]

The Epiphany story, featuring the three kings from the east, the Magi, is as widely known as the December 25TH Nativity story, with the holy family in the stable and the visit of the shepherds. They are, in fact, not two stories, but one whole story, although they are separated in the liturgical calendar, and each has its own sentiment. In the Eastern churches, Greeks and others, the Epiphany is the major feast. While in the West, our major celebration is Christmas. I didn't find among the commentators as much theological exegesis about the Epiphany as one finds about the Nativity. The Nativity is the Incarnation, a central mystery of Christianity, and so recognized and celebrated. The Epiphany has another meaning of its own: the introduction of the Messiah, and the world's redemption which the Messiah's advent means, to the non-Jewish world. To us. Did you ever think of yourselves, as Christians, who are really God's second choice? The Jews were the people blessed with the Revelation first. It came later to us, and it is symbolized for us with the discovery by the Magi of the child Jesus. It became Paul of Tarsus' assigned mission to unfold this message to the rest of the world. Thus is the standard theological significance of the Epiphany -- which by the way happens to mean from the Greek "the manifestation" of God. It lends itself nicely to illustration art and painting . . . what with three colorful mid-eastern potentates and their entourages. There are literally hundreds of classical paintings of the *Adoration of the Magi,* from the greatest of painters: Leonardo DaVinci, Albrecht Dürer, Botticelli, Filippino Lippi, the list goes on. I've copied a few of them from the Internet and posted them for you.

    The Gospel of Matthew tells the story nicely, and I need not recount it. But to gain an insight, to have an emotional grasp, to bring it into contact with our own spiritual sensibilities, I've chosen a very well-known poem, hoping it will stir feelings beyond the event's mere theological significance. It is T.S. Eliot's "Journey of the Magi."

    It is poetry. You need to listen to it with your mind completely soft and pliable, with your imagination let loose to mix with all the

images of the narrative — as the poet does. There will be symbols, and allusions, and rhythms attendant on the story as it is told. Think of movies and the flashbacks and other technical devices used to tell a story. That's what is happening here. The speaker is one of the Magi, or a member of the party, who recalls the event years later. (The speaker is also the poet, who is telling you how the event affected him spiritually.) I've given you a copy, but listen to it being read first. Your text copy is for you to study afterwards and aid you in absorbing the meaning and feeling for yourself and, I hope, for your spiritual enhancement.
[after the reading]

Poetry is written for no other reason, at least primarily, than for our pleasure. Give it thought now. It is about the journey of faith that all of us take. The journey may be difficult. There are hard times. "A hard time we had if it," the narrator says. At some point, we know that we have to give up some things, ephemeral pleasures, indulgences, excesses: "We regretted the summer places on slopes, the terraces/And the silken girls bringing sherbet." The poet, Eliot, who embraced Christianity in his baptism a short time before this poem was published, seems to take his acceptance of faith hard. "This birth was hard and bitter agony for us." That tone is felt through the entire poem, right from the opening line, "A cold coming we had of it," through to the end, "I should be glad of another death." Here is where we might depart from the poet's sensitivities. Being a follower of Christ is a challenge but not a chore, not all trial and sadness. After all, isn't the announcement of the angels positive? "I bring you tidings of great joy," etc. Add to that, "Today is born to you a savior, Christ the Lord." That should lift our spirits. We need a savior. But, as Eliot says, it means letting go of a meaningless life of worldly pursuits, with which we can "no longer be at ease." Life in Christ is a new dispensation. And the Lord makes it so easy for us to grasp with the graces available in the vision of the Infant, as the Magi found out. God, the Creator, entering history gently, allowing mankind, us, to know and embrace him as we would lift up and hold a child to our breast. The graces of this possibility are here for us now, when we gather in the Lord's presence to worship and give thanks.

There are some other images and symbols in the poem I'll point out, so you can re-read it and regain the feeling. "Three trees on a low sky," — the crosses at the scene of the Christ's death, always a factor to be dealt with and accepted as a part of our spirituality. "A white horse galloped away in the meadow" is an allusion from the Apocalypse, the last book of the bible, to the Savior's coming again, which is an article of our faith we say in the Creed at every service. The poem is packed with feeling. It will always be memorable for you each year when you celebrate the Epiphany, "the journey of the Magi." And it will be there with God's grace to stir and sanction your personal journey of faith.

Thanks be to God.

We Are All Refugees

TEXT Matthew 2: 1-14

We are all refugees. As a rule, I do not comment on or refer to matters in the national or international news in a sermon. I leave that to CBS or NBC or ABC or CNN, and the rest of the professional commentators. But I make an exception here today, because the news may help us to reflect on and understand or interpret the Sunday assigned scripture that we just read. Christmas, the birth of Jesus which we celebrate every year at this time, has some extraneous elements to it. Oh, don't misunderstand; the nativity of Jesus is as real as the birth of you and me. The life of Jesus Christ is a fact of history, a marvelous historical fact. But this part of the story, the infancy, has been simplified, condensed, embellished, so that people all over the world, in every age, in whatever culture, can grasp, can take a hold of it for the benefit of their growing faith, and for the peace of mind knowing we have a Savior who redeems the frailty and stress of our human condition.

Some of the details of the manger scene were drawn from Christian writings of the early centuries that are considered *apocryphal.* That is, unreliable sources. In one of these accounts, the Holy family lives in Egypt seven years; Jesus grows up there. Of course, there is no confirmation of that whatsoever. Also, the nativity story was written by the apostle and evangelist Matthew in such a way as to connect it to the Old Testament. Matthew wants his Jewish audience, especially, to see the allusions and the similarities in their sacred books and prophesies to the birth of Moses. In this thought, like Moses, Jesus comes to be the leader of his people, who will teach them the way to the Kingdom. Later in Matthews's gospel there is the Sermon on the Mount, in which Jesus parallels Moses again, as a lawgiver . . . now the law of the New Covenant, which Jesus will fulfill in his life and preaching, and in his sacrificial passion and death. Matthew wraps up his Christmas narrative with the following:

So he, Joseph, got up, took the child and his mother during the night and left for Egypt where he stayed until the death of Herod. And so was fulfilled what the Lord had said through the prophet, "Out of Egypt I called my son."

We cannot peg the Christmas story to an event in recorded secular history. The only account of Savior's birth we have is from the gospels. But we can corroborate the Holy Family's journey into Egypt with what was, in fact, going on in Judea at that time according to ancient world historians: Flavius Josephus, for example, a first century contemporary of Jesus, who wrote a history of the wars between the Jews and the Romans. He is among historians, ancient and modern, who identify, recognize, and regarded Harod -- at this time a mere puppet ruler assigned by Rome to the district of Judea -- as a ruthless psychopath. His slaughtering of thousands of innocents, that Matthew's gospel reports, was in the view of historians, wholly consistent with his notorious royal character. He is on record as having murdered two of his sons and their mother, because he thought they were, like Jesus as he imagined, a threat to his power.

But the gospel story of the flight into Egypt is not meant to be an historical document. Rather, like all scripture, "inspired" says St Paul, it is a lesson, a stimulus, a prompt for believers a to consider and to reflect on an aspect of their own temporal condition. We are all to recognize a truth of our existence, consider how it is played out in our lives, and then build a strong spiritual connection to the Lord. Because we understand that, like the Holy Family, Jesus Mary and Joseph, we are all refugees. There is a litany of Christian writers, holy men, theologians, whose writings on the flight into Egypt draw out this very spiritual lesson. I could mention a few names, if you bear with me, because I like these names: St. John Chrysostom, St. Peter Crysologus, St. Fulgence, St. Albert the Great, St. Anselm, St. Basil, St. Antoninus, St. Thomas, and, of course, Augustine.

If the Holy Family, in fact, had to make a long journey to seek refuge and safety from danger and political turmoil just at that time, it would not have been unusual. There were wars around. It seems, as in every century, every decade, there are wars. There is always the dire circumstance, always at some moment in time, where people are fleeing to a safer place. It may just be an archetypical factor of our existence to be up-rooted, to have to re-locate, for one reason or another, to be on the move always. Even in tranquil times, people must be moving -- a better opportunity, better job, illness, death, weather, and natural calamities, disasters and other grim circumstances require moving. We have no permanent resting place it seems. Our life's journey is, in a spiritual sense, a journey of seeking permanence in a safe haven. "The sight of the Holy Family, Joseph, Mary and the child, wandering as fugitives through the world," writes one commentator on this scripture, "teaches us that we also must live as pilgrims here below, detached from the goods of this world, which we must soon leave to enter eternity."

"We have not here a lasting city, but seek one that is to come," we read in the epistle to the Hebrews. To which St. Augustine adds, "Thou art a guest; thou givist a look and passeth on." I'll paraphrase that for you: You are only a guest here for a while. Take a look around, and then move on to your final destination, God's heavenly kingdom promised to us by Jesus. And we can add this line from Paul's letter to the Galatians: *For we know that if the earthly tent we live in is destroyed, we have prepared for us a building from God, an eternal house in heaven, not built by human hands.*

It can be a happy condition, our restlessness, our instability, our pilgrim state, because as good Christians we know where we are going, and we enjoy a certain peace and satisfaction knowing where the path, which is our life in time, leads us. And also, when we adjust and measure our lives to the Lord's. Surely it was seen in that positive light by the many artists who are drawn to this scripture and the scene of the flight into Egypt. You have pictures of such works in the insert.

Take a look. One is by Giotto, who is one of the greatest Renaissance artists, who lived over the turn of the 13TH century. The other is Henry Tanner, who lived in our time, died in 1937. And of whom it is said that the flight into Egypt was his favorite biblical story. This painting, they say, "expresses his sensitivity to issues of personal freedom, escape from persecution, and the migrations of African Americans from the South to the North. They reveal a certain human emotion and the awareness of the mystical meanings of biblical narratives." I like that.

We can look at these works and feel the security of knowing that as refugees we are in good company, and that the outcome will be good. Look to the goal. Our destination is the Kingdom of Heaven, promised by Jesus to those who love him. So we pray for the refugees of our time and our world. We can say we feel their pain. Currently in the news is a plan for an international conference to address the crisis. There are now more than a million refugees migrating to Europe. Our goal is to ask God to guide them to a safe place. As we pray for ourselves also, that God by his divine grace, lead us to the peace and security of his heavenly kingdom, our true destination and home.

I was having a difficult time finding a concise conclusion to this meditation. And then I went back to the scriptures and found the continuation of the lines quoted from the letter to the Hebrews above. It sums up the message, and is perfect for this season.

We have no lasting city, but to seek the city which is to come. Through him then, let us continually offer up sacrifice of praise to God, that is the fruit of lips that acknowledge his name. Do not neglect to do good and to share what you have; for such sacrifices are pleasing to God.

Thanks be to God.

Ordinary Time to Lent

No Need for Converts
Lamb of God Sunday
Jesus the Prophet
Learn to Preach from the Master
Questions about the Temptations of Christ
A Most Unusual Day
Jesus Prayed
"No More Mr. Nice Guy"
A Gospel Reality Show
Taking Humanism to the Next Level
Unity Through Diversity
Deals
Existential Jesus

No Need for 'Converts'

TEXT Mark 1:14-20

That title refers to something Richard John Neuhaus used to say in his efforts at bringing our churches together. Fr. Neuhaus -- if you are not familiar with him or his work -- was a Lutheran to Catholic priest activist, founder and editor of the ecumenical monthly journal *First Things*; and at the time of his death, three years ago this month, an assistant pastor at Immaculate Conception parish on the lower east side of Manhattan. In his enthusiasm for Christian unity, Fr. Neuhaus would point out that it is incongruous, at the least, to speak of *converting* from one to church to another, as we are all baptized Christians; that is, followers of Jesus and members of the church he founded. "The goal of ecumenism," Neuhaus said, "is not to create a unity that does not exist, but to bring to fulfillment the very real unity that is already there between Catholics and non-Catholics who are brothers and sisters in Christ."

I dare say that principle has been observed in the reunion recently of the Anglican church of England with the Catholic church of the Vatican, where there was no language of conversion but only of reuniting and sharing in full communion. In that Apostolic Constitution [*Anglicanorum Coebitus*], neither the word *convert* nor the word *conversion* is to be found. That is our goal: full communion. In this presentation, allow me to talk about how we are moving toward that goal, what is going on at some of the higher levels between leaders in our churches.

The need for this exposure is expressed in one of the published documents, "Together in Holiness: 40 Years of Methodist-Roman Catholic Dialogue," where the preface complains that the dialogues were not "deeply or widely" received by their respective ecclesial communities. In other words, no one has paid attention. I am going to try to change that now. While I describe some of the marvelous statements of communion that are found in the reports of these dialogues, I must state that these are the dialogues between Methodists and Catholics; but similar dialogues have been and are occurring between other groups -- between Methodists and Episcopalians, between Lutherans and

Catholics. And so forth. Of spectacular note is the Joint Declaration on the Doctrine of Justification achieved by the Lutheran World Federation and the Catholic Church in 1999, which states that "[we] are now able to articulate a common understanding of our justification by God's grace through faith in Christ." Seven years later in 2006, the World Methodist Council signed on to the Joint Declaration, establishing, in its words "a far-reaching consensus in regard to the theological controversy which was a major cause of the split in Western churches in the sixteenth century." In my view, the war is over.

In addition, lest you think this will be a theological lecture, I point out that should you read the reports you will find them to be not only thorough and clear reviews of the doctrines of our faith, but also meditations that will lift you spiritually. In fact, each report of the Methodist-Catholic dialogues begins with a meditation on Scripture. For example, the most recent, "Encountering Christ Our Savior," the 2011 report, is headed by this "scriptural meditation": Philippians 1:11 . . . that begins: *If then there is any encouragement in Christ, any consolation from love, any sharing in the Spirit, any compassion and sympathy, make my joy complete: be of the same mind, having the same love, being in full accord and of one mind.* To the point, wouldn't you say? Throughout these reports, we find statements that we can adopt to direct and further our efforts at coming together toward full communion.

The ultimate goal of the dialogues (our purpose too) is full ecclesial communion -- full communion in faith, mission, and sacramental life. The reports say that study of the historical background of the respective spiritualities leads to the conclusion that what has mattered most in both traditions has been the *reality of religion,* as it brings about the transformation of the human heart and mind in everyday life. Often cited is the conviction of John Wesley that "each human being has a duty to seek holiness and Christian perfection . . . and that the heart of the Gospel and the core of our faith is the love of God revealed in redemption." All our creedal statements, states the document, seek to proclaim this mystery: the love of God who saves us in Christ. God's purpose for creation is that human beings, opened to the gracious presence of God, commit their entire being to their Maker and Redeemer, and in communion with him become renewed in the divine image, in the holiness and happiness, which is God's intention for humankind.

Language like that should convince you of the spiritual richness of these ecumenical dialogues and their reports. It is now our turn to respond. Often quoted are the words of Pope John Paul II in his universal letter of 1995, *That All May Be One:* "Dialogue is not simply an exchange of ideas. In some ways it is always an exchange of gifts.'" There is a broad and very important meaning of that phrase "exchange of gifts"; you will hear it frequently in ecumenical conversation. In one place in the report, there are some practical examples that we may consider and adopt. Proposals for a mutual exchange of gifts:

- Opportunities for joint prayer and spiritual retreats that would testify to our shared belief that the call to holiness is intrinsic to the call to be the Church.
  (GEMs, the Greenport Ecumenical Ministries, has done this admirably for more than 10 years; and hopefully, we are advancing to the next steps.)
- Invite each other to experience different forms of worship and spiritual devotions. The Catholics have the Rosary and the Stations of the Cross.
- Methodists have Bible study groups that encourage lay people in personal reading of the Scriptures.
- Reflect upon and be inspired by the example and witness of the saints through the ages.
- Promote the sacramental ministry to the sick and dying.
- Invite Catholics to experience different forms of worship and spiritual devotion in Methodism.
- Reflect on and be inspired by the example and witness of John and Charles Wesley, the holy founders of the Methodist society.
- Lastly, to explore the sharing of the Eucharist meal, Holy Communion, in strict observance, however, of the order prescribed by the respective authorities; that is, the Methodist Book of Discipline and Catholic Canon Law.

Is there a moral to be taken away from this little theological dissertation? I believe there is, and it is this: for us Christians, pursuing unity has to be a part of our pursuit of personal holiness. The ecumenical cause is not optional or the domain only or our clergy. Unity is as paramount in our Christian way of life as is charity, caring for the poor and the sick, and evangelization. "The call to personal holiness, the call to unity in worship, and the call to mission intrinsically belong together." And in another place the dialogue document says, "For Methodists and Catholics, the call to holiness and the call to be the church belong together." The Lord commands us to preach the gospel to all nations; no less is his command to be one in unity, for which he prayed fervently at the end of his life: *that they may all be one, just as you, Father, are in me, and I in you, that they also may be in us, so that the world may believe that you have sent me.*

For the last word on this point, I will quote from the Ecumenical Directory, a document developed from the 2ND Vatican Council -- at which, by the way, there were Methodist minister observers. "Those who are baptized in the name of Christ are, by that very fact, called to commit themselves to the search for unity. Baptismal communion tends towards full ecclesial communion. To live our Baptism is to be caught up in Christ's mission of making all things one."

I began this talk by discouraging the use of the word *convert*. And I think I explained how awkward it is to speak of such conversions among baptized Christians. I should also make clear that in pursuing and achieving (in our lifetime?) the goal of full communion we will not lose the unique identities of our Christian ecclesial communities. There will always be Methodists and the Methodist society; it will have its own traditions, its own style of prayer service; but it will be Methodists in full communion with the Church of Jesus Christ. Just as today we have Anglicans in full communion and conducting their liturgy from the Book of Common Prayer. And there will be Catholics sharing in gifts of Methodism, dedicating themselves to personal holiness as John Wesley preached and learning to sing all the hymns of Charles Wesley. Take me, for example, a Catholic, and I am blessed to share one of the gifts of Methodism -- the preparation of laymen for preaching and conducting prayer and worship services. For which we say -- all together now -- Thanks be to God!

Thanks be to God.

Lamb of God Sunday

TEXT John 1: 29-34

It's a phrase that's caught on. Big time. Although not always in a spiritual context. As a Christian symbol, the Lamb of God, or *Agnus Dei,* represents Christ and His sacrifice, and is known to go back as far as the 4TH or 5TH century. It has been an inspiration for hundreds of artists and saints. In music especially, there are many many classical music settings for the Lamb of God prayer in the Holy Mass -- in the Latin, of course. Here are just a few of the composers who in their Mass compositions include sacred musical settings for the *Agnus Dei:* Bach, Mozart, Beethoven, Schubert, Gabriel Faure; plus the moderns, John Rutter and Samuel Barber, and the Jazz icon Dave Brubeck. And also some contemporary composers that you might find in your hymnal: Here is one, a favorite of mine. [sing]

    The list could go on and on. There is even a contemporary rock band -- heavy metal, to be precise -- that uses the name Lamb of God, 'though I would not recommend them at all!

    In the visual arts, the Lamb of God, or Agnus Dei, has also inspired and ignited the imaginations of dozens of artists. I include only a couple of examples here on the bulletin today.

Not to overlook every other medium of art: stained glass, stone sculpture, brass casting, embroidery, and coin. And informally: posters, greeting cards and stationary. Everywhere we turn we should not be surprised to recognize an image of the Lamb of God. It is ubiquitous, reminding us always of the Christian culture in which we live and move every day. In this morning's meditation, we will try to understand the power and the beauty and the attraction of the phrase. Importantly, we'll delve into its rich theological content, and hope to draw out of it graces to our spiritual advantage.

John the Baptist, as he was depicted in the gospel passage from evangelist John, that was read a few moments ago -- may have been the first to introduce Jesus, in those now most memorable words, as the "Lamb of God," and with the added description, the one "who takes away the sins of the world." There is no question that John had in himself, in his makeup, the capacity to utter prophetic language like this, to speak as a prophet. Like the prophets of his ancestry, Isaiah and Elias, his life, spent in austerity in the desert, was consumed by his prophetic mission. His father says of him (The Song of Zachariah), "you, my son, will be called a prophet of God; you will go ahead of the Lord to prepare the way for him."

The notion of a lamb-sacrifice in the worship of God and remission of sin is prefigured in the Passover lamb rite, by which the Jews were set free from Egyptian captivity. Says St. Paul in a letter to Corinth, "Our Passover lamb is Christ." There is also the allusion in Isaiah's poetry, the Song of the Suffering Servant, pointing to the Passion of Jesus:

> *He was oppressed, and he was afflicted,*
> *yet he did not open his mouth;*
> *like a lamb that is led to the slaughter,*
> *and like a sheep that goes before its shearers is silent,*
> *so he did not open his mouth. [Silence of the Lamb]*
> *By a perversion of justice he was taken away,*
> *For he was put to death for the sins of our people.*
> *They made his grave with the wicked*
> *although there was no deceit in his mouth.*

To this poetry of Isaiah, Augustine adds these comments: "Like a lamb, in his passion he underwent death without being guilty of any iniquity." And John Calvin in his massive theology treatise wrote of Jesus as "The Lamb, an agent of God, who in his trial before Pilate and while at Herod's Court, could have argued for his innocence; he instead remained mostly quiet and submitted to Crucifixion in obedience to the Father; for he knew his role as the Lamb of God."

In modern Christology, (i.e. the theology of Christ), German Jesuit theologian Karl Rahner continues to elaborate on the analogy ". . . that the blood of the Lamb of God, and the water flowing from the side of Christ on Calvary had a cleansing nature, similar to baptismal water. In this analogy, the blood of the Lamb washed away the sins of humanity in a new baptism, redeeming it from the fall of Adam. In those three poetic words, *Lamb of God*, is held the whole of the mystery of our Salvation."

In sum, Christian teaching has come down to us declaring Jesus the Lamb of God, who in his role of the perfect sacrificial offering, chose to suffer at Calvary as a sign of his full obedience to the will of his Father, as an "agent and servant of God." The Lamb of God is thus related to the Paschal Lamb of Passover, and is viewed as a foundation and is integral to the message of Christianity, our faith.

When a question about this scene from John's gospel -- the baptism of Jesus -- came up as to why Jesus needed to be baptized by John in the first place, we have a retort by St. Augustine that sums up in its way the mystery of our redemption. He says in one of his sermons -- 4TH century, remember: "And did the Lord need to be baptized? To anyone who asks that question, I instantly reply: Was it needful for the Lord to be born? Was it needful for the Lord to be crucified? Was it needful for the Lord to die? Was it needful for the Lord to be buried? If he undertook for us so great a humiliation, might he not also receive baptism?"

This sounds to me very much like the Creed we say here every Sunday: "Born of the Virgin, was crucified, died, and was buried." And so forth. At this point in our mediation, we can open our own imaginations and do our own search into the depth of meaning of the Lamb of God epithet John gives to Jesus. What will it tell us about him, his personality, that will help us pray? (1) *A lamb*, that he was soft: "Come to me for I am meek and humble of heart," he once said. (2) A lamb, *loveable:* "If you keep my commands, I will love you and my Father will love you," he told his disciples. (3) Lamb *of God:* powerful, who can forgive sin.

So when we pray, it is to the Lamb of God that we address our prayer this morning. And it is a plea for mercy. How perfect is this prayer for what we all desperately need. It is our condition, our human situation, frail and imperfect, that demands we cry out to the Savior for the fruits of his redemptive passion -- the forgiveness of our sins. Say it with me.

Lamb of God, you take away the sins of the world, have mercy on us.
Again:
Lamb of God, you take away the sins of the world, have mercy on us.
One more time:
Lamb of God, you take away the sins of the world, grant us peace. Amen.

Thanks be to God.

Jesus the Prophet

TEXT Mark 1: 21-28

As you may have noticed, I like to build my sermons on the gospel reading of the Sunday, supplemented with some research from the writings of the Fathers of the church, which I have found handily in this little book. [*Ancient Christian Devotional* - show book]. In today's case, all the good Fathers seem to have wanted to comment on that section of the gospel incident that features the unclean spirit, the man possessed, the devil they call him. But the inspiration that came to me was something else.

Jesus *entered the synagogue and taught. They were astounded at his teaching, for he taught them as one having authority.* Jesus was recognized as a prophet. Do you think of Jesus as a prophet? Let's look at that question, and see if we can draw a lesson from it. It is a topic of much discussion among commentators on sacred scripture and the life of Jesus. There is even the note that Muslims regard Jesus as a great prophet; yet Christians don't always think of him in those terms. The episode we read about in today's gospel would support the contention that Jesus is indeed a prophet, and was regarded as one by his contemporaries.

> *They were all amazed, and they kept on asking one another, "What is this? A new teaching --with authority! He commands even the unclean spirits, and they obey him." At once his fame began to spread throughout the surrounding region of Galilee.*

The Jewish people, his people, were familiar with prophets. Prophets had been a part of their history and their literature for thousands of years. They would know a prophet when they saw one, and they saw one in Jesus on this occasion. Like a prophet, he taught with authority, he performed signs, wondrous, miraculous deeds. Moses, their greatest prophet, taught with authority and performed miracles. Moses was the prototype, a model, by which they would recognize Jesus as a prophet. There is a very clear statement in the book of Deuteronomy, written by Moses, that we read this morning:

> *The Lord your God will raise up for you a prophet like me from among your own people; you shall heed such a prophet. This is what you requested of the Lord your God . . . on the day of the assembly . . . . Then the Lord said "I will raise up for them a prophet like you from among their own people; I will put my words in the mouth of the prophet, who shall speak to them everything that I command."*

Nowhere in the scriptures and subsequent history of the Israelites is that un-named prophet announced by Moses identified . . . except that it is, in fact, Jesus of the gospels.

You can probably remember hearing the number of times Jesus is referred to as a prophet. In John's gospel at the time he was gathering his apostles, we hear Philip say this about Jesus to his friend Nathanial: *We have found the one Moses and the prophets wrote about.* And in another place in the gospel of John, where, after Jesus fed the multitude near the Lake of Galilee, they said, *This must be the prophet who is to come into the world.* In Acts of the Apostles, Peter is speaking to the people in the Temple in Jerusalem after the passion and death of Jesus and he says, *God had his prophets tell us that the Messiah would suffer, and now he has kept that promise.* And also in Acts, in the valedictory of the martyr Stephen, Stephen tells his accusers: *Moses told the Israelites, "God will choose one of your people to be a prophet."* Oh, how these great men, Jews who were contemporaries and became followers of Jesus . . . how they knew their bible! How they recognized in Jesus that he came out of that holy tradition of prophets, who carried God's revelation to the people of Israel and then to the world at large!

And remember the two disciples, who after the resurrection, met Jesus on the road to Emmaus. They didn't recognize Jesus at first, and they began telling him about "*these things that happened to Jesus of Nazareth, about what he did and showed that he was a powerful prophet who pleased God and the people.*" But the Samaritan woman, not a Jew, who Jesus met at the well -- and he gave her a cup of water -- did recognize him: *Sir, the woman said, "I can see that you are a prophet."* And Jesus, did indeed, himself speak as a prophet and make prophesies. There was the time in what we call his eschatological address when he foretold the coming destruction of Jerusalem:

> *When you see Jerusalem being surrounded by armies, you will know that its desolation is near. Then let those who are in Judea flee to the mountains, let those in the city get out, and let those in the country not enter the city. For this is the time of punishment in fulfillment of all that has been written.*

This event, the leveling of Jerusalem and the temple by the Roman army, took place later in history, in the year 70 A.D., in the First Roman-Jewish War, about 40 years after Jesus was gone. And of course, Jesus said of himself and of his great act of redemption this prediction:

> *We are on our way to Jerusalem where the Son of Man will be handed over to the chief priests and the teachers of the Law of Moses. They will sentence him to death and hand him over to foreigners, who will . . . beat him and kill him. But three days later he will rise to life.*

What do we gain in meditating here on Jesus the prophet? We are coming out of the Christmas liturgies, where we recognized him as the Savior. We are approaching the Lent and Easter liturgies, where we recognize him as Redeemer. At times through the year, we celebrate him in our services and in our songs as King; and he often spoke about his kingdom: *the kingdom of heaven.*

What can we take away now, for our spiritual advantage from Jesus the Prophet? I have a few answers to that. First, it reminds us of the continuity and wholeness of the bible. Jesus the prophet bonds together the scriptures of the Old and the New Testaments. God's revelation and the message of Jesus cannot be grasped fully except in the light of all scripture. Jesus the prophet is a person out of those ancient holy books — like the great and holy persons of past: Moses, Isaiah, Jeremiah, the prophets . . . and there are dozens of them through the centuries. But he is greater. These holy men and women are his kin, where he comes from. To understand Jesus, we look back upon him and we see the wholeness, and the beauty and the power of God's revelation to the world.

A second thought: seeing the prophet in Jesus we know him better. All of those personal characteristics of the Old Testament prophets — courage, persistence, wisdom, closeness to God and obedience to God's message –- are in him. But we have said that he is greater. John the Baptist, himself called by Jesus a great prophet, says of Jesus, *among you stands one you do not know, he who comes after me, the strap of whose sandal I am not worthy to untie.* Like Moses and the other prophets who announced covenants with God, Jesus the prophet announced and established a new covenant between the Creator and all of mankind: *the Kingdom of God.*

It might not be a bad idea after all -- if what I have said about Jesus here as a prophet is sounding new to you -- to go to the gospels on occasion and read a chapter or two. It is amazing how much more there to Jesus than what we only have time for on Sundays. That is my experience in preparing this sermon. I am always amazed, and I always learn something. Try it.

*** Thanks be to God. ***

BRIEF INTRO.
This sermon was preached to the class at the end of my training course in qualification for my Methodist Lay Speaker's certification.
Before I begin, I want to acknowledge those two great Internet resources, Google and Wikipedia. They will make us all into great preachers. By the way, Wikipedia is a not-for-profit foundation. They ask for contributions from time to time. So do what you can; we'd hate to lose them. And now to the sermon.

Learn to Preach from the Master

TEXT Matthew 4: 1-11

Have you ever heard a discussion in which one person quotes the bible to support his argument? And then the other person counters with "Hey! Even the devil can quote scripture." Here is where that saying comes from -- the temptations of Jesus, which we read in Matthew, often on the first Sunday of Lent. The Temptation scene is also presented by the other evangelists, Mark and Luke in their narratives of the life of Jesus. It is a crucial turning point in the Lord's life. The gospel passage that precedes it is the account of his baptism. The commentators on the "Temptations" -- and they are myriad from every age -– point out that the Lord's fasting in the desert, and his encounter with temptation are the introduction to his mission, Jesus having been anointed, so to speak, by the Father's words at his baptism: "This is my beloved son, of whom I am well pleased."

As Jesus sets out on his mission of the good news and the world's redemption, he experiences what every human experiences, temptation. As one commentator says, "Jesus has to enter unto the drama of human existence, for that is the core of his mission" -- the expiation for the sins of human kind –- if he is to redeem us sinners. Thus it is explained in the Letter to the Hebrews: "Our high priest [who offers sacrifice for sin] is like us, tempted in every way . . . but of course, without sin." In the epistle reading of this Sunday, Paul expresses the whole theology of the redemptive mission of Jesus with those famous parallels of Adam and Jesus: *Just as one man's sin [Adam's] led to condemnation for all, so one man's act of righteousness [Jesus'] leads to justification and life for all. As by one man's disobedience the many were made sinners, so by the one man's obedience the many will be made righteous.*

The bible commentators as well as artists and writers have a field day with the Temptations of Jesus. Commentators give elaborate interpretations of each of the three temptations: the temptation of pleasure, the temptation to challenge God, the temptation of power. Artists and writers have depicted them in paintings, in frescos on basilica walls (St. Marks in Venice), in choral music and religious song. You can even get a ringtone for your cell phone of the Temptations of Christ song. And then there was the Temptation in Milton's "Paradise Regained" epic poem, and the Academy Award-nominated movie about the "Last" temptation of Jesus, and the Broadway play *Godspell,* with a scene of the Temptations of Jesus.

But amid all of the artistic clamor and religious excitement over this most spectacular happening in Christ's life, we may miss something . . . what I regard as of greatest importance – especially for us aspiring preachers of the Word: the Lord's knowledge of Sacred Scripture. In that notorious dialogue with the devil, he is quick to counter. He more than holds his own.

First the devil alludes to 1 Kings, where the angel of God brings food to the prophet Elijah, who has fasted for 40 days in the desert: "Command these stones to become loaves of bread," the devil says. And Jesus replies from Deuteronomy, "It is written that one does not live by bread alone, but by every word that comes from the mouth of God." When the devil tells him to challenge God, Jesus again quotes Deuteronomy: "It is written, 'Do not put the Lord your God to the test.'" And to the last temptation of power and riches, Jesus again counters with Deuteronomy, with a passage he will use often in his preaching, and phrases that sum up the whole law and life's meaning: "It is written, 'Worship the Lord your God, and serve him only.'"

There is much to note in what Matthew has conveyed to us here with his narrative. Jesus identifies himself with "the Lord Your God." Think about that. Is there any question of the divinity of Jesus in the Gospels? But I want to focus more on Jesus as the teacher, the rabbi, one who knows the holy writings of his people, the words of the prophets and holy men and women of the scriptures. We know very little of the middle years of his life, when and where he may have studied. We know that as a child of 12 he was found in the temple talking with the teachers -- a sign, no doubt, of his future calling. St. Paul, we believe, studied in a rabbinical school, possibly in Jerusalem; Jesus may have done the same.

The encounter with the devil is merely one place where Jesus shows his knowledge of scripture. There are many. You will find his whole teaching and preaching career laid out in Matthew's Gospel in the chapters that follow the account of the Temptations. He was able anytime he wished to go into a synagogue and stand up and begin giving a lesson. He was recognized as a teacher, a rabbi, an outstanding preacher. Do we think of him as this? Maybe we are focused mostly on his mission, his redemptive mission and all its dramatic circumstances. His miracles, the wonders he exhibits to the crowds who followed him, may seem to overshadow the man himself and his skill, his training, his holiness. But all these qualities are evident in this scene where he repels the attack of the devil.

And there is another thing in that scene that might go unnoticed: Jesus prays. He fasts and prays. He is alone and has gone to a quiet place where he might be free of distractions to address his Father in prayer. Later in the garden, hours before his death, there was a similar scene, Jesus praying by himself. And he taught his disciples to pray, and us too, his disciples. "When you pray, say 'Our Father may your name be honored, may your kingdom came,'" and so forth. He addresses his Father and ours, the creator God, whom all the world seeks to know and to whom all are beholden.

Jesus is the model for all his followers, Christians; but more so is he a model for us, who aspire to be preachers of his message. Bottom line: study the scriptures, know them as he did, pray, pray to the Father, and be firm in the conviction which is also your calling. "Worship the Lord your God, and serve him only."

Thanks be to God.

Questions about the Three Temptations of Christ

TEXT: Luke 4: 1-13

You may have heard the expression: "Even the devil can quote scripture." Here's where it comes from. In this passage from Luke, we have a kind of hostile dialogue between Jesus and the devil, dueling scriptures, so to speak. The first sermon I gave for my Lay Speaker class was on this scripture. I pointed out how familiar Jesus was with the scriptures of his heritage, the books of Moses, the prophets, and the Psalms. As we were a class of aspiring preachers, the point was that we should imitate Jesus in our study and knowledge of scripture. But I have a different angle on this passage today. First, I have questions about the source of the narrative. It is found in all three of the "synoptic" gospels; that is, the gospel accounts that have a similar pattern, as distinct and different from the narrative the evangelist John presents. Matthew's gospel is the most detailed; Mark's is the least. We happen to be reading Luke's account in the Sunday cycle today. It is slightly different, shorter than Matthew's.

My question is about the dialogue. Did Jesus actually report this dialogue to the gospel writers? Possibly. Matthew was one of the Apostles who accompanied Jesus on much of his mission. But there were no actual eye witnesses to the event to record the words of Jesus. We're accustomed today to having reporters carrying tape or digital recorders in order to capture the exact dialogue of a scene. Nothing like that in Jesus time! So the gospel writers would have had to create it based on accounts Jesus himself told them -- or told someone.

Some scripture commentators explain the three temptations as a parable that Jesus delivered . . . albeit it a form different from his other more explicit parables. Maybe. It is safe, I believe, to understand this event as actually having been recounted by Jesus himself; and it became an episode, a part of the oral tradition that developed and grew during his lifetime and shortly afterward. Remember that churches or communities of believing Christians had already been formed and were in place before any of the gospels were written down. We know this from Paul's epistles which antedate the gospel writings.

You can imagine this story of the three temptations having been told on some occasion when Luke was meeting in one of these churches; or Matthew, at a gathering of Jewish converts and them exchanging stories, their experiences with Jesus, then writing them down. However it happened to be transmitted, this story, this event, and the whole gospel text in which it is contained, was the precious patrimony of the Christian communities, and has been for thousands of years. The story of the temptations was remembered because it was dramatic and makes several important points about the faith in Jesus. You are convinced of it, if you consider its longevity, its staying power as a narrative, such that survived in the faith of Christ's followers for thousands of years, and has been a source of inspiration not only for saintly believers, but at the same time for many artists and composers even to this very day.

Bible commentators as well as artists and writers have had a field day with the Temptations of Jesus. Theologians give elaborate interpretations of each of the three temptations: the temptation of pleasure, the temptation to challenge God, the temptation of power. Artists and writers have depicted them in paintings, in frescos on basilica walls (St. Marks in Venice), in choral music and religious song. You can even get a ringtone for your cell phone of the Temptations of Christ song! And then there was the Temptation in Milton's *Paradise Regained* epic poem, and the Academy Award nominated movie about the "Last" temptation of Jesus, and the Broadway play *Godspell* with a scene of the Temptations of Jesus.

What an impact this event has had on our civilization, in so many areas of our culture for more than 2000 years! You have to ask what is its meaning. I have heard preachers say that by this incident Jesus shows his humanity, that like all men he is subjected to temptation. This is made clear in the epistle to Hebrews 4:15, where we read: *For we do not have a high priest who is unable to sympathize with our weaknesses, but we have one who has been tempted in every way, just as we are -- yet was without sin.*

But I have another take on it. We know that the essence of the gospel scriptures is not so much a narrative history of the Savior as it is a presentation of lessons, teachings to help us understand ourselves and our place in time, with reference to our purpose as followers of Jesus. He shows us here in this event that there is such a thing as evil, and that it is a threat to our soul, whether in the form of the devil, an evil spirit, or in a less personalized form. If it is the devil, you will know it. Either way, Jesus shows us that we must be prepared to encounter it. We are hardly surprise at that. We know evil around us; some in the very nature of human frailty: illness, suffering, and in the end, death. Some which men, including ourselves, introduce or release into the world by actions that are selfish, hostile, erroneous, lustful, stubborn, and faithless. Some evil we cannot conquer, but only bear valiantly. But there is much we can prevent: that which we are accountable for by our transgressions.

In all, we have the Lord to stand with us. Not only by his example -- as he shows as he repels the devil -- but also with the salutary effect, and his mercy, which he accomplished by his life's mission: humankind's redemption by his death's sacrifice before God. He is only beginning that mission in this scene of the three temptations, just as we are beginning its remembrance and enactment in the Lenten season. A perfect time for resolutions to increase our strength of forbearance of life's difficulties, and to fortify ourselves against temptation's threats. The means is intensified prayers, reflection on the scriptures, -- during these 40 days -- outright acts of love and charity toward our fellows.

The church will be open at times during Lent, where we may come in to pray silently in observance of the penitential season. We have a kneeler for that purpose (over there) which faces the Holy Bible -- in which Christ is present in the Word. The following Lenten prayer is printed on a card placed there. It is from the ancient liturgy of St. Mark, from the 4TH century in Christian Egypt.

We give thee thanks – yes, more than thanks, O lord our God, for all thy goodness at all times and in all places, because you have shielded, rescued, helped and guided us all the days of our lives and brought us to this hour. We pray and beseech thee, merciful God, to grant in thy goodness that we may spend this day, and all the time of our lives, without sin, in fullness of joy, holiness, and reverence of thee. But drive away from us O Lord, all envy, all fear and all temptations. Bestow on us what is good and just. Whatever sin we commit in thought, word or deed, do thou in thy goodness and mercy be pleased to pardon. And lead us not into temptation, but deliver us from evil, through thy grace, mercy, and the love of thine only-begotten Son. Amen.

Thanks be to God.

A Most Unusual Day
(Transfiguration Sunday)

TEXT Matthew 17:1-9

There are a couple reasons for the title of this sermon: A Most Unusual Day -- and not just because that's a catchy phrase . . . it's the title, in fact, of a song: "It's a most unusual day." This day is slightly, 'tho insignificantly, unusual in that Transfiguration Sunday, today, is not celebrated commonly in all Christians churches -- as are scriptural readings in most other weeks of the liturgical year. For Roman Catholics, Transfiguration Sunday is assigned to the 2ND Sunday of Lent.

But more to the point and critically, this day was most unusual in the life of Jesus -- as narrated by the gospel writers. While he had been journeying throughout his home districts -- Galilee and Judea -- preaching in synagogues, attracting and amazing followers with healings and miracles, he had not yet declared his mission or revealed his divine identity even to his closest disciples until this moment . . . and in a spectacular way. It was indeed an unusual day for Peter, James, and John, a day they would never forget. As one analyst of the scriptures writes: "The three disciples are shaken by the enormousness of what they have seen." We'll look into it with two contemporary authors of the Life of Jesus.

In his current best seller (20 weeks on the NYT list), Bill O'Reilly sets the scene. He tells us that Jesus had been traveling from Capharnaum, where earlier he had first recruited his disciples, to Caesarea-Philippi. Writes O'Reilly -- in typical O'Reilly fashion -- "a two day journey on a well-traveled Roman road . . . and they aren't too many miles up the road before Jesus feels refreshed enough to stop and relax in the sun." Then O'Reilly gives us that well-known dialog between Jesus and Peter, in which Jesus asks Peter, "Who do you say that I am?" and Peter answers, "You are the Son of the Living God."

It is shortly after that, that today's scripture begins: "Jesus took Peter, James, and John (his brother) and led them up a high mountain." If that mountain was in Caesarea-Philippi, where they were headed, it would have been Mount Tabor, an elevation of only about 1800 feet -- a

Moses, the commandments of God, but refines the law and virtually outlines a lifestyle for Christian living:

> *Love your enemies.*
> *Turn the other cheek.*
> *Be faithful in marriage.*
> *Do not be unfaithful in your heart.*
> *Do not bring your gift to the altar until you have made peace with the one you are angry with.*
> *Blessed are the merciful.*
> *Blessed are the pure of heart.*
> *Blessed are they who hunger and thirst for justice.*
> *You are the light of the world.*

We know the drill. What that most unusual day, the Transfiguration, lends to the Sermon on the Mount is absolute divine authority. The Jesus who preached the Sermon on the Mount is not a mere idealistic philosopher, whose teaching you can be impressed by, maybe follow if it's convenient. No. This Jesus is God, God the Creator's Son, come to earth to us with a divine message. The Transfiguration established that. The Sermon on the Mount is not mere good advice. As my friend, Fr. John Jay Hughes, puts it: "The Gospel is not good advice; it is good news." It is a way of life that yields closeness to God, holiness, peace and happiness in this life. Have you any doubt of its authenticity? Look up at Jesus in the Transfiguration, shining with power.

Thanks be to God.

Jesus Prayed

TEXT Mark 1: 40-45

Know what this book is? [*hold up concordance*] It's called a "Concordance to the Bible." Ever see one before? It's a great resource for Holy Scripture. Take a word, any word in the English language, look it up in this book and it will tell you every place, every text, where it is found, chapter and verse, in the bible . . . old and new testaments, every book.

Take a good look, because the concordance may be a rare book someday, as it is being replaced by the Internet. Yes, you can look up any biblical text on the Internet, just by entering the word or a phrase. I wanted to document the many times Jesus prayed, because in the scripture read this morning we see Jesus, just after his baptism by John in the Jordan, going off in the desert to pray. It was as if he were going on a short retreat before beginning his public career. He often slipped away to pray. Recall two weeks ago in the scripture we read where Jesus gets up early in the morning and goes out of town to get away from the crush of the crowds to pray. Using the concordance, I found the phrase Jesus "prayed" 13 times in the four gospels. For the word "prayer," 30 times.

Prayer was a part of the Lord's life, and that gives us a good reason to understand what exactly prayer is, and to examine its meaning in the Lord's life and in ours. We say -- everybody says -- "You are in our thoughts and prayers." Usually on a tragic or sad occasion. What does that mean? Do we really say that prayer we have promised? I remember the definition of prayer from the Catechism: "Lifting the mind and heart to God." In the gospels, Jesus, the teacher, taught us to pray. But did mankind always pray -- lift the mind and heart to God -- before the gospels? Yes, of course, the holy people of the Old Testament prayed. The psalms of David are marvelous and complete and beautiful prayers -- prime examples of lifting the mind and heart to God. The Israelites prayed to the true God, because the true God was revealed to them. Other ancient people also prayed; we know that.

It is instinctive for man to recognize his *creatureness*, and to seek out the source of his life, and to lift his mind and heart to acknowledge the creator. Prayer is a common activity of the human race, a practice engrained in humanity, and it always has been.

There is a variety of kinds and categories of prayer. Let's look at some of them. First there is the distinction between Silent Prayer and Vocal Prayer (my terms here are unofficial). Silent prayer may be simply silent, or structured meditation, or advanced contemplation. All of these are forms of silent prayer. *Simply silent* may be conscious or non-conscious praying. That latter is a kind of prayer we'll discuss in a minute, when we meet a couple of holy persons who were adept at praying.

Vocal prayer may be composed or extemporaneous. We hear composed prayers in the Sunday service read out of the liturgical prayer books. Methodist ministers are taught to offer extemporaneous prayers; and they are very good at it on all occasions. And structured meditation may be discursive or affective. We can continue with such forms as liturgical prayer, prayer of petition, or of worship, or of thanksgiving. Prayers for the deceased, prayers for peace, prayers for any occasion or cause. I happened to see a website that offers 3400 prayers "for all your prayer needs."

In our Christian heritage, we have some famous men and women who were especially known for their competency and dedication to prayer. Theresa of Avila, Spain, a woman of the Carmelite religious order, who lived in the 16th century, was an expert on every level of prayer and wrote extensively on the spiritual life. She was named a Doctor of the Church in 1970. She said . . .

- The most potent and acceptable prayer is the prayer . . . that is followed up by action.
- I would never want any prayer that would not make the virtues grow within me.
- Vocal prayer . . . must be accompanied by reflection.
- Mental prayer in my opinion is nothing else than an intimate sharing between friends; it means taking time frequently to be alone with Him whom we know loves us.

And then there is John Wesley, whom we know as the founder of the Methodist societies. He lived through the 18th century, and had a lot to say about prayer in his sermons. He makes the connection between prayer and a favorite theme of his, personal holiness.

- God's command to "pray without ceasing is founded on the necessity we have of his grace to preserve the life of God in the soul, which can no more subsist one moment without it, than the body can without air." And in his words, this is what I referred to above as non-conscious or non-explicit praying.
- "Whether we think of or speak to God, whether we act or suffer for him, all is prayer, when we have no other object than his love, and the desire of pleasing him."
- "All that a Christian does, even in eating and sleeping, is prayer, when it is done in simplicity, according to the order of God."
- "In souls filled with love, the desire to please God is a continual prayer."

John Wesley may have taken this idea from a spiritual mentor of his –- the saintly French pastor Francis DeSales who wrote in one of his sermons: *Prayer which one makes without knowing how one is doing it, and without reflecting on what one is asking for, shows clearly that such a soul is very much occupied with God and that, consequently, this prayer is excellent.*

There is much to absorb here about prayer. It is an enormous topic to consider for Christians. It is, or should become, a part of the fabric of our lives. And that is relatively easy, especially when we consider the examples of the holy persons who have gone before us, and how prayer was the key to their holiness. We have enough opportunities for prayer. The Sunday service is made up of prayers of several types: the vocal prayers we say together in the Call to Worship and in the responses in the psalm. Then we always have a few moments for silent prayer. While the formal Pastoral Payer is led by the minister, our minds can be in a state of silent meditation.

Prayer is what distinguishes us Christians from the world we move in that is being called secular, where prayer is suspect or forgotten or driven out by distractions. Here are my guidelines for adopting a lifestyle imbued with and informed by prayer: The five Cs.

- Prayer that is Consistent with the message of Jesus in the gospel. The Lord taught us how to pray: "the Lord's Prayer." His prayer is made up of all the important elements of prayer: worship, thanksgiving, petition for forgiveness, sorrow for transgressions, and the plea for the grace to avoid sin.

- Prayer that is Constant. As Paul writes to the Christians of Thessalonia: "Pray without ceasing; in everything give thanks; for this is God's will for you in Christ Jesus."
- Pray Continually. As John Wesley points out, dedicate your whole day, whatever you do, as a prayer, and it will accrue to your holiness before God.
- Pray with Confidence. The Lord's promises to those who prayer are all over the gospels. Here is just one place in John's gospel: Jesus is speaking to his disciples near the end of this life: "I tell you for certain that the Father will give you whatever you ask for in my name. You have not asked for anything in this way before, but now you must ask in my name. Then it will be given to you . . ." And I note this part in particular . . . "so that you will be completely happy." In Mark's version, it is put quite simply: "Everything you ask for in prayer will be yours, if you only have faith."
- And finally, be Comfortable in prayer. Relax. Be proud of being a person of prayer. You can show it once in a while. It distinguishes you from many in our current culture. But that's OK.

Thanks be to God.

'No More Mr. Nice Guy'

TEXT John 2: 13-22

I hope that title is not too disrespectful. It's intended to get your attention, and the fact of it -- if not the tone and colloquialism of it -- is supported by the scripture from John that was just read. What struck you from that passage? Here's the line, the verse, that struck me . . . right upside my head. *He also poured out the coins of the money changers and overturned their tables.* Have you ever turned over a table like that? You'll see it in the movies once in a while. It's violent. A crash. What was it Jesus had in mind, to do something like that? Whatever happened to "meek and humble of heart"? Where is the Jesus who would say "bring the little children to me"? The Church Fathers, who studied the gospels assiduously, had to explain it.

John Chrysostom, the 4TH century preacher extraordinaire of the Greek language, says that Jesus took this opportunity to show the religious leaders, who were standing there and who were always looking to trap him in some appearance of disrespect of the temple or blasphemy against God . . . to show them that he was a good rabbi and who would defend the sacredness of the temple. That's Chrysostom's thought.

Another commentator of that period, Bishop Theodore of Antioch, was of the opinion that by his violent reaction to the money changers and the sellers, Jesus wanted to abolish the market then and there. This idea is related to some modern interpretations that see Jesus as a radical reformer, a zealot, a political revolutionary belonging to a movement that was active at that time in Israel, and through which Jesus becomes the model for social revolutionary movements of our world today. These are serious interpretations.

Venerable Bede, the British monk and saint, of the 8TH century, who left us the *History of the Church in England,* warns that if the Lord comes down so forcefully on the evils he sees in the temple, should we not "dread with well-deserved fear lest he come unexpectedly and find something evil in us, and as a result of which we could rightly be scourged and cast out of the church." That's another way of looking at it. There is such a thing as fear of God.

But we can look at the Lord's actions, as Joseph Ratzinger does in his current book *Jesus of Nazareth,* in a more positive light. But first let's open up the scene with the aid of Giuseppe Ricciotti's *Life of Christ.*

> When he reached the temple, he saw spreading before him the usual scene that took place there especially during the great feasts. The outer court of the temple had become a stable fouled and reeking with dung, and it echoed and re-echoed with the bellowing of oxen, the bleat of sheep, the cooing of doves, and above all the noisy cries and shouts of the traders and money-changers installed everywhere within its porticoes. In that court, it was possible to hear only dimly the feeble echo of the hymns rising within the inner temple, to glimpse only faintly the pale glow of the distant holy lamps. There were no visible signs of religion in that vast enclosure, which was more like a cattle market or a convention of swindlers than an antechamber of the house where dwelt the spiritual God of Israel.

It's a scene that would rattle anyone's nerves, and according to the accounts of all four evangelists, Jesus "lost it." Apparently, his outburst did not get any movement from temple security. The commentators believe that the authorities were respectful of Jesus. He had gained a reputation among the people who thronged there. Only a few days later (according to one chronology) he would be hailed by a mob of admirers, as he entered the city again on the day we now call Palm Sunday. They gave him wide birth.

Theologian and commentator Joseph Ratzinger (aka Pope Benedict XVI) in his book -- currently an Amazon bestseller -- *Jesus of Nazareth,* gives context to the temple incident. He notes that Jesus continues on teaching the audience surrounding him and quoting from the prophets. This is not the first time Jesus, a rabbi, a teacher, taught the people from the scriptures. Here he made the point (emphatically) that the worship of God as commanded of the Jews, the Israelites, indeed of all mankind, is to be pure and focused and not mixed with commerce.

Jesus also shows who he is when he references God the Father: *Don't make my father's house a marketplace.* And this message has a universal reach, drawn from the passage from Isaiah that Jesus quotes. *Is it not written* (Isaiah 56:7), *"My house shall be called a house of prayer for all nations"?* Then, according to evangelist John's account -- which is always intent upon showing the Lord's divine redemptive mission -- Jesus makes a prediction, in somewhat mysterious terms, of his death and resurrection from the dead, after the authorities asked him to explain by what authority he should take such spectacular action. And the whole scene ends up with these verses. *He was speaking of the temple of his body. After he was raised from the dead, his disciples remembered that he had said this; and they believed the scripture and the word that Jesus had spoken.*

So the incident of "cleansing the temple" becomes not only a lesson in reverence for God's house of worship, but also a lesson in understanding Christ's redemptive mission.

We've heard all the experts, and still I am not satisfied with their explanation of the Lord's outburst. I have to go with my own exegesis, my own interpretation of the scripture here. I will not say Jesus had a temper, but I will say that he was stern, uncompromising, principled. This is the kind of steel in his bones that enabled him to go through with his Father's redemptive plan and face death. It's not a bad characteristic in his make-up for us to imitate. It amounts to strength in a faith that just might pound the table once in a while if necessary.

Through these sermons of the past few months, we have been attempting to get a reading of the person of Jesus, to better understand him, to draw from his life a model for our own lifestyle, and develop a path to personal holiness in imitation of him, our Lord. But we cannot do it in quite the same way we might of the biography of any other great person . . . say the life of St. Francis, or even of George Washington. His life is different.

"We shall never be able to ascertain a genuine evolution of character in the life of Jesus," writes Romano Guardini in his book *The Lord*. ". . . for he came to us out of the fullness of time, contained in the mystery of God. It is equally impossible to motivate the unwinding of his destiny or the manner in which he accomplished his designated mission; for their ultimate explanations are to be found only in that impenetrable territory which he called 'my Father's will.'"

In simpler phrases . . . in order to understand our Lord and Savior, to imitate him and draw close to him, we need only encounter him in prayer and study, activities that we do here today, and that we can continue privately with a commitment throughout our lives.

Thanks be to God.

Jesus Heals the Man Born Blind: A Gospel Reality Show

The title of this sermon came to me when I read the passage from John 9, and was struck by the spontaneity of the narrative. As it goes along, you don't know what to expect next. Jesus reaches down and makes mud from the dirt on the ground, rubs the mud on the man's eyes. Was the crowd that had gathered surprised by that? It was curious, indeed, according to the evangelist John who reported it. There are two other accounts in the Gospels of the Lord healing a blind man. In one of the others he also takes mud from the ground.

St Ambrose, the great 4TH century bishop of Milan, comments in a sermon that The "[only] reason for his mixing clay with the saliva and smearing it on the eyes of the blind man was to remind you that he who restored the man to health by anointing his eyes with clay is the very one who fashioned the first man out of clay, and that this clay that is our flesh can receive the light of eternal life through the sacrament of baptism."

The crowd of on-lookers can't believe it? "Could this be that blind man we knew?" "Yes, it is me." And then, in an excited way -- after all, he can see for the first time -- the man explains how it happened. Later he has to explain it again to the Pharisees, the religious establishment of the day; and he goes over the whole story one more time, in a tone convinced of the divine power of Jesus who had healed him, but then rather naively oblivious to the fact that the Pharisees were suspicious of Jesus and are trying to build a case against him. "Do you want to be his followers too?" he asks. At this, the Pharisees would have been ready to pull out their hair. The on-lookers would have laughed out loud. It was the kind of scene you can't make up? No one could have scripted it. And the narrator, evangelist John, tells it just as he witnessed it. That's why I call it a "gospel reality show." The characters are not actors; this is no set up; and they could hardly have known what was going to happen next. Everyone seemed to be stunned as each action of the incident unfolded.

There is more in this story than the miracle. It is an incident in the Gospel/Good News that reveals to us in a concrete way God's healing power through Jesus. The bible scholars count 30 or more miracles performed by Jesus, and the evangelist John writes, that Jesus *did many other things [wonders] as well. If every one of them were written down, I doubt that even the whole world would have room for the books that would be written.* That's the very last sentence of St. John's gospel.

While we are drawn to the drama of this scene and to all the miracles of the Lord's life, we have to consider that there meaning is deeper than the mere physical wonders of them. Their deep theological impact is this: God heals his people. The Lord redeems.

And then, there is so much more of substance presented by evangelist John in this rather lengthy passage. The question of evil in the world comes up. Jesus' disciples asked him a philosophical question: did sin cause this man's infirmity? Not at all. Our world still struggles with this question. How could a good and loving God permit the evil and pain and sadness that we see in our world? Is it connected to man's sinful behavior? The Lord explains:

> *Neither this man nor his parents sinned; he was born blind so that God's works might be revealed in him. We must work the works of him who sent me while it is day; night is coming when no one can work. As long as I am in the world, I am the light of the world.*

Evangelist John is always stressing in his Gospel narrative the mission of Jesus, why he has come into the world; that is, to redeem it, the mystery of our redemption: "That God's works might be revealed in him." Man's redemption, man's need for redemption is a mystery to our world . . . in a couple of ways. (1) Objectively. Through the incarnation, God's Son born as a man, visiting mankind, entering history and making the sacrifice to God that accomplishes our redemption from sin. A mystery indeed as we've been taught it, the very underpinning of our faith. (2) Subjectively. The mystery of our need for redemption: We instinctively know that something is wrong. The human condition is fraught with imperfection, with infirmities, weakness physical and spiritual, and we don't know what to do about it. The blind man in this story is evidence. The human body/human life can be flawed. The troubles and sadness we face in our lives are further evidence. Redemption. Anything. We need help. And that help comes to us in the second half of John's narrative today.

Did you happen to notice that Jesus came after the man he had healed when he learned that the Pharisees had given him a hard time, even insulted him and cursed him. "You were born entirely in sin." As if to say, "You are worthless." How wrong were they! For we know that physical flaws, physical frailty, is not the product of an individual's sin. Jesus had already/just explained that to his disciples. And then comes the encounter that every man experiences in his life. Jesus says to the man he has healed: *'Do you believe in the Son of Man?' He answered, 'And who is he, sir? Tell me, so that I may believe in him.' Jesus said to him, 'You have seen him, and the one speaking with you is he.' He said, 'Lord, I believe.'*

This is a most significant passage in scripture: where Jesus declares himself "The light of the world." *As long as I am in the world, I am the light of the world.* Further on in the story, he tells the Pharisees and the attending crowd, *I came into this world for judgment, so that those who do not see may see.*

Sacred Scripture may be viewed as a literary form in which symbols, light and darkness, are important elements for telling the story. Jesus often made use of images and metaphors -- what poetry is made of. The image of Jesus as the Lamb of God is a metaphor that is essential in the Gospel's message of man's salvation. Equally essential is the image of light. As the "light of the world," the Lord's presence in our lives, through his grace, makes it possible for us to see; that, is to believe. It is our faith. Each of us is blind from birth, so to speak, until that moment when the light of God's grace opens our eyes. Then, as with light, we are drawn closer and closer to the source; it fills us up, and the whole world of God's mercy and power and love is illuminated before us. Let us pray this morning for ourselves, and for all of the world who are in need of light and faith, and who are -- in the words of the hymn we are about to sing -- "longing for light . . . longing for truth."

> *Christ be our light;*
> *Shine in our hearts,*
> *Shine through the darkness,*
> *... Shine in your church gathered today.*

Thanks be to God.

Unity Through Diversity

*Sermon delivered at the annual ecumenical service
of the Greenport Ecumenical Ministry, January 2016.*

TEXT First Corinthians 11: v19

This Sermon – or homily, or reflection – is going to be about you . . . us. We're called "ecumenical," the Ecumenical Ministry. Ecumenical, meaning (from a Greek word) the whole world or all-inclusive. Yes, we're all inclusive. We represent nine different (our president's term) "faith traditions." We might also be seen as fractured, or -- a more benign word -- diverse. My text is from First Corinthians 11: v19 . . . and thereabouts: Paul writes:

> *I hear that when you all come together as a community, there are separate factions among you; and I half believe it – since there must no doubt be separate groups among you, to distinguish those who are to be trusted.* - Jerusalem Bible

In the King James version:

> *Now in this that I declare unto you I praise you not, that ye come together not for the better, but for the worse. For first of all, when ye come together in the church, I hear that there be divisions among you; and I partly believe it. For there must be also heresies among you, that they which are approved may be made manifest among you.*

If you know Corinthians, you know that Paul found some problems with that church, after he left it on its own and went back to Ephesus where he composed this letter. You may also know that these letters to Corinth contain some of his finest writings and counsels; and some classic and memorable phrases: *all things to all men (9:22), without love, I am nothing (13:2), We see now through a glass darkly (13:12).* And some of his most important theological statements. Examples: His counsel on marriage in Chapter 7. *Yes, it is a good thing for a man not to touch a woman; but since sex is always a danger, let each man have his own wife and each woman her own husband . . .* and on and on. Then there is this marvelous passage in Chapter 12.

There is a variety of gifts, but always the same Spirit. There are all sorts of service to be done, but always to the same Lord; working in all sorts of different ways in different people, it is the same God who is working in all of them.

We'll come back to this passage later in the sermon to make the point. What has given theologians and commentators trouble -- and there have been hundreds of them, past and present, ancient and modern -- is that verse 19 and the line: *For there must be also heresies among you. Must* is the difficult word for the theologian interpreters. Does it mean that it is inevitable that there be heresies? That would be a cynical statement for divine revelation?

If you're more curious and care to do the research (on the Internet, of course) you will find long lists of sermons precisely on this text: *There must be divisions.* Some preachers point out that, no, the word *heresy* is too strong. Others say Paul was using irony: *Why of course there are divisions: there must be heresies among you.* There is a small consensus which interprets the problematic line as a way by which the Corinthians could distinguish the righteous in their midst, from the non-righteous -- the sheep from the goats, so to speak. That consensus would include John Wesley and Ronald Knox.

Another hierarch gives us this description of ecumenism: "the sharing of gifts." That would be Paul 6TH in his encyclical on *Our Church,* 1963, the end of the Vatican Council. He wrote: "[Ecumenical] dialogue is not simply an exchange of ideas. In some way, it is always an exchange of gifts." Which brings us right back to St. Paul and Corinthians: *There is a variety of gifts, but always the same Spirit.* "In this reality," continues Fr. Ratzinger, "we receive from each other not just new insights into the gospel, but even ways of perceiving ourselves and how we stand within the apostolic tradition. The exchange of gifts becomes not only an exchange of insights on the gospel, but also insights on the way of Christian living and remaining faithful to the gospel -- insights that have developed in the intervening years and that each of us have learned though our respective faith tradition."

†With Unitarians and Universalists, we continue the quest for communion with God.
†With the Presbyterians, we are always faithful to God's

Covenants.

†We gather with Congregationalists, with whom we share our indigenous American faith.

†As Methodists, we are attentive to the Word of God, and we pass it on.

†With Episcopalians, we celebrate the beauty of prayer and worship.

†With Catholics, we bask in the purity of the True Faith.

†As Baptists we are led with the power of grace.

†Through the Jews, we have learned
to know and worship the One True God.

†And with the Lutherans, we are taught to study and love the Scriptures.

Now that we are comfortable in our diversity, is this the end of the ecumenical movement as we know it? Not at all. Although *unity through diversity* may be an acknowledgement that Christian unity is not going to be the product of negotiations by hierarchs, theological and historical experts; nor will it result from a pure grassroots movement standing alone . . . yet we can never lose sight of that unity the Lord prayed for passionately in his last discourse to his apostles. We must live our lives always conscious that a goal has been set by the words that he uttered five times in his prayer: *that all may be one.*

With that goal out ahead of us, we're called upon to pursue personal holiness within the framework of the religious experiences we are familiar with. Unity can grow only if particular diverse communities live out their faith with ultimate unity as their goal. No one can predict when this convergence will end in unity. Unity will occur when the separated communities are passionately seeking the truth together, with the firm intention of imposing nothing on the other party that does not come from the Lord, and of losing nothing entrusted to us by Him. In this way, our lives advance toward each other, because they are directed toward Christ.

We are expected to reach out for a level of holiness that Jesus commanded when he summed up the prescriptions of his Sermon on the Mount: *Be perfect, therefore, as your Father in heaven is perfect* (Mt. 5: 48). No one took that more seriously than John Wesley, the holy founder of the Methodist societies. In his sermons, Wesley explained that Christian perfection is achievable in this present life in this way:

"... because it has to do with the affections. When, by the grace of God infused into the soul through the Holy Spirit, one's love for God and others is made pure and complete, [then] we cannot help but increase in virtue, finding expression in loving, selfless actions." Faith working outwardly through love was one of Wesley's favorite biblical themes, that he offers as spiritual counsels to us.

Even though our factions are all man's doing and man's fault, there is a dimension to them, the theologian says, that corresponds to a divine arrangement. We can make reparation for them only up to a certain point through penance and conversion; but God himself, the merciful judge, alone decides when things are far enough along that we no longer need this split.

To that I must add a conclusion drawn in the report summary of 50 years of Catholic-Methodist dialogues: the statement that no one, neither Catholics nor Methodists are content with the status quo. Allow me to paraphrase St. Augustine here: *Our hearts are restless until they rest in unity.* In the meantime, we observe Augustine's rule on ecumenism (or was it Lutheran theologian Peter Meiderlin; or was it John Paul the 23RD?): "In essentials unity; in doubtful matters, liberty; in all things, charity."

I recognize that this is Lent, an annual season for intensifying our drive for Christian holiness and perfection by reflecting on the central mysteries of our Faith: the Lord's passion, death, and resurrection from the dead. Let us pray the collect of this Lenten day.

Look kindly, Lord, we pray, on the devotion of your people, that those who by self-denial are restrained in body, may by the fruit of good works be renewed in mind. In Jesus name, we offer this prayer. Amen.

Thanks be to God.

Deals

TEXT John 12: 20-33

Look at the scripture readings today. Old Testament and New. In Jeremiah we read that the Lord will make a "new covenant." This introduces a concept -- covenants -- that we are going to follow through all of today's scriptures. And believe me, a whole theology, with volumes of commentary, has grown up on the study of the bible's covenants. Jeremiah continues:

> *Says the Lord, I will make a new covenant with the house of Israel and the house of Judah; it will not be like the covenant that I made with their ancestors that they broke . . . and I will write [the law] it on their hearts; . . . for I will forgive their iniquity, and remember their sin no more.*

We learn from the Old Testament that the way in which the true God deals with the people to whom he has chosen to reveal his presence is through covenants; that is, contracts or deals, often expressed in promises to be fulfilled on conditions met. A covenant most often involves a gesture, an action that affirms and binds it. In the covenant God made with Noah, the first of the Great Covenants, the seal, the bond, the bible tells us, was a rainbow. In that covenant, the Lord promised never again to destroy mankind -- a significant stage in the interplay between the earliest revelations of the true God of the universe and its primitive denizens.

The covenant God made with Abraham was by far supreme among the Great Covenants. In this, God's promise was to bless Abraham's descendants and make them his special people. For his part, Abraham was to remain faithful to God and serve as a channel of God's blessings. The sign of the bond was, says Genesis 12, that *every male child among you shall be circumcised; and it shall be a sign of the covenant between Me and you.* This covenant formed the chosen people into the nation of Israel, out of which would come the Savior, a declaration made many times over and over in the scriptures that followed.

The three great canticles are excellent examples of that covenant being honored. Here is Zachariah, the father of John the Baptist, praising God in this song: (I edit it slightly.)

Blessed be the Lord God of Israel . . . he has remembered his holy testament, the oath, which he swore to Abraham our father . . . to give knowledge of salvation to his people, unto the remission of their sins . . . to enlighten them that sit in darkness, and in the shadow of death, and to direct our feet into the way of peace.

And at the presentation of Jesus in the temple as a child under the law, the holy man Simeon sings out praising God's covenant: *Lord, I am your servant, and now I can die in peace, because you have kept your promise to me. I have seen with my own eyes what you have done to save your people.* And not to forget the Virgin Mary, mother of Jesus, herself, whose song in Luke 1 acknowledges the Great Covenant: *He helps his servant Israel, and is always merciful to his people. He made this promise to our ancestors, to Abraham and his family forever.*

At this point, with the appearance of Jesus the Christ, we are at a new stage in the progress of covenants, in God's relationship with us. The Abrahamic covenant is about to be consummated, and a new covenant is about to be established, called by the theologians, "the covenant of grace." Channeling God voice, the prophet Jeremiah announces and elaborates it in some detail when he says, *The new covenant will not be like the covenant that I made with their ancestors that they broke . . . and I will write [the law] it on their hearts; . . . for I will forgive their iniquity, and remember their sin no more.*

We reach the term of the great covenant in that scene from John's gospel today, where the Lord realizes his role in fulfilling the promise and assuming the task that was promised. It is a stressful moment. *Now my soul is troubled. And what should I say – 'Father, save me from this hour?' No, it is for this reason that I have come to this hour.* Later, on the very night before he is to die, gathered with his disciples at the Passover ceremonial meal, he is explicit about the new covenant and its redemptive meaning, and he expresses its sign: *This is my blood which seals God's covenant, my blood poured out for many for the forgiveness of sins.*

The role Jesus has in fulfilling the great covenant is described in a theological way in the passage read from Hebrews. He is a priest, a high priest, the leader of the people, appointed to address God. There were priests throughout the history of the Israelites who led them through the years, as they awaited the covenants' fulfillment. These holy men -- and Melchizedek was one of them -- pre-figured Jesus. He would be the great high priest who addressed God directly and finally in obtaining remission of sin -- the consummation of that new covenant. And, as he says among his dying words, *It is finished.* That is, the whole plan, laid out by God and revealed gradually, for the salvation of the world, was done. The Great Covenant has been consummated and a New Covenant is declared by Jesus.

This has been a heavy dose of what they call "covenant theology." Now here is where we fit in. Let us go back in the scripture reading to discern our involvement. The word *covenant* is a derivative of a Hebrew word that means *to cut*. (How curious that we also have that expression *to cut a deal*.) We've said that a covenant is a deal, but it is a very generous deal, in which the Lord tends to be quite forgiving. The covenants God made with his holy people were often disregarded, but the Lord kept coming back to them. It is as if God's covenants always seem to have forgiveness in the fine print. In today's gospel passage, you hear the words of Jesus where he is referring directly to his death albeit with images. It is, nevertheless, an expression of covenant. *When the grain of wheat in the ground dies, it will, in the end, fulfill its promise and yield much fruit.* That is, the Lord's death and resurrection closes the book on the Great Covenant promised to Abraham, and accomplishes the redemption of mankind, the forgiveness of sin that we need so badly.

As the Lord Jesus was true to the loving deal God made for us, the "covenant of grace," I see little covenants required of his followers. As we sometimes say, "here's the deal": *Those who love their life lose it, and those who hate their life in this world will keep it for eternal life. Whoever serves me must follow me, and where I am, there will my servant be also. Whoever serves me, the Father will honor.* That's a promise. That's a deal.

It is not so difficult to interpret this lesson: To love your life in the way it is to be understood here, as a contract, means an inordinate self-love . . . the kind of self-love that gets you in trouble and leaves you impervious to everyone else, unavailable for any true charity. But to hate one's life, in the way it is to be interpreted here, means to deny yourself, to have moral discipline and adhere to God's commandments . . . which, says Jeremiah, God has written in our hearts.

Here now is the payoff. In the letter written to the Hebrews there is the line: *God is not unfair. He will not forget the work you did or the love you showed for him in the help you gave and are still giving to your fellow Christians.* And in another place, (Ex 19: 4), Covenant faithfulness is the condition and means of receiving covenant benefits, and there is nothing arbitrary in that; for the blessings flow from the relationship . . .. *As I carried you on eagles' wings and brought you to myself, now if you obey me fully and keep my covenant, you will be my treasured possession.* We are ready to do the deal.

Thanks be to God.

Existential Jesus

TEXT John 12:1-8

I wasn't sure how I should title this sermon: *Existential Jesus*, as I've written for the bulletin or *The Dinner Party* . . . because that's what is actually happening in this very brief passage from John's gospel. And although the narrative is brief, it contains all the features of a lovely dinner party. They are all dear friends: Lazarus, a co-host with his sisters, Martha and Mary, whom we have met in earlier episodes -- a memorable one in which Jesus called Lazarus from the grave where one of the bystanders remarked, "See how he loved him." The 8TH century British Benedictine monk and church historian, Venerable Bede, says that Jesus went to Bethany "so that the raising up of Lazarus might be imprinted more deeply in the memory of all."

A few of his close disciples were with him at the dinner party in Bethany: John, the evangelist, who recorded the event, and Judas also who had a part in it -- 'though an infamous part. And there may have been elements of the crowds who followed him . . . nearby, if not at the dinner table.

Mary's gesture of extreme hospitality is what is most strikingly dramatic in the course of the evening -- the highlight of a sensational scene. John writes, *Mary took a pound of costly perfume made of pure nard, anointed Jesus' feet, and wiped them with her hair. The house was filled with the fragrance of the perfume.* What's the word? -- Sexy. And this scene is included in every bible play or biblical movie that was ever made.

But look at the very last line of the passage . . . or the next to last line: *Leave her alone,* Jesus says with reference to the precious nard: *She bought it so that she might keep it for the day of my burial.* Jesus is conscious of his death. Often, he had predicted to his disciples that he would suffer at the hands of the authorities. This happened more than once when he was approaching Jerusalem.

> (1) He said to them, "The Son of Man is going to be betrayed into the hands of men. They will kill him, and after three days, he

> *will rise." But they did not understand what he meant and were afraid to ask him about it.*
> Mark 9.
>
> *(2)* The third prediction in <u>Matthew 20</u> specifically mentions crucifixion: *Now as Jesus was going up to Jerusalem, he took the twelve disciples aside and said to them, "We are going up to Jerusalem, and the Son of Man will be betrayed to the chief priests and the teachers of the law. They will condemn him to death and will turn him over to the Gentiles to be mocked and flogged and crucified. On the third day, he will be raised to life!"*

But the thought of his death, his mentioning it here, at the dinner party, is different. It is an *existential expression*. It is Jesus aware of and understanding his life in the view of its end. That is the existential attitude. Existential Jesus. Let me explain. The word, multi-syllabic, sounds scientific; it is not really so strange or unfamiliar. They toss it around in the media these days with the meaning of *real* or *immanent*. This or that, say a flood or severe weather, is an "existential threat." That's not exactly correct usage. The term has a more subtle and pervasive meaning than that. It comes from a philosophical movement of the last and prior century, which has had and continues to have significant influence on our society today. Which is why I've chosen it as a topic this morning. It is a concept that is hard to pin down, and can have various relevancies, some quite pessimistic, some that could be positive and useful. Simply put, the existential thinkers insisted that what is real, only, is day-to-day experience in itself and the choices we make. Such experience has no reference to principles or ideas other than what is felt at the moment. Nor do choices one makes have any reference beyond what is perceived here and now, personal advantage. Our immediate feelings are all we have to make sense out of life. Life's meaning, as best it can be discerned, is nothing more than the sum total of all of these experiences and choices, adding up in the end to . . . what? Do'no. Nothing.

Some, in the present age, who feel to be a part of this thought, conclude that life turns out to make no sense at all, to be, in their analysis, (an off-used word) absurd. What life in this view adds up to is *nothing;* particularly when one considers where it leads; namely, to death. The end. For some people that's OK. What can they do about it? Nothing. Nil. Nihil.

In Christian thought, we cannot be satisfied with that answer, life=*nothing*. It makes no sense. It is unreasonable. It insults our intelligence. As Christians, we may likewise examine our day-to-day experiences and the choices we make, and total them up and try to make sense of them. They may at times seem to border on the absurd. And we are aware of our death, as we say our prayers. But we know that our lives do make sense, because they are lived within the framework of divine grace, or in the context of the way of life Jesus taught and exemplified by *his* life. This is our Faith. Sure, he was aware of his death, and he says so at this diner party. He was not unmindful of the meaning of his life. His life's meaning is defined by his mission to provide redemption for the world and assure it of life beyond death.

> *I have come from heaven to do the will of the one who sent me. And it is the will of the Father who sent me that whoever sees the Son and believes in him shall have eternal life and I shall raise him up on the last day."* John 6: 38

Jesus is aware of his mission at that dinner party. He has thoughts of his death, when he refers to his burial in his response to Mary. In a sense, his attitude is that of the model existential man. He knows his life's meaning is to do the will of God his father, and that it leads to his passion and death, and to his burial and resurrection . . . and, as we say in the creed, to his place at the right hand of the Father. That is the glorious outcome . . . and it is there for us too. Adopting a *Christian existential way,* in imitation of Jesus, while it includes the thought of life's temporal condition ("Life's too short," is a popular expression.) it is a way of defining and taking hold of our life's purpose. It is not nihilist gloom, but is positive and bright. Jesus, on the eve of his death, would insist in his final address to his closest disciples: *I have told you this so that my joy may be in you and that your joy may be complete.*

There are advantages in our Faith, and in having a bit of an existential attitude. It makes it easy for us to dismiss many of life's complexities -- the day-to-day world-weariness, the surrounding distractions and troubles -- as truly insignificant and, if you will, meaningless in the context of our life's true meaning and its direction to be with the Lord in his kingdom as he promised. All else, as the philosophers like to say, is absurd. And they are right, aren't they . . .

when you consider a good portion of our experiences in Faith? Mindful of this Faith, let the day-to-day experiences that define us be experiences of our relationship to Jesus through prayer. And let us chose Jesus every conscious moment of our life. Amen.

In my reading in prep for this sermon, I came across this passage in the memoirs of Louis Bouyer, a devout theologian, trained as a Presbyterian minister in Paris, who later as a priest contributed at the Vatican Council. His words are uplifting, and I leave them with you.

> "Indeed, the closer I come to the end, the more I feel that there is meaning to our life; the hand of God guides us, using all things for His purposes: the failures, the disillusionments, as well as, nay rather more than, the successes, the happy times – or those that strike us as such; and which is more surprising even our glaring faults." -- *Louis Bouyer*

Thanks be to God.

Holy Week and Easter

'Words Have Meaning'
The Main Mystery
"Today you will be with me in paradise."
[Sixth Word] "It is finished."
"Father, into your hands I commend my spirit."
Easter Sermon: Love Exposed
Proof Positive
Jesus, We Hardly Knew Ye
Dispelling and Urban Myth
Faith 101
The Man Born Blind
Trinity Sunday or How We Know God

'Words Have Meaning.'

TEXT John 6: 51-59

That title comes from my favorite teacher in the seminary. It was a point he insisted on in epistemology class. *Epistemology,* a high-priced word, refers to that branch of the study of philosophy in which we examine knowledge, and how we get knowledge. Is it possible to know? Some *avant guarde* philosophers would answer that question in the negative. Or, "We're not sure." But my professor taught us emphatically that unless you assume from the start that it is possible to know, there is no sense in having a philosophical inquiry. You have to start with the premise that you *can* know, and that you can learn and acquire knowledge, that words have meaning.
Agreed?
In the passage we read from John this morning, Jesus restates his teaching several times.

> *I am the living bread which has come down from heaven.*
> *Anyone who eats this bread will live forever;*
> *And the bread that I shall give*
> *is my flesh for the life of the world.*

And when they start arguing about what he said, he reiterates:

> *I tell you solemnly, if you do not eat the flesh*
> *of the Son of Man and drink his blood,*
> *you will not have life in you.*

Any questions? What part of this don't you understand?

If some of the bystanders did not understand, the Christian community, our Church, from the beginning, understood. Here is Cyril of Alexandria, a Father of the Church, a bishop, writing commentary in the 5TH century: "Failing to understand his words spiritually, they were offended and drew back . . . [their thinking confined to the old covenant.] In the New Covenant there are the bread of heaven and the cup of salvation which sanctify body and soul . . . . Do not think of them as mere bread and wine. In accordance with the Lord's declaration, they are body and blood. And if our senses suggest otherwise, then let faith confirm you. Do not judge the issue on the basis of taste; but on the basis of faith, to be assured beyond all doubt that you have been allowed to receive the body and blood of Christ."

Jesus did not make this most exciting declaration out of the blue, the evangelist tells us. He had been preparing his disciples and the large crowd of followers all along. He was in the vicinity of Capernaum, where -- as we've read in our scriptures over the past few weeks -- he crossed the lake in a boat, and when the crowds gathered and he saw that they had not eaten, he gave them an abundance of bread and fish, in a miraculous feat. Feeding them in this fashion, set them up for announcing the food from heaven. He even alluded to the feeding of the Israelites in Moses' time, and tells them:

> *It is my Father who gives you the bread from heaven, the true bread; for the bread of God is that which comes down from heaven and gives life to the world. "Sir," they said, "give us that bread always." Jesus answered: "I am the bread of life. He who comes to me will never be hungry."*

In this long and magnificent discourse on the "bread of life," reported by the evangelist, Jesus continues in the most affectionate language, protesting his love for the Father -- the love that binds him to the Father, and the Father to us. And then he says that rich and holy and mysterious metaphor that delivers hope to us: "I am the bread of life." Climaxing it with

> *. . . and the bread that I give you is my flesh . . . Anyone who eats my flesh and drinks my blood has eternal life, and I shall raise him up on the last day. For my flesh is real food and my blood is real drink. He who eats my flesh and drinks my blood lives in me and I live in him.*

I quote this discourse of Jesus at length, because it is so direct, so emphatic. It does not need interpretation. These words have meaning, indisputable, unambiguous meaning. Later, on the night before his death, taking the Passover meal with his disciples, he shows us how he will give us his flesh to eat, his blood to drink. The scene, recognized as the institution of the sacrament of the Eucharist, is reported by the three synoptic evangelists. Here is Luke's version:

> *Then he took some bread, and when he had given thanks, broke it and gave it to them saying, "This is my body which will be given for you; do this as a memorial of me." He did the same with*

the cup after supper, and said, "This cup is the new covenant in my blood which will be poured out for you. Do this in remembrance of me."

The Anglican Benedictine theologian, Gregory Dix, has written a passage about the Eucharist that makes a point we should always have in mind: "Was ever another command so obeyed? For century after century, in every continent and country, among every race on earth, this action has been done in every conceivable human circumstance, for every conceivable human need, from infancy and before it, to extreme old age and after it." And he goes on at length telling us that it is this Eucharist, which is at the heart of Christian living; it is what makes us holy. It is what draws together and binds "the holy common people of God."

Since its institution on that fateful evening, the celebration of Eucharist -- the taking of the Lord's body and blood in the appearance of bread and wine -- has had a most compelling history. St. Paul in his first letter to the community he organized at Corinth, the Corinthians, describes how the Eucharistic service is conducted, almost word for word in the way it is described in the gospels. And he adds an admonition that, "Anyone who eats this bread and drinks the cup of the Lord unworthily will be behaving unworthily towards the body and blood of the Lord."

There were times in the history of the Eucharist in the Church that Christians took to heart deeply these words of Paul, and out of feelings of unworthiness, rarely would partake of the sacrament . . . to the extent that in the 13th century the church authorities (the Fourth Lateran Council) had to make a rule that Christians *must* receive the Eucharist at least once a year at Easter.

During the years of reform, 16th century, Martin Luther thought it appropriate that Christians receive Communion frequently. Other reformers, however, so distorted the practice of the Eucharist that its true essence became confused . . . even lost. Ulrich Zwingli, the Swiss theologian reformer, for example, taught his people that it was only a *symbolic presence.* And many Christian communities today have allowed this interpretation or something close to it. "You may receive the bread and wine as the Lord's body of blood, or however you may wish to understand it," a minister would say.

Our patron, John Wesley, an ordained priest in the Church of England, would have taught his followers Christ's *real presence* in the bread and wine. Charles Wesley wrote dozens of "Eucharistic Hymns," and the Wesleys advocated and practiced frequent reception of Holy Communion. What has happened, however, is that in order to be distinguished from the Catholic Mass, and to place major emphasis in their service on the importance of preaching the Word of God (where Christ is truly present also), full understanding of the meaning of the words of Jesus is not insisted on. [The Mass is *in se* the enactment of the Eucharist (the word means "giving thanks"), that is, the memorial of the Lord's Supper, in which Jesus gives us his body and blood, and at which moment this sacrament was instituted.]

Please bear with this sermon, if you think it is sounding like a lecture. I will now close it with a prayer, because my purpose is to lift our spirits and foster personal holiness by these considerations. Let us pray:

May we find, through God's grace, an understanding of Christ's words in the fullness of their meaning, and develop in our religious practices a consistent reverence for this most holy sacrament -- his body and blood under the appearance of bread and wine. This we ask through the Lord Jesus Himself, who gives Himself to us in the Eucharist each time. Amen.

Thanks be to God.

The Main Mystery
You gotta problem wid dat?

TEXT John 3: 14-21

So much of our faith, with its mysteries, if you put your mind to it, can easily be grasped . . . and embraced. Oh, some people get hung up on the virgin birth of Jesus. A mystery at the point of the Incarnation. But I always say: If God can make a squirrel, a virgin birth should be no problem. Yes, that leads us to creation, in itself a mystery, but a mystery that is easy to grasp. We need only look to the stars and know there are planets and more stars beyond. Or consider biological intricacies, the mysteries of life itself, in all the creatures of the world. Again, easy. We accept these "mysteries" and live with them, because we are a part of them. We ourselves a creation, creatures.

Now turn to Jesus, whose life we know from the gospels. We've -- many of us -- been baptized into our faith, and we've learned to know and love the Lord. No problem. We pray a lot, and we know that we have to pray; and we feel good about it. But now turn to today's gospel. In John 3, Jesus is answering the sincere man, Nicodemus, who asked him about the meaning of being "born again." In his answer Jesus says,

> *And just as Moses lifted up the serpent in the wilderness, so must the Son of Man be lifted up, that whoever believes in him may have eternal life. For God so loved the world that he gave his only Son, so that everyone who believes in him may not perish but may have eternal life.*

In the apostle/evangelist John's report of this incident, we have Jesus alluding to the Old Testament scripture -- a passage that so clearly prefigures and explains in a way the redemptive act of Jesus, his suffering and death. The 7TH century British monk Bede, whose sermons we have, wrote this: "In the raising up of the bronze serpent is prefigured our Redeemer's suffering on the cross." By *prefigured* we are to understand that there is wholeness in sacred scripture's revelation to us; its parts are connected to produce a continuity that helps us understand some of the mystery of Christ's life. Venerable Bede goes on: "The Redeemer of the human race did not merely clothe himself in sinful human flesh, but entered into the likeness of sinful human flesh, in order that by suffering death on the cross, in this likeness, he might free those who believed in him from all sin and even from death itself."

We're heading toward the heart of the mystery of Redemption, but we're not there yet. We have to ask this question: Why did Jesus have to suffer and die, to redeem us (that is, buy us back) from sin. This, I say, the *why*, is the "Main Mystery" of the title of our sermon today. The mystery of Redemption, expressed in that question. Why? Could there not have been an easier way -- yes, a more humane action, that would have sufficed, appeased, and satisfied? It's hard to imagine one at this late date, but the suffering and death of Jesus -- the grisly fact of it -- is not something easily grasped, even with deep faith.

"Do not let your hearts be troubled," Jesus would often say to his faint-hearted disciples. There is an answer to the question, and it is a reassuring answer. And there are clues to that answer throughout the gospels. There is this line in the passage we just read from John . . . that "God so loved the world that he gave his Son." The operative word is *loved*. And the Lord has said this about love: "There is no greater love than to lay down one's life for one's friends." I think we are getting close to the answer to the question . . . about the mystery of Christ's suffering as the act of Redemption. But first, let's set the scene, get some context, see the backdrop, assess the human situation.

All the scriptures read this morning are about sin. That's a subject we are all familiar with, not only as Paul will point out, personally: "All of us once lived among them in the passions of our flesh, following the desires of flesh and senses, and we were by nature children of wrath, like everyone else." (Eph. 2:3) But also in our human environment -- there is, to say the least, a problem that has its roots in disorder and alienation. Sin. It would not be unrealistic for us, to recognize as the Israelites did who came to Moses, and say: "We have sinned by speaking against the Lord and against you; pray to the Lord to take away the serpents from us." The consistent condition of our humanity is to be in the need of redemption. Something is wrong that needs righting, correction. Something is missing that needs fulfillment. Someone needs to take away from our world the deadly serpents.

The presence of Jesus the Christ, or Messiah, in the world is the relief the world needs. He is the one who said, "I am the good shepherd and the good shepherd lays down his life for his sheep." And Paul in Romans 5 sums it up: "God demonstrates his own love for us in this: while we were still sinners, Christ died for us."

If still we do not understand the answer to the question of the Main Mystery, we need only return to the scene of Jesus on the eve of his death, and hear how he explains it himself to his disciples.

> *I have loved you, just as my Father has loved me. So make sure that I keep on loving you, just as the Father keeps loving me because I have obeyed him. I have told you this to make you as completely happy as I am. Now I tell you to love each other, as I have loved you. The greatest way to show love for friends is to die for them. And you are my friends if you obey me.*

The greatest way to show love for friends is to die for them.
There it is again. Are we beginning to grasp the answer to the question? . . . to grasp the Main Mystery and understand Redemption? The apostles to whom he spoke these words -- according to John, who was there -- understood. They got the point, and they took Jesus up on it. Each and every one of them who was there died, was martyred, gave up his life for their love of Jesus, the faith. We may not need to go to that extreme in fact. But we can imitate Jesus by returning his love: "If you love me, keep my commandments." As you listen to his words and understand them, feel the effect of his love, feel the effect of Redemption -- that comes with peace and love of neighbor; in short, living the Christian life of faith.

In the 3RD epistle the apostle John wrote (He is credited with three epistles/ letters, in addition to the gospel narrative.) . . . he wrote this:

> *My dear friends, we must love each other. Love comes from God, and when we love each other, it shows that we have been given new life. We are now God's children, and we know him. God is love, and anyone who doesn't love others has never known him. God showed*

his love for us when he sent his only Son into the world to give us life. Real love is not our love for God, but God's love for us. God sent his Son to be the sacrifice by which our sins are forgiven . Dear friends, since God loved us this much, we must love each other.

It could be that in Sunday school, or on the first page of the catechism, we remember learning that God is all powerful, omnipotent, all knowing, all-seeing, and so forth. Maybe they didn't teach us what John wrote -- God is love -- because we were too young to understand it. Now we do understand the meaning of love. We know it when we see it in the lives of others, and when we experience love in our own life. Where does that love come from? Like everything, it comes from our Creator. And not only did love come into the world through the creation of the world and mankind, but it was manifest in the person of Christ Jesus, God coming into the world in the form of a man. "Love came down," as Christina Rosetti states it in her Christmas poem. And to go one step further in the expression of love, Jesus demonstrated love in his redemptive suffering and death. "There is no greater love." That's the answer to *why*. And it is our faith -- and our hope, what we are called to, and our goal.

Thanks be to God.

"Today you will be with me in paradise."

Let us pray:
> *Gracious God, bless now the words of my lips and the meditations of our hearts. Breath your Spirit into us and grant that we may hear and in hearing be led in the way you want us to go. Amen.*

TEXT Luke 23: 43

When preachers study the popular devotion of the "Seven Last Words" of the Lord on the cross, they take note of the different audiences to which each phrase is directed. The dying Jesus addresses his Father in heaven (twice). He addressed the apostle John, and his mother Mary in a gentle and solicitous way, and he calls out to the crowd of bystanders when he asks for water. And he addressed the thief hanging with him to his right . . . so the evangelists tell us. There is one difference in the words to the thief. (He's called the *good thief*). It is a dialog going on here. There is an exchange between the two thieves. And then the good thief begs Jesus, and Jesus responds: "Yes, today you will be with me in Paradise."

All the great spiritual writers, the Fathers of the Church, in their sermons and writings have made commentaries rich in spiritual insight on this scene. They interpret it in many ways that give us lessons for our spiritual growth. In the view of Origen, a very early (2ND century) theologian, the good thief is cast in contrast to Adam, who in sinning caused the gates of Paradise to be closed; and here the gates of Paradise are opened again to the good thief . . . who is the first to know the freedom of Christ's redemptive action.

Another Father, Ephrem, a Syrian, writes that "through the mystery of the water and blood flowing from the Lord's side, the robber received the sprinkling that gave him the forgiveness of sins." And Leo the Great, pope of the 5TH century, taught us in a sermon: that (quote) "in a brief moment of time, the guilt of a longstanding wickedness was abolished. In the middle of the harsh torments of a struggling soul fastened to the gallows, the thief passes over to Christ, and the grace of Christ gives a crown to him." (end quote) How unusual the faith of the good thief that he recognizes the majesty of Christ, his power and glory, even at this moment when the Lord is beaten and in the midst of his redemptive passion. And with a burst of God's grace this "good thief" confesses Jesus as his Lord and Savior.

This scene, and how it unfolds in the narrative of the evangelists, has made a deep impression on the Christian consciousness for centuries. Tradition as far back as the 4TH century recorded a name of the good thief, Dismas, and elevated him to the height of sainthood. [I had a friend and classmate by the name of Dismas, although it is not a popular name today. He was given the named in religious life as is the custom. Dismas Hoolihan, God bless you, Dismas, wherever you are.] In the liturgical calendar of the Eastern or Greek churches, the feast of St. Dismas is celebrated on March 25. That would have been last Monday. And there is a prayer to St. Dismas that tells the story:

Glorious Saint Dismas, you alone of all the great Penitent Saints were directly canonized by Christ Himself; you were assured of a place in Heaven with Him "this day," because of the sincere confession of your sins to Him in the tribunal of Calvary . . . you whose face was closer to that of Jesus in His last agony, to offer Him a word of comfort, closer even than that of His Beloved Mother, Mary -- you who knew so well how to pray, teach me the words to say to Him to gain pardon and the grace of perseverance; and you who are so close to Him now in Heaven . . . pray to Him for me that I shall never again desert Him, but that at the close of my life I may hear from Him the words He addressed to you: "This day thou shalt be with Me in Paradise." Amen.

There is plenty here in the story of good thief Dismas to edify us, and ply us with rich graces and a renewed devotion in our pursuit of holiness. Jesus engages in a dialog with the supplicant, the good thief. The Lord is personal and responsive. What's new about that? How many times have we read in the scriptures that Jesus responds to someone who asks him for a favor? The woman at the well: *Sir, give me a drink of that water . . . and I will never have to come to this well again;* the Official whose son is sick: *Sir, please come before my son dies;* the leper on the road in Galilee: *Lord, if you will, you can make me clean.* These were individual and personal appeals. The Lord was not demonstrating his divine power in a public way, but rather his compassion in a personal way. The list goes on. What about Lazarus, of whom his sisters, Martha and Mary, beg the Lord in their distress?

And yet, there is a secular mind that doesn't think of a God that is personal, a God that cares for us in a personal way, and would respond to our needs. (pause) There was another thief in that scene on Golgotha who did not recognize Christ as Savior. "Don't you fear God?" his fellow said.

One of the ancient Church Fathers, Augustine, draws a parallel between this scene and the judgment that Jesus spoke of shortly before his "Palm Sunday" entrance into Jerusalem. Augustine writes: "The one robber was like to those who would be on the left; the other like those who would be on the right, as in that parable when it is said that he will place the goats on his left and the lambs on his right." And Augustine goes on, "He who was being judged was anticipating the final judgment."

Good Christian believers, like us, have no hesitation about where we want to be at that point in time: with Dismas, on the right. But there is no reason we should want to be like Dismas, that is, *in extrimis*, in our final moment. We pray and prepare. For we have the advantage of knowing of the Lord's mercy well in advance of that; and we make it the basis of our peace of mind. It should also be the basis of our love of the Lord. The good thief, Dismas, did not have the graces of knowing Jesus during his lifetime, but he knew enough and had that powerful burst of grace, was favored by God, to find a secure place for himself, knowing life was about to end.

Paradise. This is the only time in the scriptures Jesus mentions, actually names, Paradise. Many many times he spoke of the kingdom of heaven; that was a major theme of his teaching. Recall: "You are blessed, Simon son of John, because my Father in heaven has revealed this to you." Or: "Look at the birds of the air: they neither sow nor reap nor gather into barns, and yet your heavenly Father feeds them."

A contemporary theologian tells us that this too is a mysterious saying, but it shows us one thing for certain: Jesus knew he would enter directly into fellowship with the Father -- that the promise of Paradise was something he could offer *today*. He knew he was leading mankind back to the Paradise from which it had fallen, and into fellowship with God as man's true salvation. So, in the history of Christian devotion, the good thief has become an image of that promise -- an image of the consoling certainty that God's mercy can reach us even in the final moments; that even after an imperfect or misspent life, a plea for his gracious mercy is not made in vain. So let us finish with a reprise of the prayer to Dismas:

Glorious Saint Dismas, you who alone of all the great Penitent Saints were assured of a place in Heaven with Him "this day," teach us the words to say to Him to gain pardon and the grace of perseverance; that we shall never again desert Him, but that at the close of life we may hear from Him those same words: "This day thou shalt be with Me in Paradise." Amen.

Praise to you Lord Jesus Christ, King of endless glory!

Thanks be to God.

[Sixth Word] "It is finished."

Gracious God, bless now the words of my lips and the meditations of our hearts. Breath your Spirit into us and grant that we may hear and in hearing be led in the way you want us to go. Amen.

TEXT John 19: 30

It is finished. *Consumatum est.*

What's finished? Do you know that there are many who do not accept or understand redemption? What is *finished* here, in the words of the Lord, is the work of mankind's redemption. Charles Wesley declares it a hymn:

'Tis finished! the Messiah dies,
cut off for sins, but not his own,
Accomplished is the sacrifice,
the great redeeming work is done.

The work of our redemption had begun centuries earlier when God called Abraham out of the Ur valley and revealed to mankind the true God -- unknown up to this time in man's history, and confused with many concepts, but none that rightly explained creation of man and the world.

What about the scene now, the crucifixion of Jesus? In the eyes of many it is absurd . . . that God would require the sacrificial death of his "beloved son." The "folly of the cross," St. Paul calls it. And the Lord himself has doubts: on the night of his trial he went off by himself and prayed: "Father, do not let this happen to me."

It *is* absurd, the very thought of it. But then, who is to say what is folly and what is not. Is war absurd? Disease that wantonly takes a life away . . . does that make sense? The weakness of men that allows us to drift into every kind of aberration and confusion, when we sin against one another. Something is wrong with our world, and in the quiet hours when we reflect upon life, we know it. We need redemption, whether we profess faith or not. The poets of the bible, the psalmists, were able to capture our feelings: *Out of the depths, I cry to you O Lord . . . for the Lord is kindness and with him is plenteous redemption; He will redeem Israel from all their iniquities.*

But redemption is not the crucifixion of Christ only. It is the whole of the coming of God into the world in the person of his Son, Jesus. It is the birth of the infant, Jesus, when the angels announce "a savior is born for you; he is Christ, the Lord." It is in the beginning of his public mission at his baptism when the Father's words are heard: "This is my beloved Son." And when John the Baptist says, "This is the Lamb of God, who takes away the sin of the world." Redemption is throughout the life of Jesus, teacher and preacher, who taught us what is the true nature of God; who taught us how to live and how to navigate our way through this somewhat crazy world, and how we can survive to live beyond this life: "I am the light of the world; I am the way and the truth; who believes in me and keeps my commandments, will have life everlasting."

But most of all, he revealed to us that God, our Creator, knows and loves us. In the Lord's parting words to his disciples on the evening before his trial, he spoke of love:

> *Let my teachings be a part of you. When you are faithful disciples of mine, the Father will be honored. I have loved you, just as the father has loved me. If you obey me I will keep loving you, just as my Father loves me because I have obeyed him. I tell you this to make you happy as I am happy. Now I tell you to love each other as I have loved you. The greatest way to show love for friends is to die for them. I have told you everything the Father has told me. God the Father loves you, because you love me and believe in me. And now I am leaving this world to return to the Father.*

And from this point, he went to his death to complete the work of redemption, his mission. It is finished now. We are the beneficiaries . . . if we believe, if we need it, improbable as it is. I don't mind using the word *absurd*. There is plenty of absurdity in our experience here . . . and by this act, his crucifixion, it is neutralized. The mystery of the Lord's redemptive death on the cross is the mystery that makes sense out of all of life's mysteries. It is finished. Done. There is need for no further questions, only faith and devotion, for which the Lord gives us ample grace. And that is why we sing with gusto, "Let us ever glory in the Cross of Christ our salvation and our hope."

Coda

Today happens to be "Earth Day," the time we are reminded to look out for our environment. I've heard of some theologians who are working on a theology of the environment -- after all, the earth is the object of God's creation . . . like us. But environmental theology does not appeal to me. We might, however, tie the idea in with our message in this way: Our earth is not perfect, but flawed, and very much out of control at times. I need not mention the earth's terrible record of what we call "natural disasters." Is this not analogous to our human situation? . . . flawed and in dire need of correction, of redemption. That's about as far as I'll go with Earth Day -- except that at times we might reflect on the beauty of the earth. On Sunday morning, some of you may go to the beach front to watch the sun rising from the east, our neighboring ocean's spectacular daily display. It is a metaphor for the Risen Lord, whom the Father rewarded for his work, and who sealed our redemption and our passage to the promised life, which he accomplished on the cross. It is truly finished. And we rejoice with our Easter alleluias to share it.

Lest you ever forget you are a redeemed and holy people, here is a prayer, ancient in its origin, which St. Francis favored and left to us in his last testament.

Adoramus te.
We adore you, most holy Lord Jesus Christ, here and in all the churches in the whole world, and we bless you; because by your Holy Cross you have redeemed the world. Amen.

Thanks be to God.

"Father, into your hands I commend my spirit."

TEXT Luke 23:46

In this final prayer, Jesus quotes psalm 31. It should not be surprising that the words of scripture were on his lips at this fateful moment. *You have redeemed me, O Lord, faithful God,* is the rest of that verse of the psalm of David. It is likely that he had prayed this psalm many times before. Think of the number of times we have read in the gospels that Jesus went off by himself to pray, the many times he quoted the sacred scriptures. He was a man of prayer. In his ministry, he was a teacher of the sacred books. He taught his followers how to pray. And at this moment, near death, he could call upon his prayer resources to express his feelings, and draw near to God his Father. I am going to say that these last words are a prayer of *affection,* an expression of deep love for the Father, and a sigh of comfort, knowing he will soon be in his Father's arms.

In the "Last Words" meditations we consider today, three are addressed directly to the Father by Jesus. Others are spoken to John, to the thief, to bystanders, and one in a general way. If we go back and read through the gospel life of Jesus, we will see how his affection and reverence for his Father is frequently expressed, and how it builds in intensity to the emotional pitch we witness in the garden of Gethsemane.

When he first started out in his ministry, when he met his cousin John (Baptist) who was his pre-curser, who in a sense introduced him, the Father entered the scene with an expression of love for Jesus. *This is my beloved son. I am proud of him.* Shortly after that, when the crowds approached John and asked about his background, he said, *I am not the Christ, the Messiah, I am the one who has been sent before him.* And John continues in a long answer, describing Jesus: he says, *He whom God sent speaks God's own words. God gives him the Spirit without reserve. The Father loves the Son and has entrusted everything to him.* "The Father loves the Son." This relationship becomes most evident as the scriptures continue.

There would be a second time when the Father's voice is heard. Jesus took Peter and James with him to a height on Mount Horeb in Galilee, and his mysterious divine nature was revealed in a dazzling light with those same words: *This is my beloved Son, in whom I delight.* John Wesley comments: "We have here a glorious manifestation of the ever-blessed Trinity: the Father speaking from heaven, the Son spoken to, the Holy Ghost descending upon him. *In whom I delight . . .* What an encomium is this! To the pleasure, the delight of God, this is praise indeed; this is true glory; this is the highest, the brightest light that virtue can appear in."

And there was an occasion later on with Jesus and his disciples when he comments on the Father's way of revealing things. *At that time Jesus said, 'I praise You, Father, Lord of heaven and earth, that you have hidden these things from the wise and powerful and have revealed them to the little ones.*

Once in Jerusalem he explained his mission to his followers in these words: *These works I do I do in my Father's name . . . I and the Father are one . . . the Father is in me and I am in the Father.* That is intimacy, a divine bond, the *mystery* surely. This latter statement aroused opposition among his listeners, and he barely escaped before they would have stoned him.

While we concentrate on the close bond between Jesus and the Father, we ought not lose sight of our participation in this love.

John 17:24. *Father, I want those you have given me to be with me where I am, so that they may always see the glory you have given me, because you loved me before the creation of the world. Father I have known you, and these have known that you sent me. I have made your name known to them, and will continue to make it known, so that the love with which you loved me may be in them and so that I may be in them.*

This is where love comes from -- to us and to the world, from God, from Jesus, from the gospel. Love comes down into the world through the passion of the Son and Savior. You really have to read the Prayer of Jesus in the 17TH chapter of St. John, and you will know of the depth of feeling in this love. And while you are at it, go to evangelist John's first letter, where he writes, God *is love, and showed his love for us by sending his Son into the world, so that we might have life through him.* The expression of love between Jesus and the Father is the model of love for us to absorb and emulate. As John's letter continues, *Dear friends, if God so loved us, then we should love one another.*

Should you have reservations about the nature of this love . . . that it is ethereal, abstract, too divine, not laden with the emotion we know of love in our experience of human love, then go to Gethsemane where love prostrates itself on the ground and weeps, where you hear the cry *Abba,* Father. Here Jesus' prayer shows both his unique relationship of oneness with his Father, and at once conformity to the will of the Father in self-sacrificing love. Jesus endured his agony so that he could reveal his union with the Father and their profound love for the world: *Father, into your hands I commend my spirit.*

Indeed it is an emotional prayer, springing from the love of Jesus for the Father. On this note, we can close this Lenten season of penitential manners, and be lifted up and be happy with him. Here in his final moments he knows his work is done, and that next he will be in his Father's arms. We should be so blessed. As the prayer of that psalm 31 concludes, [Father,]
Let you face shine upon your servant;
Save me through your steadfast love.

Thanks be to God.

An Easter Sermon: Love Exposed

TEXT Luke 24: 13-35

Every well-traveled gentleman should have a song he can sing and play on his guitar or piano. And every Gospel preacher should have a good Easter sermon in his repertoire. This is mine. My text is from the Emmaus story: In Luke, Chapter 24.

> *Did not our hearts burn within us while He talked with us on the road, and while He opened the Scriptures to us?*

The Emmaus story -- recall it? -- is a treasure of Gospel mystery, and red meat for Scripture scholars and theologians. The incident illustrates for the second time the Eucharistic ritual. As he did the evening before his arrest and execution, Jesus (not recognized yet by the two disciples) takes bread and blesses it and gives it to them, and instantly they realize who it is. The description of the Eucharist here becomes consistent -- from the days of the early church when Paul writes to the Christians at Corinth and instructs them with virtually word for word the evangelists' account of the Last Supper -- consistent through 20 or more centuries, and up to this very day in the Mass or Holy Communion. "Do this in memory of me," Jesus had instructed, and, writes Anglican Benedictine monk Gregory Dix:

> "Was ever a command so obeyed for century after century in every continent, among every race on earth, for kings at their crowning and for criminals going to the scaffold? This action has been performed . . . by an old monk on the 50TH anniversary of his vows, by an exiled bishop in a prison camp in Siberia (now I'm going to skip a little of this famous passage) -- faithfully, unfailing across all parishes of Christendom, the pastors have done this just to make holy the common people of God."

For this, the little village of Emmaus, as Luke says "about seven miles outside of Jerusalem," now vanished, became universally famous.

And then there is Emmaus as evidence of the Lord's resurrection from the dead. It is one of 12 appearances Jesus makes that are recorded by the evangelists. According to a tradition, apocryphal perhaps; that is, based on unreliable sources, the disciples in the story were said to be related to Jesus: his uncle, Cleophas, Joseph's brother, and his son, who would have been the first cousin of Jesus. Should they have been able to recognize Jesus? St. Augustine sounds impatient toward them in a sermon: "O, my dear disciples, you had hoped! So now you no longer hope? Look, Christ is alive. He was at one and the same time seen and concealed. I mean, if he wasn't seen, how could they have heard him questioning them and answered his questions? He was walking with them along the road like a companion and was himself the leader."

And according to Luke, during that peripatetic (a walk) conversation, *He [Jesus] explained everything written about him in the Scriptures, beginning with the Law of Moses and the books of the prophets.* We know that Jesus was well-versed in the scriptures of the bible, as we have read many accounts of him speaking *with authority* in the synagogues, even as a child. Remember? He was, after all, a rabbi. They called him "teacher." Here, his human and natural life on earth completed, he sums up its meaning and purpose one more time. But is it enough? Do we still have questions? The disciples at Emmaus wanted him to stay longer and tell them more. He left them.

Had they been able to recall, Jesus told them many times about what had just occurred -- his death and resurrection. Here is evangelist Matthew's 16TH chapter:

> *From that time on, Jesus began to explain to his disciples that he must go to Jerusalem and suffer many things at the hands of the elders, the chief priests and the teachers of the law, and that he must be killed and on the third day be raised to life.*

He deliberately went to Jerusalem following the prophesies, knowing it was dangerous, and although he agonized over it, he willingly went to his death.

Why? This he did not explain to the disciples at Emmaus. What is the reason mankind's redemption (assuming such a thing was needed . . .

and it was) had to be accomplished by the torture and death of this man, Jesus. Could there not have been another scenario? Philosophers have called the life and death of Jesus absurd. And rightly so.

It has to do with love. "What's love got to do with it, you ask? I think there is an answer to that, and we can find the answer once again if we go back over the Gospel accounts of his life and listen carefully to what he said to his followers -- to his apostles in particular on private and intimate occasions. On a day, after he had explained it in a parable: the good shepherd lays down his life in love for his sheep -- he tells them outright:

> *For this reason the Father loves Me, because I lay down My life so that I may take it again. No one has taken it away from Me, but I lay it down on My own initiative. I have authority to lay it down, and I have authority to take it up again. This commandment I received from My Father.*

There is this relationship here, revealed over and over again in the gospels of the love between Jesus and God the Father. Love comes from God. It is God's nature. Writes Apostle John in an instruction to the early church: *God is love . . . God showed his love for us when he sent his Son into the world to give us life.*

I thought I would have a difficult time trying to express the practical and relevant point of this, and then I found this passage in the first epistle or letter of John that says it all. *Dear friends, since God loved us this much, we must love each other. No one has ever seen God, but if we love each other, God lives in us, and his love is truly in our hearts.*

The great theologians do a riff on passages like this in the bible. St. Bonaventure, in particular, a 13TH century scholar teacher from the University of Paris tries to explain: "The knowledge that Christ died for us does not remain knowledge but necessarily becomes affection, love." "It's over," Jesus said at the moment of his death. It had been the supreme act of love, the only way God's love could be adequately demonstrated to us -- through the sacrifice, Old Testament style -- of the sacrificial lamb: "*Greater love has no one than this: to lay down one's life for one's friends,*" he says of himself to the apostles in his farewell to them on the night before his death.

Why did the savior need to die in this plan of man's redemption? Because there is no greater way to show love than to give one's life. But there is more. As we said above, he was seen at least 12 times after his resurrection from the dead. These were happy encounters. It was over, and now is the time of that complete happiness he had promised them. Love has been exposed. The love that emanates from the very nature of God, our creator, through the Son, and is showered down from the Trinity through the Holy Spirit of God, is *exposed* by an act of sacrifice that resulted in securing life eternal for mankind. Us. That's our celebration of Easter . . . why we say alleluia! Now we understand as the Emmaus pilgrims did. Our eyes are opened. And our hearts can burn within us. And we want more.

Thanks be to God.

Proof Positive
The "Doubting Thomas" Story

TEXT John 20: 19-31

This is a most memorable passage from the gospels, because of the drama, the dialogue, the symmetry. We remember it from childhood, because it is a winning scene. Thomas doubts, then he is set up, and Jesus comes directly to him. Jesus convinces. Proof positive. We like that. It is a scene we have recourse to in our faith all our lives. And we say it often: "I believe . . . on the third day he rose from the dead and ascended into heaven." This whole tenet of faith is called to mind and reinforced in our (and the world's) language where we have the expression, "doubting Thomas."

It should not surprise you that a long, long list of the great Fathers of our Church, the holy men of the early Christian centuries -- Chrysostom, Clement of Alexandria, Ignatius of Antioch, Origin, Pope Gregory the Great, the list goes on -- have taken to commenting on this scripture. Here are a couple of samples of how they saw it.

First, from Ammonius of Alexandria, a Greek philosopher and a Christian who wrote commentary on the gospels, 3RD century. This is from his commentary on John.

Thomas was charged with being a real curiosity seeker, because he thought the resurrection was impossible. Thomas was searching for him [Jesus]. Thomas wanted to see the wounds all around Christ's flesh, as well as his flesh itself, to see if he had risen. It fit God's purpose that Thomas did not believe, so that we all might know through him that the body that had been crucified had been raised.

From Gregory the Great, a pope during the 6TH century, famous for many achievements too numerous to list. A prolific writer, this is from one of his homilies or sermons.

> Why then, when Thomas saw and when he touched, was it said to him, *Because you have seen me you have believed . . .* and the following: *Blessed are those who have not seen and have believed.* Certainly, this saying refers to us, who keep in

our minds One whom we do not see in his body. It refers to us, but only if we follow up our faith with our works. That person truly believes who expresses his faith in his works.

Because this scripture is an anchor of our faith, let us examine the whole scene more thoroughly, in the scriptures and in the traditions of Christian believers. This particular detailed scene is not reported by the other gospel writers, only by John; although in the New Testament books there are mentioned nine such appearances of Jesus after the resurrection. In another one, Luke's, there is the same realism, with Jesus taking and eating broiled fish which is offered to him. Theologians are at pains to explain that these appearances of Jesus are not "ghosts." And although they are patently physical, they are not naturally biological. On all of these occasions, Jesus abruptly "appears": *They were still talking about all of this* [A couple of disciples had reported meeting Jesus on the road to Emmaus.], *when he himself stood among them and said to them, "Peace be with you." In a state of alarm, they thought they were seeing a ghost,* writes evangelist Luke.

Once we have, by our faith, grasped, with Thomas, the fact of the Lord's resurrection, we look to the broader meaning of this phase of the narrative of his life. And we find that meaning in other parts of the passage from John. Over all, the Lord's message to his disciples is that now their work begins. He has finished his mission from the Father, the act of redemption, a sacrifice carried out just as it was outlined and described in detail through the writings of the prophets. The implementation of the that redemption is to be carried out by the disciples. *As the Father has sent me, so I send you.* I don't think they were aware at that point of what their role was to be. It was to be a colossal undertaking that they were to be a part of. Although later [Pentecost] they would be reinforced by the infusion of the powerful graces of the Holy Spirit -- as Jesus had assured them. At the moment, they were still shaken by the events they had witnessed, fearful they might be next . . . the reason why *the doors of the house where the disciples had met were locked.*

He had prepared them, in that endearing farewell discourse the night before his passion and death: *I tell you solemnly, whoever believes in me will perform the same works I do myself, and he will perform even greater works (John 14:11). I commission you to go out and to bear fruit, fruit that will last (15: 16).* And of course, the Great Commission, as recorded in Matthew's gospel.

> *All authority in heaven and on earth has been given to me, Go, therefore, make disciples of all the nations; baptize them in the name of the Father and of the Son and of the Holy Spirit. And teach them to observe all the commandments I gave you. And know that I am with you always; yes, to the end of time.*

Making clear exactly what this mission is and what its purpose is; that is, the redemption, the sparing, the absolution of fallen mankind, he instructs them as shown in this passage in the grace-yielding action of forgiving sins:

> *"As the Father has sent me, so I am sending you." After saying this, he breathed on them and said: "Receive the Holy Spirit, for those whose sins you forgive, they are forgiven; for those whose sins you retain, they are retained."*

Thus, the institution of the Sacrament of Penance or Reconciliation, the assurance of the forgiveness of sins as practiced today in the Catholic Church.

The take-away from this sermon is two-fold. First, let your precious faith be reinforced by the scripture we have reflected on this morning. Think of this scene with Thomas each time you recite the creed (affirmation of faith) on Sunday service, or at any time in your prayers. Second, recognize that there is also another message in that scripture: namely, that we have inherited that same mission to make disciples of all men -- if not by actually undertaking a foreign mission as the apostles did, then at the very least by living an exemplary Christian life. As one of the commentators said: "That person truly believes who expresses his faith in his works." To be recognized as a follower of Christ goes a long way toward conveying the gospel message. Finally, in addition to his giving us the gospel narrative -- the life of Jesus with this scene after the resurrection -- John (we call him the evangelist) has nicely summed it all up in this opening paragraph from his letter; that is, the 1ST Epistle of St. John, which I read:

Something which has existed since the beginning, that we have heard, and we have seen with our own eyes; that we have watched and touched with our hands: the Word, who is life. That life was made visible; we saw it and we are giving our testimony, telling you of the eternal life which was with the Father and has been made visible to us. What we have seen and heard we are telling you so that you may be in union with us, as we are in union with the Father and with his Son Jesus Christ. We are writing this to you to make our own [and may I add] *and your joy complete.*

Thanks be to God.

Jesus, We Hardly Knew Ye

TEXT Luke 24: 36b-48

Read any good books lately? I refer to the books of the holy bible, of course. Or books *about* the bible. This is just a lead question to get me into the topic of today's sermon. First, I confess that I have not read through one book of the bible, the gospel, from beginning to end in a long time. But that's going to change (before I finish writing this sermon). For sermon preparation, I use some books *about* the gospels from the Fathers of the Church. The Fathers of the Church are so named, and are so very important for reasons that will become evident shortly.

They are holy men, most of them declared saints, scholars, preachers and/or bishops who lived in the centuries of the early Christian movement. They are men (all men in the earliest centuries; the women Doctors of the Church come along later) . . . men who are devout followers of Christ, who studied the sacred writings, and who were the leaders and teachers of the Christian church at its beginning. Note that in those centuries there was no printing press. The sacred books were read from hand-copied manuscripts. During these centuries the earliest monasteries were founded, where much of the manuscripts copying was done.

I will mention St. Augustine a few times this morning; he was a scholar, a rhetorician like his idol Cicero, who after he became a Christian at first joined one of these monasteries in North Africa. The Fathers of the Church gave us, in their sermons and writings, commentaries on the scriptures that help us interpret and understand the gospels. And we have many of these writings available to us -- 1500 to 1600 years later -- for study today! I should mention that all of the sermons of Augustine when he was bishop of Hippo in North Africa, and the sermons of John Chrysostom, Archbishop of Constantinople in the 4TH century (that's Istanbul today), are not only available, they are, thanks to our marvelous technology, to be found online! So, by the way, are the sermons of John Wesley, holy father of the Methodists.

In his commentary on the scriptural passage from Luke that was read this morning, Augustine says, the disciples were "flustered with joy; they were rejoicing and doubting at the same time. They were seeing and touching, and scarcely believing. What a tremendous favor grace has done us! We have neither seen nor touched, and we have believed." This is the assurance we Christians today like to hear and have always needed -- that like Augustine we are called upon to be believers of faith.

Bede, who by his reputation was known as Venerable Bede, an English Benedictine Monk living in the 7TH century, famous for his *Church History of the People of England*, was a prolific commentator on the gospels. About the scene recounted in Luke this morning, Bede wrote, "When the Savior appeared to his disciples, he immediately imposed on them the joys of peace. He repeated that same thing that is a part of the celebrated glory of immortality, that he gave as a special pledge of salvation and life when he was about to go to his passion and death." Bede refers here to the Lords last discourse to his disciples. Bede's commentary continues from this point and becomes a clear and direct theology of the divine plan of our salivation, the teaching that we profess today.

Another, Cyril of Alexandria, bishop of Alexandria (Egypt, at the time was a part of the Roman Empire.) in the 5TH century, interpreted the scene in this way: "To produce in them [the disciples] a more firmly settled faith in his resurrection, he asked them for something to eat. They brought a piece of broiled fish, which he took and ate in the presence of them all. He only did this to show them that the one risen from the dead was the same one who ate and drank with them during the whole period of time when he talked with them as a man."

You could get the impression from the way this scene unfolds, and from some of what Jesus said and their reactions, that the disciples were surprised to see the Lord; that is, they had not anticipated what actually happened. Jesus chides them gently. He says: *These are my words that I spoke to you while I was still with you -- that everything written about me in the Law of Moses, the prophets, and the psalms must be fulfilled.* And only a few days ago, on the last evening he was with them he said: *I will go away, and then I will be with you again and your joy will be full.*

Even so, I understand the apostles' confusion. Who, of course, could have expected a man to come alive after death. When you read all the accounts of this scene in the evangelists -- and all of them write about it -- you get the impression that there was chaos, to the point that even the evangelists themselves did not know how to describe it and make it credible. But they did make it credible . . . in the very awkwardness of it. The Lord moves to settle them by asking to share a meal with them. Then he gives them their mission instructions, together with a promise of the Holy Spirit. Luke continues: *He helped them understand the scriptures. He told them:*

> *The scriptures say that the Messiah must suffer, and then three days later he will rise from death. They also say that all people of every nation must be told in my name to turn to God, in order to be forgiven. So beginning in Jerusalem, you must tell everything that has happened. I will send you the one my Father has promised, but you must stay in the city until you are given the power from heaven.*

His disciples were devout Jews but mere yeomen, not scholars. They may have missed the prophesies of their holy books. But you have to wonder how they could have missed the signs Jesus himself gave them while he was with them for 20 or 30 months. At least three times, the Lord predicted his death and its circumstances and the glorious outcome of his rising out of the tomb. Sometimes his words were metaphorical . . . but even so. The first time was while he was preaching in the north early in his mission; he spoke to his disciples privately and said: *The nation's leaders, the chief priests, and the teachers of the Law of Moses will make the Son of Man suffer terribly. He will be rejected and killed; but three days later he will rise to life.* Then Jesus explained clearly what he meant. This was the time Peter took Jesus aside and told him emphatically that he would not let that happen.

Of this scripture, Cyril, in a sermon, ties the Lord's prediction of his suffering with the apostle's mission: "It was the duty of the disciples to proclaim him everywhere. They must also proclaim the cross, the passion, and the death in the flesh. And they must preach the resurrection of the dead, that truly glorious sign . . . by which he utterly abolished death . . . and took away the sin of the world."

Not long after that, also reported by Mark, as Jesus moved south through Galilee, his home region, he again warned *that the Son of Man would be handed over to people who would kill him; but three days later he would rise to life.* And Mark adds, *The disciples did not understand what Jesus meant, and they were afraid to ask him.* John Chrysostom comments that "[the disciples] knew that he was soon to die, for they had continually been told. But just what this death might mean, they did not grasp clearly . . . nor that there would be a speedy recognition of it, from which innumerable blessings would flow. They did not see that there would be a resurrection. This is why they were sad."

The third prediction, in the Gospel of Matthew, specifically mentions crucifixion:

> *Now as Jesus was going up to Jerusalem, he took the twelve disciples aside and said to them, "We are going up to Jerusalem, and the Son of Man will be betrayed to the chief priests and the teachers of the law. They will condemn him to death and will turn him over to the Gentiles to be mocked and flogged and crucified. On the third day he will be raised to life!"*

Of this, an anonymous writer from the period of the Fathers, whose commentary on Matthew, although incomplete, was widely regarded as a valuable resource writes: "Jesus announces to them his future death, so that when that day of suffering arrives, it might not disturb them, since they were aware that these things were about to happen. Nevertheless, when he was arrested, they were all scandalized and they fled."

Where does this leave us? I have let the Fathers of the Church do the commentary on today's gospel reading. There is not much more to add to it. They impress on us, by their study of the gospels, the continuity and authenticity of our faith. They help us understand the amazement of what was happening in the days (of Easter) after the resurrection. They also persuade us not to be in our lives today confused by it — indecisive or scared or unprepared to encounter the Lord. We now have plenty of opportunity of knowing Jesus in study of the gospels and in prayer. At the beginning of this sermon, I said I would read from beginning to end one of the gospels. I did, Mark. And how enlightening it was. I urge you to do the same sometime. There is so much more about the Lord than what we get from the passages read once a week. You too may be happily enlightened and inclined to say prayerfully, "Jesus, we hardly knew ye." Let the risen Lord come into the room. He will assure you with his peace.

Thanks be to God.

Dispelling an Urban Myth

TEXT Luke 24: 36b-48

Or an "old wives' tale" may be a more precise term. The myth I'm talking about is the notion that people say that the Old Testament of the bible is read by Protestants and the New Testament of the bible is for Catholics. Every hear that? Before I begin my dispelling, I want to apologize and say how uncomfortable it is for me to use terms like "Protestant" and distinguish Catholics as a "denomination." Many of you may have heard me say, yea insist, that Jesus Christ established one church. It was fractured a while ago, only 400 years or so, and we're now trying to put it back together. There is no more *protesting* as such, and the only sense that it is *catholic* is, as we say in the creed every Sunday, that it includes everyone -- or is intended to include everyone in the world.

Now back to the myth. It is not true, but patently false. And to the extent that anyone might believe/hold it, they are not only wrong, but they are missing the thrust of God's revelation in the bible -- the whole bible. That is, the Old Testament and New Testament, the story, the narratives, the poetry, the history written in the bible are one whole message of revelation; and they point to one man and his life and the redemption he achieved. This is evident so often whenever Jesus teaches, as he does in today's gospel reading:

> *Then he said to them, "These are my words that I spoke to you while I was still with you -- that everything written about me in the law of Moses, the prophets, and the psalms must be fulfilled." Then he opened their minds to understand the scriptures.*

You see, in this statement, he ties together the Old Testament and the New Testament. Maybe that *urban myth* is only something of our post-Reformation age. The Christians of the first century understood rightly. Writes one scholar/author on the life of Jesus:

> It is important for the whole approach taken by the early Church toward the facts of Jesus' life. What the risen

Lord taught the disciples on the road to Emmaus now becomes the basic method for understanding the figure of Jesus: everything that happened to him is fulfillment of the Scriptures. Only on the basis of the Scriptures, the Old Testament, can he be understood at all. With reference to Jesus' death on the Cross, this means that his death is no coincidence. It belongs in the context of God's ongoing relationship with his people, from which it receives its inner logic and its meaning.

A striking example of this connection between the Old and New Testaments is in St. Peter's famous sermon to the people of Jerusalem recorded in the second chapter of the Acts of the Apostles. We read a part of it this morning. Peter is explaining the meaning of the Lord's death and resurrection and he quotes a psalm of David. "What David said are really the words of Jesus," says Peter and then he goes on to quote the psalm at length:

> *Because of this my heart will be glad,*
> *my words will be joyful, and I will live in hope.*
> *The Lord won't leave me in the grave.*
> *I am his holy one, and he won't let my body decay.*
> *He has shown me the path to life.*

Pick up one of the gospels and begin reading it, and when you come to a passage in which Jesus quotes or refers to the scriptures, go back and look up his reference; you are then making the connection. You will be informing your faith, elevating your spiritual life, gaining a hold on the holiness and the joy promised in that psalm: "The Lord has shown me the path to life and his presence will fill me with joy." (Acts 2:20 etc.) The scripture scholars who study these things report that there are 78 references by Jesus to the Old Testament. (We say the "Old Testament." In the Lord's time, it would be known as "the books of Moses and the prophets.") His references include quotes from 24 books of the bible -- mostly the psalms, Deuteronomy, and Isaiah. "Jesus is the greatest Old Testament scholar of all time" in the opinion of scriptures scholars.

Here are some examples. While preaching a parable to the people in the temple he quotes psalm 118 in reference to himself: "The stone which the builders rejected has become the cornerstone." This is interpreted as meaning that although at first rejected by some of his contemporaries, in God's plan, he, Jesus becomes our redeemer. Paul, writing to the Ephesians, picks up on that same reference and says, interpreting the psalm, that Jesus "is the cornerstone of the edifice of the church." And long before his own death and resurrection, Jesus taught his disciples about life beyond the grave. He referred to a story in Exodus, God speaking to Moses; he said to them concerning the resurrection of the dead, "have you not read what was spoken to you of God saying 'I am the God of Abraham, the God if Isaac, and the God of Jacob. God is not the god of the dead, but of the living." The disciples would come to understand this, seeing the resurrected Lord. He continues to teach his disciples at this moment of today's scripture reading, after his resurrection, just as he had taught them in the past when he had quoted Isaiah: *It is written in the prophets, and all of your children shall all be taught by God. Therefore, everyone who has heard and learned from the Father comes to me.*

Were the apostles ready for the risen Jesus? No, according to Luke's account. Luke writes: *They were startled and terrified and thought that they were seeing a ghost.* As the encounter continued and Jesus went on to convince them, first showing them his wounds, and then taking something to eat, the evangelist says they were thrilled at seeing him; but they remained in a state of wonder until he pointed out that his life, with its passion and its death and resurrection from the grave, had been foretold. If only they had paid attention (!) True, they were fisherman, laymen. Not students of sacred scripture as he was.

He made it a point to instruct them very often.

> *"These are my words that I spoke to you while I was still with you, that everything written about me in the law of Moses, the prophets and the psalms must be fulfilled." Then he opened their minds to understand the scriptures and he said to them, "thus it is written that the Messiah is to suffer and to rise from on the third day, and that repentance and forgiveness of sins is to be proclaimed in his name to all nations beginning from Jerusalem. You are witnesses of these things."*

Over that long period after the death, burial, and resurrection, until the Lord leaves them, leaves the earth -- about 40 days -- the apostles must have gradually begun to realize what it is they had witnessed all these years traveling with Jesus. There must have been for them an *ah-ha* moment. An *ah-ha* moment is when you realize the meaning of an experience you have been having over a period of time, or a deeper meaning of something you've known for a long time but didn't understand. "Ah-ha," you say, "now I understand." We can have these moments in our lives. They may occur during prayer or at church. For the apostles, everything came into focus at Pentecost, with their experiencing the power of the Holy Spirit. They were still confused in that upper room in Jerusalem where they were huddled together. But by the end of the day, the Spirit's enlightenment came in the form of what evangelist Luke in Acts 2 described as "the sound of a mighty wind and tongues of fire." And with enlightenment came wisdom and courage. And every one of them, the apostles, went on to a life of preaching the gospel and sacrifice for the love of God. But that's a story for another time.

May there be *ah-ha* moments in our experience, when we understand the wonder of our redemption . . . how it meets our desperate needs, and becomes the source of our peace and happiness. That's a simple prayer to make this morning. Be confident in the graces in this Easter season. Realize that we have a share in Christ's resurrection. And lift the words from that psalm of David that Peter quotes. "Because of this, my heart will be glad, my words will be joyful, and I will live in hope. The Lord has shown me the path of life, and his presence will fill me with joy." Are you convinced? No more of that nonsense about who reads what testament of the bible.

Thanks be to God.

Faith 101

TEXT John 20: 19-31

I've used the title, "Faith 101," because you need only read that selection from evangelist John 20 and you have, in a short span of bible verses, a compendium of the substance of what all Christians profess. A first semester course in faith. Let's make a list.

(1) Jesus is alive, resurrected from the dead after his passion and crucifixion. To underscore that, I'm going to quote here from Cyril of Alexandria, a bishop in the 4TH century who wrote a two volume treatise on the gospel of John. "By his unexpected entry through closed doors, Christ proved once more that by nature he was God, and also that he was none other than the one who had lived among them. By showing his wounded side and the marks of the nails, he convinced us beyond a doubt that he had raised the temple of his body, the very body that had hung upon the cross. He restored that body which he had worn, destroying death's power over all flesh, for as God he was life itself."

(2) The message of Christ; yes, the message of Christianity is "peace." More from Cyril: "When Christ greeted his holy disciples with the words 'Peace be with you,' by peace he meant himself; for Christ's presence always brings tranquility of soul." *(end quote)* This was the peace St Paul picked up on when he assured the church at Philippi, the Philippians: *The peace of Christ which surpasses all understanding will guard your hearts and your minds.*

(3) Knowledge of Christ is joy. *The disciples rejoiced when they saw the Lord.* Recall the Lord had said to his disciples on that last evening with them: *A little while you will not see me, and then a little while later you will see me . . . and your hearts will be filled with joy that no one can take away from you.* Here now, in the secure room, is that later moment, that "little while later." It is the moment when the legacy of true *joy* becomes the characteristic of his followers, us: *The joy of Christian faith.* Let us never lose it or forget it. It comes with our faith.

As the Father has sent me, so I send you. When he had said this, he breathed on them and said to them, "Receive the Holy Spirit. If you forgive the sins of any, they are forgiven them; if you retain the sins of any, they are retained."

Let us dissect this faith-rich passage:

(4) The Trinity is named. *The Father has sent me;* that is; I am the Son of the Father. And *he breathed on them and said to them Receive the Holy Spirit.* Thus, the Triune God: Father, Son and Holy Spirit. Just as has he had promised on that earlier evening when he was with them. He said: *The Holy Spirit, whom the Father will send in my name, will teach you all things and will remind you of everything I have said to you.*

(5) Next, here is the power to forgive sins: *If you forgive sins they are forgiven.* Just as we confess in the Creed: *[We] believe in the forgiveness of sins . . ..* That is what the Lord's passion, death on the cross, and resurrection from the grave, the action of redemption, was all about -- the forgiveness of sins of an alienated and broken down mankind.

(6) And one more thing, or theme, in that passage: *evangelization: As the Father has sent me, I send you.* The apostles are sent on the mission of preaching the Lord's message and building a community of his followers. We Christians too are always evangelists, even if we do not go on the mission; that is, we are called to spread the gospel by our example, and in our services, and in our generosity toward others in temporal or spiritual need.

There is more: At the end of this passage John writes: *But these [signs] are written so that you may come to believe that Jesus is the Messiah, the Son of God, and that through believing you may have life in his name.* The essence of the Creed we profess is just that: Jesus of Nazareth is the Christ, the Son of God, the Messiah promised throughout the Old Testament histories, to the people chosen to receive him . . . in my favorite phrase, "The desire of the everlasting hills." He is the one.

The final word in our Creed is "life everlasting" and the final word of this scripture passage is *life.* That is our hope and our reason for believing. This gospel, when it was read on Sunday -- what with the drama of the Apostle Thomas and the exchange between him and the Lord -- always makes a great impression on us [on me as a child.] It was so graphic, so palpable, who could not be believe. Forever in our language we have the phrase and the character of "doubting Thomas." Some commentators say there was a strategy in Thomas's demand: He knew he would be preaching Christ and Christ crucified someday, and he wanted to have evidence, something he could convince his hearers with. So he could say, "I was there." For us, the story with its drama is an anchor of our faith.

I have to say a few words about that Creed. The Apostle's Creed we say -- have been saying since we first were in Sunday school, or first picked up a catechism -- or the Nicene Creed. They are virtually, essentially, the same faith. But they were not so easily come by. In fact, it took about four centuries, 400 years after Jesus lived/died, for the formulation of the Creed to be firmly clarified, established, and promulgated. It has the name Nicene Creed, because the language was developed at the Council of Nicea in the year 325. (Nicea was a harbor town, now the modern Iznik of Turkey, about 100 miles SW of Istanbul). There the leadership of the Christian communities, bishops from various regions in Asia Minor and beyond -- including Egypt, Georgia, Armenia, Syria, Greece -- got together (as many as 1000) to deal with some controversies and confused teachings circulating, and hammer out a statement that would be consistent with the gospel revelation. They were not dealing with enemies, but with some of their own bishops who for decades were leading some of the churches in error. *Heresies* we call them now. Was Jesus of Nazareth really God, the Son of God? Equal to the Father? Did Jesus have a physical body and a human will? Can we say "Mary, the Mother of God"? What about the sacrament of penance/forgiveness? Is it valid?

The Council of Nicea was virtually unanimous (900 out of 1000) in affirming the Holy Trinity intact, the central mystery of Christian belief. And we confess its exact words in the Creed today. Not that heresy was wiped out once and for all. There were many skirmishes in later centuries, and they were not mere quiet disagreements. A favorite saint of mine and a giant of Christian history and theology, John Chrysostom, a bishop in Constantinople, a good guy, once found himself in exile, banished because of his defense of orthodoxy, the true gospel. The point being that the faith handed down to us has been tempered as of steel in many battles and heated debates to guarantee and secure the fullness of its truth through the valiant efforts or our Christian forefathers. It calls for our reverence and devotion each time we stand to recite the Creed.

There is final note. In this faith-loaded passage from John, the Lord makes a clear distinction. There are those who have seen and believe, and those who have not seen. Those who by God's plan have seen are the apostles, the women, Mary the mother of Jesus, Mary Magdalene and others, the disciples on the road to Emmaus. And the then there are the others: Us. To whom . . . did you notice? . . . the Lord imparts his special blessing.

Blessed are those who have not seen and yet have come to believe.

The blessing of the Risen Lord! That's something to embrace and cherish and build our Christian faith on.

Thanks be to God.

The Man Born Blind

TEXT John 9: 1-4

"Tell me, so that I may believe in him."

Have you ever seen a man so guileless (my word) as this man, the man born blind, who is a central character in this narrative by evangelist John about Jesus in Jerusalem? I mean, a simple man. And Jesus said at one time "you must become as children to enter the kingdom of heaven (Matt. 18: 1-5). This man is that model. Confronted by some who were skeptical about Jesus he says —- if you will bear with some contemporary idiom -- "Hey, you got a problem with this man? Wadda ya want from me? All I know is that I was blind and now I see." And later, when he meets Jesus again, not realizing in whose presence he is, even though Jesus has just restored his sight, he asks who is the Lord, the Messiah, "Tell me so that I may believe in him."

There are several accounts of Jesus curing blindness, but none match the ironies and theological depth as this account by the apostle/evangelist, John. When John wrote this scene, he filled it with much detail and dialogue. He was there. Remember, this scene began with the disciples asking Jesus why the man was blind. They were there near the temple and a crowd was following Jesus. As an eye witness, John could recount the use of mud rubbing the eyes of the man, the words Jesus spoke, even the statement of the parents of the blind man in their encounter with the leaders in the temple. John would have followed the scene into the temple, where it was played out with considerable drama -- the blind man getting testy with those who kept pressing him about the incident, and him repeating what happened three times: "I have already told you . . . why do you want to hear it again?"

We have a broad choice of how we might make a lesson for ourselves out of the event. The disciples want to know about what we call the *problem of evil* in the world, and Jesus explains that, no, bad things like this do not happen as punishment for sin. It doesn't work that way. There might also be a theme of Christ's mission. He repeats several times that God's works are revealed in him, and that he has come to be the light of the world. "I must do the works of Him who sent me.

As long as I am in the world, I am the light of the world." Jesus "the Light of the world" makes a marvelous theme, and there is so much light symbolism in this narrative; as later in the scene he tells those skeptics that they are blind, they do not see the light, they are in the dark when it comes to receiving the promised Messiah. Light and darkness images, blindness and sight images are throughout.

The writer, John, wrote these words late in his life, when he was an old man, who had many years to reflect on and understand his experience with Jesus. And it was John's intention to present a profile of the Lord that identified him without question as the Son of God, the Messiah, who was sent for the world's redemption. It is more than safe to say that John would have his readers interpret his writings on many levels, as evidence of the divine power in Jesus' presence. I mean such things as blindness and sight, darkness and light, sin and faith.

The purpose of John is also evident in the Lord's miracles, and the way they always seem to have an extra mysterious feature in them. In this case, the mud rubbed on the man's eyes, and his washing in the pool of Siloam. Another time in John, Jesus mysteriously wrote in the sand with his finger on the ground when he was confronted with some hostile members of the leadership, and when he dismissed the troubled woman who was about to be stoned.

There is so much in this episode to choose from for explication and for our spiritual edification. I think the evangelist would approve of my choice: To take a closer look at the blind man's actions and reactions and extract a message from that. In what sense is he a model for Christians, for us who are followers of Jesus? As I suggested, in his simplicity and in his willingness to believe. Once he learns that Jesus is indeed the Messiah, expressed as "the Son of Man," he worships him, the evangelist says. All the man needs are the Lord's word, and he's on board, devout, committed. Of course, it is more than just the Lord's word; it is the very presence of Jesus up close, and the fact too that he has blessed him with a miracle, his sight.

Except for the physical presence of Jesus, is not this our experience too? We have heard the Lord's word; we have felt his blessings; so let us respond without hesitation as the blind man did -- with heart and mind committed to the Lord. It may be that distractions, some necessary and some not so necessary, come between us and our sense of God's presence in our lives. But we could take a lead from the stubbornness and toughness of the man born blind. Brow-beaten by the leaders, he stood up to them; without the support of his family, he faced them; and single minded, his focus was on the Lord. You could say that Jesus, God's grace, gave him that courage, and also the light of faith to recognize his Savior. He was a simple man, he had suffered, but this was his lucky day. It is a beautiful story.

And are there some bad guys in this story? Oh, yes . . . the professional scholars of the scriptures, the Pharisees. Jesus is not gentle with them. They have been harassing him all day, testing him and trying to trap him. He is direct with them (in so many words): You know better. You are not handicapped, not blind as this man. And so for that very reason, you are sinners for your failure to recognize God's presence here in your lives. This is a harsh indictment, one we surely wish to dodge. Instead, we'll go with the blind man: Tell me, Lord, and I will believe. As simple as that.

Thanks be to God.

Trinity Sunday
or How We Know God

TEXT John 16: 12-15

Last year I wrote and delivered a sermon using the title of a book by Thomas Cahill: *Desire of the Everlasting Hills,* a long book-length commentary on the gospels in the New Testament. Anyone remember it? Thomas Cahill is a New York based scholar, an expert in ancient languages, Latin, Greek, Hebrew. I mention him because I want to call your attention to another book of his on the bible, that made an enormous impression on me: opened for me a clear understanding of the Old Testament for the first time, despite my many previous years of study of those scriptures. That book was called *Gifts of the Jews*, an essay-style commentary on the Old Testament. Its thrust is this . . . that the Jews, the Israelites, God's favored tribe, were chosen by the world's Creator to reveal himself: the One True God. Operative word here is ONE. When the ancient peoples of the world grappled with those existential questions of man's origin and the world around them, they came up with a theology of a many gods: a god for every phenomenon of their experience . . . one for the sea, another for the sky, another for the earth, and so forth. The pantheon -- *pan* meaning *all, theo* meaning *god.* It could be cumbersome and confusing, but it served their purpose, although it was not entirely satisfactory.

In contrast, the Jews, holding to their one true God revelation, were unique, special. But their situation was risky, and often over the centuries they had to struggle with their allegiance to God, and at the same time defend themselves against the many polytheistic adherents (pagans) surrounding them. Thus, the occasional alienations, the wars, the captivities we read about in Old Testament history. They did prevail, however, and they alone passed on to civilization the basic knowledge of the one true God -- the *Gifts of the Jews.* This included, through their prophets, their religious leaders, also, the promise of their God paying them a visit to protect and defend them against their enemies.

The New Testament story that Thomas Cahill gives us under the title *Desire of the Everlasting Hills* opens up this revelation to the fuller knowledge of who the one true God is; that is, with the incarnation of that God in the person of Jesus of Nazareth. Now we were to learn more about our God. In the revelation, which is the books of the New Testament we learn that our God is a Trinity: the Father, Son, and the Holy Spirit. It is Jesus who teaches us this. Hundreds of times in the narratives of his life we hear him speak of his Father and of the Spirit, while declaring himself to be "one with the Father." Scripture scholars, some who are actually scripture statisticians, can tell us how many times in the New Testament the Trinity is mentioned. I'm only going to cite a couple. First, at his baptism in Matthew 3:16-17 we read: *Jesus was baptized. And as soon as he came out of the water, the sky opened, and he saw the Spirit of God coming down on him like a dove. Then a voice from heaven said, "This is my own dear Son, and I am pleased with him."* John Wesley, in a sermon, declares emphatically that this is a clear revelation of the Holy Trinity.

Second, in the scripture passage assigned for today's reading, Jesus is delivering his farewell address to the disciples. *All that the Father has is mine.* And *The Spirit will guide you into all the truth.* There is no other way to understand these scriptures except that Jesus is revealing to us the Trinity: Father, Son (himself) and the Holy Spirit. Trinity was not an easy notion to grasp, even for the first community of Christ's followers who were his contemporaries. It took time to process it, understand it, and establish it as a tenet of faith. Some people got it wrong. The priest Arius, in 3RD century North Africa, for example, had a following of Christians who were taught that Jesus is an inferior being. (Arius must have skipped that passage in John 10 where Jesus says, *I and the Father are one.*) The movement (heresy) of Arius lasted even into the fourth century after a Council of 350 bishops had condemned it. The Emperor Constantine, who had made Christianity the official religion of his empire, organized that Council to try to bring about peace and tranquility among his battling citizenry. This was the Council of Nicaea [or Nicaea], a city in the north of today's Turkey, that gives its name to the affirmation of faith they hammered out: The Nicene Creed.

Should we need a hero for this story, one is readily available. He is Athanasius of Alexandria. From a prominent family and well-educated, as a young man, a deacon and an aide to the bishop of Alexandria, he had attended the Council of Nicaea. He subsequently succeeded his mentor and was bishop of Alexandria for 45 years. These were years of turmoil over that persistent Arian heresy, which must have tested him spiritually and physically. As leader of his church, he was a prolific writer and polemicist in defense of the proclamations of the Council. In those years in the Roman empire, the religious and political authorities were intertwined in such a way that if you were not -- to use a modern phrase -- *politically correct,* you could be banished. This happened to Bishop Athanasius four times. He sought refuge in Germany while the erroneous doctrines of the priest Arius had the favor of whichever Roman emperor was in power -- and that power together with Christian orthodoxy swung back and forth over several imperial / political administrations.

We'll come back to Athanasius at the end with a prayer. But here we have to come up with a response to the doctrine of the Trinity. Jesus will help us. He had to answer that question more than once, and his answer was always the same: *You have only one Lord and God. You are to love the Lord your God with all your heart and with all your soul and with all your mind and with all your strength. That's the first commandment.* Then he elaborated: *And the second commandment is this, that you should love others as you love yourself.* Plain and simple, wouldn't you say? As to how this is done, Jesus has said repeatedly: (John 14:15) *If you love me, keep my commandments.* And (John 15: 10) *If you keep my commandments, you will abide in my love, just as I have kept my Father's commandments and abide in his love.* And what is love?

High-capacity super theologians drill down in the theology of the Trinity and will teach us that the very notion, the substance, the idea of love which is in the world's consciousness emanates (not from Hollywood or from romance novels) but from the Trinity. There the bond, the essence of the holy relationship between the three persons, Father, Son, and Holy Spirit, is love. That's what love is and where love comes from. And it is given for us to share. Something deep to think about, and pray about -- as we make sure our love is with all our heart, with all our soul, with all our mind, with all our strength.

As promised, we will close with this prayer, invoking the name of St. Athanasius:

Almighty ever-living God, who raised up the Bishop St. Athanasius as an outstanding champion of your Son's divinity [and the integrity of the Divine Trinity] mercifully grant, that, rejoicing in his teaching and his protection, we may never cease to grow in knowledge and love of you. Through our Lord Jesus Christ, your Son, who lives and reigns with you in the unity of the Holy Spirit, one God, for ever and ever. Amen.

Thanks be to God.

Pentecost and Ordinary Time

A Big Day [Pentecost Sunday]
The Kingdom Option
'Faith Comes through Hearing'
Jesus and His Friends
The Good Samaritan Story
Social Jesus
'It's a Jungle out There.'
Matthew's Mission
Feast Day of Peter and Paul
A One-on-One with Jesus
'A Hard Rain is Gonna' Fall'
Desire of the Everlasting Hills
Getting to Know Peter
490 -- Do the Math.
The Blue Haze: Divine Mercy
Mark's Gospel: Voice of the Lion
The Lord Plays Favorites.
Back to Basics
Philemon
'If I Were a Rich Man'
Jesus as the 'Boss'
Slogans and Mottos
Corragio
Jesus in a Somber Mood

A Big Day
[Pentecost Sunday]

TEXT John: 15:26-27; 16:4b-15

That uninspired sermon title refers to the fact that we celebrate today the Memorial Day holiday, the un-official beginning of summer; and also Pentecost, the official end of the liturgical Easter season. I shall attempt to draw these themes together in my sermon. But first I must add to this complexity the presence this morning of the Southold Town High School Navy Junior ROTC -- that is, Reserve Officers Training Corp. The unit is led by Major Bill Grigonis USMC Retired, and has been present at our Memorial Day service for more than a decade. Welcome once again. And thank you for looking so good.

St Paul in that passage read from Galatians, which happens to be an alternative selection for today's scripture, is quite explicit about the rules of living the Christian life. He is sounding like a drill sergeant: ("This is how we do it in the Navy.") He writes,

> *I warn you brothers and sisters, live by the Spirit and you will certainly not gratify the desire of the flesh.* And then he goes into detail. *The works of the flesh are obvious: immorality, impurity, lust, idolatry, sorcery, hatreds, rivalry, jealousy, out bursts of fury, acts of selfishness, dissentions, factions, occasions of envy, drinking bouts, orgies, and the like. I warn you as I warned you before, those who do such things will not inherit the Kingdom of God.*

The Galatians were not an especially wicked community, that Paul should issue such a stern warning. It was a Christian community that he founded in his travels in that part of Asia Minor, in the vicinity of Antioch today. It included many converts from paganism, as well as some Jewish converts. He wrote this letter to them only a short time later after moving on, having heard rumors that they might be slipping back into their old ways and losing their focus on the true *Way*. And so, he explains with great detail and emphasis.

Following the *Way*, the Christian life, is a not easy. It would have been a new challenge to some of the converts from Galatia. People do slip back into those old vices he names; or they don't pay attention and get into bad habits. In fact, you might suspect that it is humanly impossible to live a life of Christian perfection. But ah! Key word there is "humanly." Here is where God's grace comes into play. To the Galatians, Paul began his letter by saying, *Live by the Spirit.* This is not a vague pep talk. Paul means the Holy Spirit, the Spirit God sends, most spectacularly, at the event known as Pentecost . . . in Greek, "the 50TH day"; that is, after the Lord's Resurrection.

The Apostles were gathered together in hiding, fearful that the same hostile forces that killed Jesus would go after them too. And then the risen Lord appeared. Evangelist Luke describes what happened next: strong winds, a rumble sound, tiny flames appearing above each of the disciples. *Receive the Holy Spirit,* Jesus says. It was as he had promised them dozens of times before:

> *When the advocate comes whom I will send you from the Father, the Spirit of truth that proceeds from the Father, he will testify to me. And you also will testify because you have been with me from the beginning . . . . He will guide you to all truth.*

You may recall that the Apostles were common men, yeomen, not the type likely to be heroes. At a time during the Lords' trial, Mark ran away. Peter didn't even have the guts to say he knew Jesus. So when you hear the outcome of Pentecost, the years that followed, how these disciples of Jesus took up that command he had given -- *Make disciples of all nations,* and *You also are to testify because you have been with me from the beginning* -- and they literally went to the ends of the earth, faced all kinds of danger, preached, organized communities, led churches, and in the end all of them gave up their lives for the cause, for Christ, you must ask: What power came over them on that day that made them capable, more, made them heroic? It is the Holy Spirit, the power of God's loving care for us through grace, God's assistance that makes it possible to keep the rules, to sidestep what Paul had called the works of the flesh.

Even so, I doubt that the apostles, those in that room on that night, although empowered by the Spirit, ever found living for Christ easy. It required courage and discipline; they had to keep in spiritual shape and be stubborn in their faith in order to succeed.

Does this not describe our situation, as we work our way toward the goal of authentic Christian identity? It can be done. As you walk in the cemetery today to place flowers on a grave, or as you reflect in your mind on friends and family who have gone before you, consider the lives of Christians who have succeeded and who now have realized the promise of everlasting life as Jesus promised . . . and demonstrated in his own resurrection from the dead.

There are mysteries here. In that account of what happened at Pentecost, the Trinity and the Resurrection are revealed in a single sentence. *My Father,* says Jesus, *the Son risen* from the dead, *will send you the Holy Spirit.* We affirm them every time when we say our creed together.

It may have all been new and astounding to the Galatians, and maybe they didn't grasp it completely, which is why they were backsliders and had to be bucked up again by Paul. It happens. But Paul could be convincing, and he doesn't leave the Galatians only with a scold. Look at the next part of his letter. *The fruit of the Spirit is love, joy, peace, patience, kindness, generosity, faithfulness, gentleness, self-control.* Who would not trade this list for that other list mentioned above? You can catch the enthusiasm of the Spirit again today. The same Spirit and its fruits are as available to you as they were on Pentecost day, when they empowered Peter and the Apostles.

†

So, how did we do blending Memorial Day and Pentecost into the sermon? Can I hear an "Amen"? Now I want to make some distinctions. Memorial Day is a day of remembering. It began more than 150 years ago, with children from the southern states bringing flowers to the graves of soldiers who fought and died for the Confederacy in the Civil War. After the war, the day was dedicated to honoring soldiers of the Union too; and then in the early 20th century it became a national holiday for remembering all members of the Armed Forces who had given their lives. Today it is our practice to visit and place flowers on the graves of all deceased friends and family. Memorial Day is a stable day of remembrance. But Pentecost is a dynamic day of grace -- not so much for remembering as for celebrating. Its effect and power continues. It is the day the full effects of mankind's divine redemption, through the life and death and resurrection of Jesus Christ, were distributed to all the world for all times. It is the designated point in time at which the Christian era begins. It is the commencement of A.D. *anno domini,* the "year of the lord." It is the point at which God's helping hand, grace, is made available to us . . . to the world.

As it was promised by Jesus, shortly before his death, he told his disciples:

> *If you love me you will do as I command. Then I will ask the Father to send you the Holy Spirit who will help you and always be with you. The Spirit will show you what is true. You will know the Spirit who is with you and will keep on living in you.*

Memorial Day passes, and we will come back to it again next year. Pentecost prevails, and is ever present for us to collect what we need to pursue the Christian life of virtue and integrity and personal holiness. It is up to us to reach for those graces, the powers of God's helping hand, reach out and hold on to it to the end . . . when *we shall* someday be remembered on this day.

Thanks be to God.

The Kingdom Option

TEXT: Matthew 21: 23-32

Which "kingdom" shall you choose?
There's an expression we often use referring to others . . . or to ourselves: "He's in a world of his own." What do we mean by that? -- that someone just doesn't get it, is not tuned in to the reality of the situation at hand? I am using that phrase and notion to try to understand the Lord's teaching about the Kingdom of Heaven. Is it like being "in another world"? What.

It is not to be taken as a mere figure of speech. The Lord made it a part of his teaching, particularly in the parables, over and over again.:

The kingdom of God is like a mustard seed.
The kingdom of God is like a pearl of great price.
In my kingdom there are many mansions.
The kingdom of God is like the king who settled his accounts with his servants. (The gospel we heard last week.)
Unless you become as little children you cannot enter the kingdom of God.

In the sermon on the mount, the very first beatitude is "Blessed are the poor in spirit, for theirs is the kingdom of heaven." Before Jesus began his ministry, John the Baptist preached, "Repent for the kingdom of heaven is at hand." There are also mentions of God's kingdom in many books of the Old Testament. And the kingdoms of Solomon and of David may be interpreted to pre-figure the kingdom Jesus announced so consistently. In today's reading, Jesus names the kingdom in a more indirect way: "Truly I tell you, the tax-collectors and the prostitutes are going into the kingdom of God ahead of you." He was directing this remark to the local religious leaders who simply failed to accept his message. We have to understand this. The commentators on the gospels have grappled with the concept for centuries, trying to understand what Jesus meant. From St. Augustine to Pope Benedict and in between, even the protestant theologian Calvin. At one end of the spectrum of interpretations is the sense that the kingdom of God is only in your mind, very subjective. At the other end is the idea that the kingdom of God will be at the conclusion of this world.

Here is how one interpreter writes that I think comes close to what I wish to say this morning. We can understand the Kingdom of God as God's intention for the universe: "God has revealed that God's intention for our world is that all humans live as brothers and sisters, as sons and daughters of God. (Is. 2:2-5, 11:6-9, 40:4-5; Eph. 1:3, 1:9-10). In the relevant passages, he cites from Isaiah, the prophet describes in poetic language a peaceful kingdom in which "a new king will arise," and goes on in the familiar verses of the liturgy of Christ's nativity: "the hills will become a plain . . . the glory of the Lord will be revealed." And verses from Paul to the Ephesians cited describe a plan of God to be carried out though Christ's coming "to bring creation together, everything in heaven and on earth . . . giving us "every spiritual blessing in the heavenly world." Our thoughts and actions can either be in tune with God's intention or not. Only by being in tune with God's intention will we ever know true fulfillment or happiness in this life. Prayer, discernment and knowledge of God's revealed Word are needed to discover how one can be in tune with God's intention." (*Fr. William Barry SJ*)

I like this interpretation, because it gets us involved. The kingdom of God is God's intention, and our actions can either be in tune with God's intention or not, with the outcome being the possibility of happiness and peace. When we are in tune with God's intention . . . I guess that means a response to Jesus who said, "If you love me, keep my commandments." . . . we are tuned in to the reality of the situation at hand. We're in a world of our own, but it is not an unconscious world of our own. It is a world in which we are very conscious of our responsibilities as Christians. We know where is love and happiness can be found, and we feel the boundaries of the kingdom of God. This is the kingdom of God that is not an illusion in our mind, nor is it the great hereafter.

We sense that we are in the kingdom of God as we sense our identity as Christians. We may also know that there is surrounding us a world that is apart, not within the safe parameters of God's kingdom and, sadly, not aware of it. Rather more like the group Jesus scolds: "John came and you did not believe him; now I come and you do not believe me."

There is another thing (There are many things about the kingdom of God throughout the gospels.), but we can learn about the kingdom of God in this passage. You don't have to have any pure qualifications. There is only one test. Belief in Jesus and his message.

Thanks be to God.

'Faith comes through hearing.'

TEXT Matthew 13: 31-33,44-52

How many parables are there in the Gospel of Matthew? We just heard five of them. I researched and counted 38 all told in Matthew. Some of them are also in the other evangelists' gospels. I'm sharing my research with you in that chart inserted in today's Sunday bulletin. It gives you a strong impression of how the Lord delivered his message. He was intent on teaching with parables . . . at least that's how Matthew represents him.

Parable is from a Greek word that sounds almost the same. It means an illustration, an object or a story that has a second meaning. Many speakers use parables as a rhetorical style to make a point. This morning we have the parable about the mustard seed, about yeast, about a pearl, about a hidden treasure, and about a net thrown into the sea to catch fish. All teaching us about The Kingdom of Heaven. There are also parables that are stories. Everyone knows the parable of the Prodigal Son. It's famous. Parables have been used by others, and are found in literature besides the New Testament. You may have heard the parable of "the blind men and the elephant": a group of blind men touch an elephant to learn what it is like. Each one feels a different part, the trunk, or the leg, or the tusk; and then they compare notes and learn that they are in complete disagreement. Ever heard it? It sounds familiar, but I don't recall the point of it.

Jesus was a teacher, a rabbi, trained in the scriptures of his people. He spoke in the synagogue often times, as here in Capernaum; and he spoke out in the countryside -- the Sermon on the Mount, for example. (This would put us in mind of John Wesley, whose preaching career was made out in the fields, rather than in the churches -- for which he got in some trouble). At times, as we hear at the beginning of this Gospel chapter (13), Jesus got into a boat to be free of the crowds, and he preached off shore.

Matthew says of Jesus that he always "spoke to the crowds in parables; indeed, he would never speak to them except in parables. This was to fulfill the prophesy." At one point his disciples asked him, "Why do you talk to the people in parables. And he answered with a quote from the prophet of Isaiah. *'Here is my servant whom I have chosen, my beloved, the favorite of my soul. I will endow him with my spirit and he will proclaim the true faith to the nations.'* And then he explained further: *The reason I talk to them in parables is that they look without seeing and listen without hearing or understanding.* And then he quotes Isaiah again: *[As it was written] you will listen and listen again, but not understand, see and see again, but not perceive . . . their ears are dull of hearing, and they have shut their eyes for fear they should see with their eyes, hear with their ears, understand with their heart and be converted and be healed by me.* And then he says directly to his disciples *But happy are your eyes because they see, your ears because they hear.* And toward the end of explaining the parable of the wheat and the weeds, he says in summary: *Anyone who has ears, listen!*

That's what I want to talk about today. Let anyone with ears listen. Because there are some who are not listening. In fact, a lot of the world we encounter every day is not listening. Why not? The message of the gospel is Good News: joy and happiness and the promise of life eternal. Who does not want to listen to that?

There are a couple of reason for those "without ears," who are not getting the message of Jesus and God's grace and salvation. Maybe it has never been broadcast to them. It is the duty of all of us, true believers who *have* listened, to have a part in proclaiming the Good News to others. We do that mainly in the lives we live: "Let your light shine before men," Jesus said; let the world know we are Christians. "They will know we are Christians by our love," as a children's song says. Living the Christian life is a virtue, a good habit that gets easier the more we pursue it . . . although we have to work at it and ask for the Lord's graces all the time.

Some in our Methodist society also do foreign mission action. The theme of the Methodist Conference this spring was "Setting hearts and lives afire for mission work." Not satisfied with their own capture of the blessings of the Lord for themselves, they are bursting to tell others. Some brethren ante-up their dollars; some give their time by weeks and months, even years, carrying the message of Jesus to others in the world who have ears -- but have not heard it yet. That's a good thing. A cousin of mine, my godchild in fact, has gone on a mission to Haiti every summer for several years. The foreign missions are a large part of the Methodist way . . . following the command of the Lord: "Make all nations my disciples."

But what about persons who have ears, and who also have the message of the Lord's words broadcast all around them, and yet their ears are "dull of hearing." Either there is too much static in their lives, or they just don't want to hear the message. Or they don't understand it. Here is where Jesus steps in with his parables. He has made it simple and clear.

In our time, there are those who live in the culture of salvation, but are not aware of it. They do not listen, or their ears do not hear. Or they are not receptive, and say it is too mysterious; or they don't have time for it, because it interferes with some other purposes they have in their lives. But they really can't say they don't understand the Gospel message of life. Reason alone tells us that there is something more to life than this. This life has its limitations; that's obvious in many ways. "Life's too short" is a popular expression. We desire more. And the Christian culture we live in directs us, who listen, to a better life and peace.

When Jesus delivered his message, he explained it to anyone who didn't get it. We have ears to hear. And we have eyes to see. And we have minds to think. The matter of life and its purpose is not a theoretical question, not a philosophical problem, left for scientists or philosophers to grapple with. It is something that affects every aspect of our daily lives.

A holy man like St. Bonaventure, who was an associate of Francis of Assisi, would say that we have eyes to see God's message all around us . . . in the earth of creation -- the sea, the stars, the moon, the people of every land. We need only to listen in a prayer to hear. We do it. It is easy for us, who are people of faith. But we must keep our ears sharp, be attentive and hold on to that message of salvation that the coming of Jesus to earth delivered.

In the parable in which Jesus describes the Kingdom of Heaven as a net that was thrown into the sea and caught fish of every kind, he teaches that there is a system of justice in God's plan in which the righteous are separated from the evil, for whom there will be a punishment: "the weeping and gnashing of teeth." We want to be on the righteous side of that justice. We want to be like the apostles who, when Jesus asks "Do you understand all these things," answered, "Yes.

We do." We want to be those of whom the Lord says, "The righteous will shine like the sun in the kingdom of their Father."

So let's end this as the Lord ends his explanations of his parables in Matthew's Gospel: "Let anyone with ears listen!"

Thanks be to God.

Jesus and His Friends: A Family of Faith

TEXT Luke 10:38-42

The gospel reading assigned this week, and on which I should base my sermon, is among the briefest: Only 4 verses. The narrative is, in fact, so sparse, so literarily economical, you might think it was written by the evangelist Mark . . . or by Ernest Hemingway. Yet it is also one of the most memorable scenes. For me especially. This passage was often referenced around my home when I grew up. My mother's name is Martha, her mother's name, that is, my grandmother, is Martha, my sister's name is Martha Mary. My aunt's name is Martha Mary -- a religious sister, who is now in heaven after 60 years in religious life. (They are all in heaven, now that I notice.)

The story is simple enough. It is not a parable. Jesus did not set this scene up (nor did the evangelist) to make a point. He does make a point, however. "Mary has chosen the better part." But he may not have convinced everybody. There has always been some back and forth among commentators as to which is the better pursuit: good works or prayer. This may even be the root, in an analogous or parallel way, of a contemporary controversy: should a woman stay at home and care for her household, or should she go out and make a career for herself in the workplace? Should the modern woman be a Martha or a Mary, so to speak? But we're not going there today. I said that Jesus may not have clearly convinced everyone on this issue. Although he says outright that, "Mary has chosen the better part, which will not be taken away from her," it could be argued as Augustine points out in a sermon (That's back in the 4TH century), that Martha's love was more fervent than Mary's, because even before Jesus arrived, she was making preparations for him. Another commentator, John Cassian, a theologian and monk in Rome in the early church (5TH century), comments that Jesus was in no way criticizing Martha, he just meant that her role of taking care of his bodily needs (preparing the meal) "can only last as long as the human being is there, whereas the zeal of Mary for spiritual nourishment can never end."

I was surprised that I could not find more commentary on this passage in the writings and sermons of the early Fathers of our church. So I will offer a commentary and an interpretation of my own. Something I think the Fathers may have missed. These were friends of Jesus. Visiting their home was not a casual encounter. Martha was making preparations for him as an invited and expected guest. They were a family of longtime and loving friends. There had been an earlier occasion when, according to the evangelist John, Mary washed the Lord's feet as a gesture of respect and affection. Recall that time later when Jesus goes to their home in Bethany, the town in which they lived, after the death of Lazarus, their brother. The people who had gathered to console the two sisters, could not help but remark at how much Jesus loved Lazarus. He wept as he approached the burial place, deeply feeling in that existential moment the loss of a dear friend. Martha, Mary, Lazarus: These were a family of Jesus' closest friends. They knew him, because of their faith in him. "Yes, Lord, I believe," Martha says to him. And throughout the whole drama of the petitions of both Martha and Mary and the raising of Lazarus, this relationship of friends is narrated in the context of faith. "Everyone who has faith in me will live," he tells Martha. And he says a little while later, "If you had faith you would see the glory of God." There was never a question about the relationship of Martha and Mary and their family, including Lazarus; they were friends, a family who knew Jesus because they were a family of faith.

When Jesus speaks of faith, as he does here, he is speaking from the great tradition of biblical Israel, into which he was born and in which he was schooled as a teacher: He could reference the faith of Abraham and of the other great men and women of his people. The bond which established the people chosen for God's revelation was faith. When the God of the universe reveals himself, he speaks to Abraham. Abraham does not see God, but hears his voice. Faith takes over immediately. Abraham is a man of faith who assumes the role God has for him by putting himself in the hands of the God who is faithful. Augustine explains: "Man is faithful when he believes in God and his promises; God is faithful when he grants to man what he has promised." Thus in faith was the covenant established through which the nation of Israel was formed, and from which the Savior would come forth for man's redemption and glory. It all happened through the power, the dynamic of FAITH.

There are those out there in the world who do not understand this dynamic. They see faith more as a gallant quest to find meaning in their lives and no more. But the faith that comes out of the bible, out of the history of the chosen nation, the faith which Jesus speaks of to Martha and Mary is something far more and on a much high higher level than is a gallant quest. Faith is a light that obliterates the darkness and all the hazards of a shadowy quest. "I have come as light into the world, that whoever believes in me may not remain in darkness." The light of faith is unique; it is capable of illuminating every aspect of human existence.

I like the King James version of the definition of faith in Hebrews 11: *Faith is the substance of things hoped for, the evidence of things not seen.* Faith is not blind, notwithstanding that phrase "blind faith." No more groping. Faith is not something we struggle with. Faith is a given ... in the truest sense of the word ... given to us by God's favor toward us, or grace. A contemporary theologian writing on faith tells us that, "A light this powerful cannot come from ourselves, but from a more [transcendent] primordial source; in a word, it must come from God. Faith is born of an encounter with the living God, who calls us and reveals his love, a love which precedes us and upon which we can lean for security and for building our lives." He goes on: "Transformed by this love, we gain fresh vision, new eyes to see; we realize that it contains a great promise of fulfillment and that a vision of the future opens up for us." This future is pointed out clearly to Martha:

> *I am the resurrection and the life.* Jesus tells her. *Those who believe in me, even though they die, will live, and everyone who lives and believes in me will never die. Do you believe this? She said to him, "Yes, Lord, I believe that you are the Messiah, the Son of God, the one coming into the world."*

Our faith in the word of Jesus is the engine that drives our spiritual life forward, by which we are able to express devout prayer and worship, by which we can discern what is right and what is wrong; it is the support on which we base our acts of charity toward others and build up our generosity toward the needy, and by which we follow the command to love our neighbor. It is everything to us. In our prayer, we thank God every day for it . . . . But then we move on, because it is also the foundation of our inner peace. Faith makes it happen that we know

Jesus as Martha and Mary knew him, and we can become like them, his friends.

To petition that, I close with the collect or general congregational prayer from the liturgy of Sts. Martha and Mary in the Episcopal calendar on July 29, their feast day.

> Generous God, whose Son Jesus Christ enjoyed the friendship and hospitality of Mary, Martha and Lazarus of Bethany, open our hearts to love thee, our ears to hear thee, and our hands to welcome and serve thee in others, through Jesus Christ our risen Lord; who with thee and the Holy Spirit lives and reigns, one God, for ever and ever. Amen.

The last word: The final verse of that passage in John sums it up: *Many of the people who had come to visit Mary saw the things that Jesus did, and they put their faith in him.*

Thanks be to God.

The Good Samaritan Story
"It's in our DNA."

TEXT Luke 10: 25-37

As many times as I've looked at paintings or prints of Vincent VanGogh's work, I had never seen, nor was I aware, of his painting of the Good Samaritan. It is marvelously expressive, is it not? The detail follows  Luke's narrative closely: the Samaritan helping the wounded man onto his horse. The painting is approximately 2 x 2.5 feet in dimension, (That's about the size of your desk top.) and is displayed in the Kröller-Müller museum in Otterlo, Netherlands, a town about 50 miles from Amsterdam.

What always strikes me when I look as something like this, art, is the impact incidents in the gospels in the life of Jesus, have had on our civilization and culture. The world's greatest artists have found them subjects for their art. Not only painting, but also music, and drama. I'll let you think of some examples. (1) Christ's baptism, by Giotto -- among literally hundreds of other artists who painted this holy subject. Giotto also did the (2) Flight into Egypt. (3) The death of John the Baptist is rendered in paintings and in an opera . . . Richard Strauss' *Salome,* with the famous "Dance of the Seven veils." And there is much poetry inspired by the scene of Jesus in the garden of Gethsemane. Poems by Kipling, Ella Wheeler Wilcox, Rosanna Eleanor Leprohon.

This is what I mean about the gospel's impact on our culture. And only the Christian gospel imbues in us, yea, demands of us -- as today's gospel parable illustrates -- love of neighbor, love of fellow man. Jesus explained that commandment many times in the course of his preaching. To a scribe who questioned him, he said, *It is most important that you love others as much as your love yourself* (Mark 12:31). In Matthew 5: 43, he goes even further with this: *But I say unto you, love your enemies, bless them that curse you, do good to them that hate you, and pray for them which persecute you.* In the story we hear today, Jesus tells us emphatically and exactly who our neighbor is, and how we ought to act. No exceptions, no distinctions. Paul reiterated in the scripture of a couple of Sunday's ago, in Galatians: *For the whole law is summed up in a single commandment, "You shall love your neighbor as yourself."* There is no such mandate in the beliefs of other cultures. Only Christianity, and it is in our DNA.

With respect to the attitude toward one's neighbor in other religions, I am only aware that some of them focus more on self, looking inward rather than outward, concentrating on perfecting themselves by meditating inwardly. And at least one can be, is often, hostile to others, violently hostile. But for us followers of Jesus, who are committed to him and who take his words to heart, that is why, we have and we are -- whether we reflect on it as religious or not -- first responders, volunteers who rush to a neighbor's aid, Christian believers who make sacrifices to start up hospitals, (There is Good Samarian Hospital here on Long Island.). It is our civic policy to shelter the homeless -- just exactly as the Samaritan did in this parable: he took out two denarii, gave them to the innkeeper, and said, *Take care of him; and when I come back, I will repay you whatever more you spend.* There is a so-called "Good Samaritan law," that is supportive of persons who come to the aid of someone in an emergency. And our government leaders direct us to -- and we do so willingly -- share our prosperity, our advantages with others around the world who have less. All of this is the Good Samaritan effect. It's in our DNA.

From the very inception of the Christian movement, Christians have responded willingly to the Good Samaritan story. I like to examine the earliest commentaries. Most focus on the realistic details of the story -- how a kind man (who happens to be a foreigner) has pity on a person he finds in distress on the highway, having been robbed and beaten. The commentators take note that a couple of professionals pass him by . . . could not be bothered. It's a fairly clear-cut and straight-forward parable, in which Jesus makes the point that the great commandment to love one's neighbor means just that: make time for it, do it at your expense; not any particular person is your neighbor, but all of mankind. Got that, counselor? (It was a lawyer who asked Jesus the question.)

Interestingly, other experts, early Fathers of the Church, see an allegory here. The assault victim is the image of Everyman; the Samaritan can only be the image of Jesus Christ, God himself who for us has set out to take care of his wounded creatures. God has made himself our neighbor in Jesus. He pours oil and wine into our wounds, a gesture seen as an image of the healing gift of the sacraments. And he brings us to the inn, the Church, in which he arranges for our care and also pays a deposit for the cost of care.

In some ways, the cost of care is the cost Jesus incurred by his sacrificial death in order to heal us . . . mankind's salvation.

Interpretations like this show the richness of inspired scripture. While it offers us a simple literal/realistic message, at the same time there is also deeper meaning in it, to reiterate and underscore truths of our faith. That may be why the story of the Good Samaritan has staying power over the centuries, and why its message in imprinted on our psyche and becomes a part of our Christian DNA, our faith.

In this scriptural richness, we cultivate our faith. We hear the word of God repeated in the Good Samaritan story, and we gain confidence in our good works. It may be that our good works, sprung from our DNA, lead us to faith, to a stronger faith, to an enlightened faith for the first time. That's how powerful the grace of God's message is. We understand that our efforts to reach out, our generosity gains us God's favor, graces, and bonds us with Jesus. Writes a contemporary spiritual writer and gospel commentator: "Everyone is called to be become a Samaritan -- to follow Christ and become like him. When we do that we live rightly. We love rightly when we become like him, who loved us first." And it should be easy. It's in our DNA.

Thanks be to God.

Introductory Note. *To begin, let me thank Pastor Ann [of the Orient Congregational Church] and the Church Services committee for inviting me to preach. It is an honor I welcome and appreciate very much.*

Having the service outdoors is pleasant at this time of year. But I should mention that John Wesley, who is credited with founding the Methodists, was a priest of the Anglican Church, and he got in trouble with his superiors for conducting services and preaching in the open air outside of the church. One more thing: You will hear me quoting from the Fathers of the Church in this sermon. I am not a scholar of ancient Christian documents. However, you will find that in our day and age we have the sermons of St. Augustine and St. John Chrysostom available online. And many others, no doubt. I am happy to tell you that without Google, Wikipedia, and this little treasure: Ancient Christian Devotional, this sermon would not have been possible!

Social Jesus

TEXT Luke 10:38-42

There are a number of ways to draw lessons from this gospel: Luke's account of Jesus' visit to the home of Martha and Mary. Evangelist John gives another account of a visit to their home, and names the place as Bethany, a few miles from Jerusalem. Lazarus, their brother, lived with them. And John writes in his account, "Jesus loved Martha and her sister [Mary] and Lazarus." They were friends, dear friends.

In the interest of full disclosure, I must confess that this story got much play around my childhood home. My grandmother's name was Martha, my mother's name was Martha, an aunt's name was Sr. Martha Mary, and my sister's name was Martha Mary. How many times I heard that famous scripture line! *Martha, Martha, you are worried and distracted by many things . . ..* They are all in heaven now, I hope supporting me here this morning, making sure I do right by this scene.

There is ample commentary on this story in the early church. Although Jesus, himself says that, "Mary has chosen the best part," one writer, Ephrem of Syria, a poet and composer of hymns in the 4TH century, writes that, "Martha's love was more fervent than Mary's, because before Jesus arrived she had prepared to serve him . . . and later when the sisters called Jesus because of their brother's grave illness, Martha ran ahead eagerly to meet him." You may choose among yourselves which of these ladies is your model. But there is consensus among early Christian commentators that there is in this scripture a valuable lesson. In the words of Church Father John Cassian, a 4TH century Christian monk and theologian, it is "to cling always to God and to the things of God -- this must be our major effort; this must be the road the heart follows unswervingly."

There are a number of occasions like this in the gospel narratives . . . Jesus accepting hospitality, attending a social party. He was a celebrity, in a sense. People not only followed him from town to town and listened to his preaching, but they also sought his intimate personal friendship. Often he seemed exhausted by the crowds; he goes off in a boat with his disciples for some relief; or he slips away to a mountain retreat for some quiet and prayer. No doubt he welcomed invitations where he could not only escape the crowds, but also enjoy the quiet company of close friends. This was one of those occasions. There were others. Jesus was at a diner of a prominent Pharisee when he cured a man and was criticized for healing on the Sabbath. And another time he was invited to dinner at the home of a Pharisee, and the women washed his feet with a sweet fragrant balm. To Zacharias, a man of short stature, who climbed up on a tree to get a glimpse of Jesus over the crowd, Jesus says, "Hurry and come down; for I must stay at your house today." He had a reputation of eating at table with what his critics regarded as common people -- "sinners," they said. Events like these, that the gospel writers chose to provide for us, are on the surface social events, not formal settings for preaching as in a synagogue or on the mountain side. And yet note that Jesus delivers a message, somewhat casually, but a message nonetheless that has become a part of the fabric of our Christian faith. Perfect example: "Mary has chosen the best part." Comments Augustine, "Mary was enjoying the truth"; that is, the words of Jesus, his promises, eternal life. And Ambrose of Milan, the mentor of Augustine, writes in his commentary on Luke's gospel, "Let the desire for wisdom lead you as it did Mary. It is a greater and more perfect work. Do not let service divert the knowledge of the heavenly Word." (I think Ambrose sides with Mary.)

It was a repeated interpretation among Church Fathers that what Mary was drawn to was the Word of God, reflecting the teaching of Jesus that *Man shall not live by bread alone, but by every word of God* (Luke 4:4), and *the words that I speak to you are spirit, and they are life* (John 6:63). In sum, the obvious message of Jesus here is that spiritual values are more important than material business . . . such as, as illustrated symbolically in this context, preparation of a meal.

This may be lesson enough. But I want to comment further and focus on how the Lord's human personality, his personal character, comes through this story; and its implications for us his followers. One contemporary commenter, on an Internet blog, notes the number of dinner parties Jesus attended and concludes that it's a sign Christians should have some fun once in a while. But I'm not going there. I don't think we need that kind of encouragement. There is an aspect of this story that happened to strike me during the week I was preparing to preach this sermon. I visited a friend in the San Simeon nursing facility here in Greenport, where I saw not only my elderly (98) friend but a room full of others like him. There is an age, I once read about in an article by a psychiatrist, whose patient, an elderly woman, very elderly, described her unhappy situation in a complaint as "the age of misery." There is infancy, youth, middle age, old age – and after that, perhaps as an unintended consequence of modern medicine and wonderful healing technology, *the age of misery:* persons well-beyond old age physically, with no imminent terminal disease, but helpless, often immobile, and, worst of all, having outlived, out-survived many in their family and social circle, alone.

Floyd Memorial library was hosting a monthly movement - group call the Death Café, people sitting around with coffee and cake and talking about this inevitable topic. When my turn came around to offer an idea or comment, I described this stage of life and asked what is the solution for these people. Several around the table answered rather promptly: "Have someone take care of them." That seemed so simple. And it was the right answer. At this difficult stage of life every person needs someone else. Oh, the nursing homes take up some of the problem, but not all of it; and theirs is a very special and medically intense solution, with long-term residents in beds requiring constant attention. But there are many others, persons in their homes. Alone, bearing the misery of that post-old age age, who need someone. In this gospel story we should not miss the setting that Jesus was a visitor. Martha and Mary were alone, living with their brother who was gravely ill. I think the inspired evangelist chose to tell this story to show us *Jesus the visitor.* More than a simple social visit, this time they called him because their brother Lazarus was *in extremis,* dying. And here evangelist John reveals to us not only the Lord's humanity, writing that *Jesus wept,* but also his divine power, and the life of Lazarus was restored.

As Christians, we are called to pursue holiness -- John Wesley insisted -- by studying the life of Jesus and emulating him. In episodes like this one, we observe his social instincts and are drawn to him by his humanity, at the same time that we are awed by his divine prerogatives. It is the mystery of his incarnate humanity that attracts us. Like us, in all but sin, Paul said. We live today in a real-time environment, this time and place, where Christian virtues are in great demand, and imitating the Lord's human sensibilities and adopting his social instincts would serve us well . . . aware of and ready to seek out our neighbors in need -- as he did Martha and Mary -- and console and help them . . . and recognize Jesus in them. We always have these words of his to assure us we are doing the right thing.

Truly I tell you, whatever you did for one of the least of these brothers and sisters of mine, you did for me.

Thanks be to God.

'It's a jungle out there.'

TEXT Mark 6:14-29

It is challenging each Sunday to have to compose a message that is a commentary on the gospel passage, as that passage is somewhat randomly assigned to us by the Lectionary. The Lectionary is a directory, used by all or most Christian congregations to assign the Bible readings for the day. And the assignment of the scripture passage for today – when I first looked at it – was most challenging: the execution of John the Baptist.

While the event this passage describes may be a challenge for preachers, it certainly stirred the imagination of artists throughout history: There is the play by Oscar Wilde, *Salome*; and then the opera, *Solame,* based on Wilde's play, by Richard Strauss, featuring the famous "Dance of the Seven Veils," -- which was then taken up by Rita Hayworth in the movie version, "Salome." Plus, there was an earlier movie version of the story with Yvonne DeCarlo in 1945: "Salome, Where She Danced." On YouTube, if you are curious. (Neither of those movies, as I recall, was I allowed by my mother to see.)

But I have seen some Caravaggio, the Italian master who produced two magnificent 'though gruesome oil paintings of "The Beheading of St. John the Baptist"; one hanging now in a London museum, the other in Madrid. (You can also look at them online.) And there is another 16TH century Italian masterpiece on the topic: Titian's "Salome with the Head of John the Baptist."

It's a great story. It has everything: royalty, politics, intrigue, infidelity, sex and violence, even war between Herod and his brother over the adultery John condemned. This is the stuff movies are made of. But how do *we* handle it? I'd like to offer that this story is a sign to us that being associated with Jesus entails risk . . . to say the least. John was the first casualty of the gospel -- although we know that prophets of the Old Testament were summarily executed before the coming of Jesus, the Messiah, into the world.

When Jesus learned of John's death, Matthew tells us, he went off by himself to be alone. To morn. John was kin. They had been together on the mission, when Jesus accepted John's baptism. [As an aside, the Fathers of the Church, early Christian Bible commentators, go to great lengths explaining this theological anomaly. Jesus, of course, had no need for baptism, since he was sinless. St. Jerome gives an explanation with three reasons: First, because Jesus was born a man, that he might fulfill all the justice and humility of the law. Second, that by his baptism, he might confirm John's baptism. And third, that by sanctifying the waters of the Jordan through the decent of the Dove, he might show the Holy Spirit's coming in the Baptism of the Spirit." But that's for another sermon.]

Back to risk assessment at being a Christian. I do not intend to alarm anyone. However, in fact, there are Christians dying for the faith these days in Egypt, in Iraq. A few years ago, a church was destroyed . . . and in many places on the continent of Africa, where wars always seem to involve attacks on Christians because they are Christians. Not to mention China, where Methodist missionaries have labored for years, and which has never been a safe place for Christians.

"It's a jungle out there." And it was ever thus. And as a result, we have litanies of saints martyrs going back to the Apostles, who were the first wave.

My friends, we are most fortunate here in America to have a society that protects Christians from violence and extreme prejudice. It was not always so. Blood was shed for the cause of Christ right here in our state in the 17TH century: the killing of eight French Jesuit missionary preachers, upstate near the Mohawk Valley town of Auriesville, the birthplace of the Indian girl Katherine Tekakwitha, whom the Jesuits baptized and who died with them. Just a reminder that by our Christian baptism we did not join a benign social club.

We are not likely in our day and age -- at least here in the United States -- to meet a fate like John the Baptizer or any of the others. But we would do well to understand that we must cultivate a personal faith that is hardened, a faith of steel, that will sustain us if not against physical threat, against spiritual attack . . . which is not that remote.

You see, there is another aspect of the killing of John the Baptist that we might reflect upon. He was not killed by brigands or outlaws, but rather by "the authorities." The issue he defended was moral truth, God's law. Christians are never safe when truth is at stake. We stand for the truth, we have the truth, we are not searching for the truth. Jesus said not only *I the way*, but also *I am the truth*. A social environment that questions truth, or disregards it, or feels incapable of finding truth and throws up its hands cynically, saying "What is Truth" anyway? . . .

what does it matter? . . . is always a potential threat to us Christians. Remember, Jesus said "I am the Truth." It was the other guy who was skeptical: John 14: *Therefore, Pilate said to Him, "So you are a king?" Jesus answered, "You say correctly that I am a king. For this I have been born, and for this I have come into the world, to testify to the truth. Everyone who is of the truth hears my voice."*

We Christians, who are of the truth, who hear the voice of Jesus) must always be shoring up our faith, hardening it against threats, building it on a solid foundation through prayer and worship, reinforcing it each Sunday as we declare it with a full heart . . . if we are to qualify, if not as martyrs, at least as having a martyr-worthy faith.

All the Fathers of the Church, whom I rely on for direction in preparing my sermons, take a different tack in their commentaries on the killing of John the Baptist. They focus on the sensuality of what was perhaps the most notorious birthday party in all of history: [quote] "The birthday party that becomes a funeral, the banquet that turns into a bloody killing." . . . in their words. Their interpretation and lesson, 'though differing from mine, may, nevertheless, have some value in studying. It makes the point that is made evident in Herod's party scene: sensuality will undermine reason and faith. Hillary of Poitiers, a 4th century Bishop in France (then a part of the Roman Empire) comments eloquently: "Virtue is undesirable to those who are immoral; holiness is abhorrent to those who are impious; chastity is an enemy to those who are impure; integrity is a hardship for those who are corrupt; frugality runs counter to those who are self-indulgent; mercy is intolerable to those who are cruel; as is loving kindness to those who are pitiless, and justice to those who are unjust."

In this horrific scene, *amid the delight of corporeal things*, virtue is compromised. So our faith, if not hardened against excess, will be in jeopardy. That's always a problem, and another reason to be constantly strengthening our faith as we strive for the personal holiness John Wesley preached and exemplified. At the same time, we are called to pray for our fellow Christians who face real physical danger because of their faith. Awareness of their real plight today -- in our time – should make us understand how precious our faith is. And so we act to protect it and embrace it, in all its sweetness, and with all its risk.

Thanks be to God.

Matthew's Mission

TEXT Matthew 13: 1-9, 19-23

When's the last time you read the Gospel of Matthew? I mean from cover to cover, 28 chapters? Not lately. I'm sure I read it during my years in the seminary. But don't you find that when you go back to Scripture, you often discover something new. I re-read Matthew, all of it, in preparation for today, because I wanted to get a feel for it, get his point of view and style . . . and because for the next 16 weeks, the Gospels we read at the service are from Matthew. It started back in June on the first Sunday after Pentecost, and will continue until November. We really should take a look at what Matthew is all about.

He was one of the Lord's 12 close companions, the Apostle Matthew. Jesus met him in Capernaum, a village on the coast of the Sea of Galilee, about 25-30 miles from Nazareth where Jesus came from. It's not there now, but is the site of excavations, where ruins of a synagogue have been found -- perhaps the synagogue in which Jesus preached at the start of his career. Peter and Andrew were from Capernaum, fishermen. Matthew was not a fisherman but a tax agent, kind of white-collar, we'd say.

Matthew's objective in writing his narrative about Jesus was to show that Jesus was, indeed, the person promised in the sacred scriptures, in the words of the prophets, that his readers were familiar with. Over and over he writes, "just as the prophet Isaiah had said," or "So God's promise came true, just as it was written, or "This was to fulfill the prophesy."

Mathew gives a most comprehensive picture of Jesus as a teacher. In reading Matthew, you keep coming on lines that have become aphorisms in our language: "No man can serve two masters," "The birds of the air neither sow nor gather into barns," "Watch out for false prophets," "you are the salt of the earth." And many more. The fullest narrative of the famous "Sermon the Mount" is found in Matthew. It is found also in Mark and Luke, but not in its entirety. Matthew is filled with Jesus' parables, one right after another. It was his style of preaching. The parable we read today, the parable of the sower, is the one parable Jesus explains -- just in case you didn't get the point.

Commentators for centuries have gone over and over it, explaining its message of faith and how faith in the Lord begins and develops ... and also how it could die away and fail. We don't need to add more commentary at this time. Anybody who doesn't get the point of the parable of the sower? No?

I'd rather go to what is the secondary objective Matthew seems to have in mind in writing his version of the Good News. It is this: while many commentators and secular scholars might regard Jesus as a great philosopher, and a great leader of a movement, they miss the point that is so very evident in the Gospel according to Matthew. The words and sayings of Jesus are not merely for academic study and erudite analysis. And they are more than a moral code for ethical humanists. Jesus requires of his followers holiness, the adoption of a lifestyle that reflects discipline, love and respect of others, but always in the context of duty toward worship of God.

John Wesley picked up on this. He saw his Christian faith as not merely adherence to a line of thought, but as demanding personal and deep holiness. When he first came of age in college (at Oxford) he formed a club with his brother and their fellows to foster holiness, and to study how to be holy; that is, how to be Christ-like, observing every directive Jesus gives. They called it the Holiness Club. He preached in one of his most well-known sermons, *The Almost Christian,* that "In every age there are those who will not go all of the way to Christ. They are almost persuaded to be Christians, but they falter at some point. Not only this, but the Church is full of almost Christians who have not gone all the way with Christ."

And this is not merely keeping the ancient commandments That's a given. But also listening to the counsel of the "beatitudes" Jesus gives in the Sermon on the mount: "You must be pure of heart; you must be merciful; you must be peacemakers." When he came down from the mountain, he raised the bar:

> *You have learned how it was said to our ancestors, 'You must not kill.' But I say this to you, anyone who is angry with his brother will answer for it. You have learned how it was said You must not commit adultery.' But I say this to you: If a man looks at a woman lustfully, he has already committed adultery with her in his heart. You have heard it said, 'An*

> *eye for an eye and tooth for tooth,' But I say this to you: if anyone hits you on the right cheek, offer him the other as well. If any man orders you to go one mile, go two miles with him and more: I say this, Love your enemies and pray for those who persecute you."*

This is what one of my theology professors called "pure ozone" Christianity; and what the saintly pastor Dietrich Bonhoeffer called the "Cost of Discipleship." It is a high standard, indeed; and there have been interpreters of Christ's words who have gone to extremes. The Russian novelist, Leo Tolstoy in his later life was a literal interpreter of the Lord's words. "If your eye causes you to sin, cut it out and throw it away." Hyperbole, the commentators say. We must allow Jesus some hyperbole in his preaching style to make his point. They say that we may interpret the Lord's words holding to their general thrust, but less for their specifics. They draw a distinction between being a good Christian and perfection.

What should our stand be? After all, the Lord's words were (and I quote) "Be perfect as your heavenly Father is perfect." Hyperbole? We strive for perfection in most things we do, in education and learning, in health and physical fitness, even in pleasure and enjoyment. We always strive to go all out. Why not in our Christian commitment? Don't you think we owe it to our Methodist heritage, at least to go for the level of holiness that John Wesley speaks of all the time. Holiness is God-like. Paul says "be imitators of Christ." That's holiness.

At least we must be above average. So it can be said about us in a paraphrase of what Garrison Kieller says of the children of Lake Wobegon. "We are a church. . . where all the Christians are above average." In the next several weeks, we will be going through the Gospel of Matthew. It could be called our "how to" gospel, where we hear many counsels on how to be holy and above average Christians. Let's pay attention to that. Or better yet, why not pick up the Gospel of Matthew yourself in your spare time and see what it takes . . . directly . . . from the Lord himself?

Thanks be to God.

The Feast Day of Peter and Paul

TEXT Mark 4:35-41

This Sunday we celebrate the great apostles, Peter and Paul... together. In the course of the Lectionary calendar, each saint has his own separate day: Peter, in the calendar on January 28, when his *Confession* of the divinity of Jesus is commemorated. The scene is described in the three synoptic gospels (Matthew, Mark, and Luke). Jesus is with his disciples near Caesarea Philippi in the north, and he asks them, *Who do people say that I am?* After several conjectures by the disciples, Peter, characteristically, speaks up: *You are the Christ [Messiah], the son of the living God.* I'd say he earned special recognition with a day of his own for that bold statement. It was also on this occasion that Jesus said, referencing Peter's future role: *On this rock I will build my church, and the gates of Hell will not prevail against it.*

Also in January, the church calendar has a separate day for Paul, marking that crucial event of his life, his conversion. Evangelist Luke, who composed the Acts of the Apostles, tells the story in this way: *When Saul had almost reached Damascus* [Saul was Paul's former name], *a bright light from heaven suddenly flashed around him and he fell to the ground and heard a voice that said, "Why do you persecute me?" "Who are you?" Paul asked. And the Lord answered "I am Jesus."* The Lord then directed Paul on his way, and we know the rest of the story.

From very early on, the Christian church celebrated Peter and Paul together on June 29, commemorating their martyrdom in Rome. The date chosen marked the anniversary of the removal of the saints' remains to secure them, at a time in the 4TH century when Christians were undergoing sporadic persecutions under the Roman Emperor Valerian. In a 1968 excavation, evidence of Peter's burial was found in a tomb beneath the basilica built in his honor, the famous St. Peter's Basilica. There is also a magnificent basilica in Rome honoring Paul. It is called "St. Paul's Outside the Wall," because, yes, it is outside the old walled city.

As great as these men were in the eyes of Christians, indeed, of the world, they were not born saints. Peter for all his bluster, a leader explicitly chosen by Jesus, who once drew his sword to defend Jesus, failed the Lord at a critical time when he was arrested and put on trial. Tradition tells us that Peter repented deeply for that lapse of courage. *He wept bitterly*, wrote evangelist Matthew. But he seems to have recovered his composure and self-confidence sufficiently to be there after the Resurrection in a most tender scene: Jesus asked him, referring to his former name, *"Simon, son of John, do you love me more than the others do?" Simon Peter answered, "Yes, Lord, you know I do." "Then feed my lambs,"* Jesus said. The question was repeated twice more and finally Peter said, *"Lord, you know everything, you know I love you"; and the Lord then said, "feed my sheep."* This scene is interpreted as a commission to Peter to be the leader. It was not long after that that Peter did in fact assume leadership of the Christian community in Jerusalem, and he delivered there to the Christian converts one of the greatest speeches in the whole bible. It's recorded in Acts 2. At the end of it, his listeners said, *Friends, what shall we do?* And Peter replied, *Turn back to God! Be baptized in the name of Jesus Christ, so that your sins will be forgiven. Then you will be given the Holy Spirit. This promise is for you and your children.* By now Peter was operating empowered by the Holy Spirit of Pentecost.

Paul in his letters often wrote of his life before his conversion; he was not especially proud of it. *You know how I used to live as a Jew (under the Law of Moses), and I was cruel to God's people, the Church, and I even tried to destroy it*, he wrote to the Christian community in Galatia (Gal 1:13). *I made trouble for the church*, he told the Philippians, (Phil 3:6). And in 1 Cor 15: 9, he wrote modestly, *I am the least important of the apostles. In fact, I caused so much trouble for God's church that I don't even deserve to be called an apostle.* And note what he adds: *But God was kind! He made me what I am, and his kindness was not wasted. I have worked very hard as an apostle, although it was God's kindness at work and not me.*

There was a time when Peter and Paul were together in Jerusalem, in what is regarded as the very first church council. It was about 14 years after Paul's conversion and is reported by Luke in the Acts of the Apostles book. On the agenda were issues and policies that had to be ironed out with respect to converts to Christ's way; some who were

Jews represented by Peter, and some who were Greeks, represented by Paul. Both Peter and Paul spoke to the assembly there on that day. The question was ultimately resolved that converts to the Lord's way who were not Jews would not be required to follow all the Mosaic laws; i.e. circumcision.

Years later, Peter and Paul were in Rome during the reign of the Emperor Nero, who waged a bloody persecution against the Christians and condemned and executed Peter and Paul. Their martyrdom for the cause of Christ is what we commemorate and celebrate today. There is much important and marvelous history in the lives of these men, too much to even sketch it in our limited time. Read that book again, the Acts of the Apostles, by evangelist Luke. And be impressed that Paul and Peter were both great men -- "They were giants in those days" -- so filled with the Spirit and love of Jesus that they presented their lives to the executioners for his sake. Pillars, we call them, for they truly established the foundation of the Church of Jesus we thrive in today. Through their lives and their writings we have an abundance to study and learn about our faith. As I remarked earlier, Peter and Paul were not born saints. We've seen how they had to resort to the Lord for his mercy. And from that point forward they became exemplary, nay, heroic followers of Christ.

For centuries, Christians have honored with deep reference the lives of their holy men and women; saints we call them. And we celebrate them in our liturgies. Here are our reasons. In the first place, we recognize them as larger than life. In the instance of Peter and Paul, especially. They are of the stature of the greatest men in world history, having been the virtual founders of Christianity. No one compares to them in that regard. (Jesus, of course, is the actually founder of his WAY.) Secondly, we regard the saints as models by whom we can fashion our lives as Christians. We could study and gain much confidence from the pattern of the lives of Peter and Paul. The Lord chooses us to follow him as he did Peter and Paul -- if in less spectacular fashion. And if, like them, we have a need for forgiveness and mercy, God insists that we carry on. And his love and guidance will be there to direct us.

Thanks be to God.

A One-on-One with Jesus
or
Facetime with the Lord

Introductory Note.

According to an accommodation between Christian churches, the scriptures assigned for Sunday reading are always the same, on a three-year cycle, which promotes optimum exposure to the word of God for their congregations. We happen to be in cycle B this year. For example, the gospel passage read today from John 3 is also being read at the Congregational church up the street and in Greenport at Holy Trinity and . . . well, there are exceptions, and at St. Agnes today they are reading a passage from Matthew. I note this because you may wonder why the following passage is read on Trinity Sunday. It's my job to explain.

TEXT John 3: 1-17 Trinity Sunday

> *Now there was a Pharisee named Nicodemus, a leader of the Jews. He came to Jesus by night and said to him, Rabbi, we know that you are a teacher who has come from God; for no one can do these signs that you do apart from the presence of God.' Jesus answered him, 'Very truly, I tell you, no one can see the kingdom of God without being born from above. Nicodemus said to him, "How can anyone be born after having grown old? Can one enter a second time into the mother's womb and be born?" Jesus answered, "Very truly, I tell you, no one can enter the kingdom of God without being born of water and Spirit. What is born of the flesh is flesh, and what is born of the Spirit is spirit. Do not be astonished that I said to you, 'You must be born from above.' The wind* blows where it chooses, and you hear the sound of it, but you do not know where it comes from or where it goes. So it is with everyone who is born of the Spirit." Nicodemus said to him, "How can these things be?" Jesus answered him, "Are you a teacher of Israel, and yet you do*

> *not understand these things? Very truly, I tell you, we speak of what we know and testify to what we have seen; yet you do not receive our testimony. If I have told you about earthly things and you do not believe, how can you believe if I tell you about heavenly things? No one has ascended into heaven except the one who descended from heaven, the Son of Man.* And just as Moses lifted up the serpent in the wilderness, so must the Son of Man be lifted up, that whoever believes in him may have eternal life. For God so loved the world that he gave his only Son, so that everyone who believes in him may not perish but may have eternal life. Indeed, God did not send the Son into the world to condemn the world, but in order that the world might be saved through him.*
>
> The Word of the Lord.

"How can these things be?" Nicodemus says to Jesus. He's perplexed. Jesus has just presented him with a lesson on how to enter the Kingdom of heaven; that is, how to become a faithful follower. But it is not a wonder that Nicodemus is confused. The Lord speaks in images; and in this instance an image that is filled with theological/spiritual truth: Being born again, that is, by water and the Holy Spirit ... baptism. *Very truly, I tell you, no one can enter the kingdom of God without being born of water and Spirit.* Jesus himself, was baptized by water and the Spirit by John at the start of his ministry. [Lk 3:21] *After everyone else had been baptized, Jesus himself was baptized. Then as he prayed, the sky opened up and the Holy Spirit came down upon him in the form of a dove. A voice from heaven said, "You are my own dear son, in whom I am most pleased."* John Wesley says of this scripture that it is a clear declaration of the Blessed Trinity: Jesus the Lord, the Holy Spirit in the form of a dove, and the voice from the heavens of the Father. That's one point in connecting today's scripture reading to Trinity Sunday.

Back to Nicodemus: Jesus goes on to reinforce and elaborate this revelation with more images ... of the wind and the sound of the wind, and Nicodemus is further confused. But you have to respect Nicodemus; he approaches the Lord directly and gets a one-on-one experience, even if he is a little sheepish about it, coming as he does to Jesus in the night time. Already, Jesus was suspect and under surveillance by those who didn't like to hear his message. He expresses disappointment at that, if not outright frustration. Nicodemus is, after all, someone who should be paying attention to God's revelation: *You are a teacher of Israel, you should understand these things.*

There is among theologians and commentators on scripture a notion they call Luther's Rule. It is this: As God has come to us through Christ the Lord, we should go to God through Christ the Lord. The action of Nicodemus seems to follow that axiom. He has a few questions, he puts them directly to Jesus. Isn't that a good rule to follow, for us? In matters of faith, for example, today the liturgy calls our attention to the Holy Trinity, the mystery of God's nature and inner life. Not an easy tenet of our faith to grasp. Like Nicodemus, we might be perplexed: How can these things be? But then we look to Christ the Lord. Time and time again he announced the Holy Trinity in so many words. For thousands of years the Jews/Israelites had clung to their faith in the one true God. At times it cost them dearly. Now, Jesus the Messiah, who they were told to expect, reveals more about the one true God, God's nature, a Holy Trinity.

- At his baptism in the Jordan, in the beginning of his ministry, as we have already noted.
- Remember when the apostle Philip approached Jesus and asked: [John 14:9] *"Lord, show us the Father." And Jesus answers: "Philip, I have been with you for a long time. Don't you know who I am? If you have seen me, you have seen the Father... don't you believe that I am one with the Father..."* And a little further along in that same section, he says, *"If you love me, you will do as I command. Then I will ask the Father to send you the Holy Spirit who will help you and always be with you. The Spirit will show you what is true."* There it is again: Father, Son, and Holy Spirit, the Trinity.
- And after his resurrection from the grave and he is giving final instructions to the apostles he says [according to Matthew 28:19] *"I have been given all authority in heaven and on earth! Go to the people of all nations and make them my disciples. Baptize them in the name of the Father, the Son, and the Holy Spirit. And teach them to do everything I have told you."*

In the early centuries of the Church, church leaders, teachers, saints, bishops descended in a direct line from the apostles, had to clarify what we confess as the doctrine of the Trinity. There were debates and arguments in their meetings, until it could finally be declared as the universal belief of Christians: Father, Son, and Holy Spirit make up the Godhead; three persons, equally God, one God, as we recite in our creed every Sunday. The Holy Trinity, a mystery. The pre-eminent mystery of our faith.

While we see here the Trinity of the Godhead revealed to us through Jesus Christ in his own words, you might be surprised to hear that there is a school of thought among theologians that argues that even prior to the revelation of Christ, *before faith,* men could discover the Trinity of God or at least a vestige or trace of it through experience and observation of the world around us.

Think about what we know and experience. There are *three* dimensions of reality evident in creation. St. Bonaventure says they are *power*, the force behind creation, *wisdom*, the order and design of creation, and *goodness*, the beauty of creation. Power, Wisdom, Goodness 1,2,3, a trinity in its own right. Elements we are able to observe in our experience. Traces, vestiges , footprints of the Creator. And Bonaventure points out more patterns of trinity in experience that are traces of the divine Trinity . . . which point us in the direction of God. How about these: land, sea, sky; or the dimension of things: width, length, depth. And within us, our interior make-up: three powers: to know, to will/love, and to remember. Bonaventure's thought is thus described: "Within ourselves or our soul we find the Memory, Intellect, and Will stamped with and leading to illuminations from above. With the Memory's capability of remembering past, present, and future it becomes an image of eternity where all is present. The Intellect must be enlightened by eternal Truth to have certitude. The Will is stamped with and seeks the highest Good."

Or, perhaps, in terms more familiar: In modern psychology our mind is described as: Ego, Super Ego, and Id. Traces, vestiges, imprints of the Trinity? We might think about it.

While we are commanded in the very First Commandment to respect and honor "the Lord thy God" exclusively, and admit no others as our God, it is the Trinity that we worship. Not an easy concept;

philosophers, theologians and saints have grappled with that mystery for centuries. But in the end, they have found the Trinity to be an easy object of devotion and love. Throughout the gospels, whenever Jesus speaks of his Father or of the Holy Spirit, it is always with the language of love. [John 14:31] "I obey my Father, so that everyone in the world might know that I love him." And in Paul's letter to the Romans 5:5 we read: "For we know how dearly God loves us, because he has given us the Holy Spirit to fill our hearts with his love." When we re-examine our faith, and know that it demands in the very first instance, Commandment One, allegiance and worship of God before anything else, yes, the Holy Trinity. Be reminded that it was inscribed on our forehead at our baptism with water, when we became Christ's follower: "In the name of the Father, of the Son, and the Holy Spirit." Yes, the Blessed Trinity.

Nicodemus didn't get it. But he had the right idea. We might take a cue from him in our prayer, which is, after all one-on-one, facetime, with the Lord.

Thanks be to God.

A hard rain is gonna' fall.

TEXT Luke 12: 49-56

When I first read the scripture assigned for this Sunday, I was unnerved. Its meaning was inscrutable/unfathomable for me. Maybe that's why Bob Dylan's song popped into my mind. A title also inscrutable . . . and dire. *"A hard rain is gonna' fall."* It's a warning, isn't it?

The church historians tell us that the occasion for these statements by Jesus was at the time of the Jewish feast of the Dedication. An observant Jew, Jesus would go up to the temple on this day. It is the memorial celebration of the recovery and rededication of the temple in Jerusalem by the victory of Judas Maccabeus and his forces over Syrian occupiers, who had desecrated the sacred place. This was about 150 BC, 150 years before the birth of Jesus. The feast was celebrated every year in Jesus' time, and is still celebrated today. We call it Hanukah.

There were pockets of hostile groups (we might call them violent demonstrators today) among the crowds who followed Jesus along the way to Jerusalem, and listened to his teaching. The case against him was building up and he was aware of it. It was about at this time that they threatened to stone him, and for a second time, as recorded in Luke's gospel, he was able to escape. Is it any wonder that his nerves might be frazzled, and that he was losing his patience -- frustrated by the stubbornness of listeners who refused to grasp what he was telling them about the Kingdom of God . . . what its character is, and how it would affect them, and how they should respond to it? But they would have none of it!

He was beginning to realize that his life was seriously at risk. This chapter of Luke's gospel is prelude to the sacrificial passion and death of the Lord. In his preaching, we've been reading, he stressed the temporal character of life, of the world: If we follow the sequence laid out by evangelist Luke, we heard Jesus' warnings in parables of the rich man who stored up his wealth only to lose it all when *on this very night the demand will be made or your soul. You must stand ready, because the Son of Man is coming in an hour you do not expect.* And in a parable of the servant unprepared for the return of the master, who *will be cut off and sent out to the same fate as the unfaithful.*

In each of these parables was he is talking about life's most distinctive condition, its inevitable and unpredictable term. He may have been in a reflective mood, about himself too, looking to what was ahead of him . . . a period of stress that would climax in the garden of Gethsemane: *There is a baptism I must receive, and how great is my stress until it is over.* All of the early centuries' commentators say that this "baptism of fire" is his passion and sacrificial death.

We may feel his angst, as he tells how the Kingdom of Heaven, that he had been preaching on this journey, may impact people. *Do you suppose that I am going to bring peace on earth?* ("A hard rain is gonna' fall.") *No, I tell you, but rather division.* For some it would not be easy.

> I met a young woman whose body was burning
> I met one man who was wounded in love
> I met another man who was wounded in hatred
> I heard the sound of a thunder that roared out a warnin'
> I heard the roar of a wave that could drown the whole world.
> And it's a hard, it's a hard, it's a hard, it's a hard
> And it's a hard rain's a-gonna' fall."

Often Jesus had warned about people who would not hear and/or get the message of the Kingdom of God. And what the dire consequences would be. In the parable of the three servants, the one who does not manage his accounts properly is banished: *As for this useless servant, throw him outside in the darkness; there he will cry and gnash his teeth.* In the parable of the sheep and the goats, he says of those on his left, the ones who did not give food or drink to the hungry, who did not recognize Jesus: *Away from me you that are under God's curse! Away to the eternal fire which has been prepared for the devil and his angels.* And from John 12: 47: *Whoever rejects me and does not accept my message has one who will judge him. The words I have spoken will be his judge on the last day.*

"And it's a hard rain's a-gonna' fall."

I think his frustration may have reached a fever pitch in this passage. It is a warning in the tradition of the Old Testament jeremiad prophets . . . those who prophesied in warnings. How could they have missed his message? He scolds: *When you see a cloud rising in the west, you immediately say, "It is going to rain"; and so it happens. And when you see the south wind blowing, you say, "There will be scorching heat"; and it happens. You hypocrites! You know how to interpret the appearance of earth and sky, but why do you not know the meaning of the present time?*

"A hard rain is gonna' fall."

Assume with me that these dire warnings need not be aimed at you and I. We have studied the Kingdom of God in his words in the gospels, and we seek to belong, as we worship and pray at each Sunday service. We say "thy Kingdom come" in our prayer.

We can be more at ease with this inscrutable gospel, with another interpretation . . . which says that the fire -- *I came to bring fire to the earth* -- is "the saving message of the gospel and the power of its commandments." Cyril of Alexandria, bishop and patriarch, in North Africa in the 5TH century, one of the great Doctors of the Church, proclaims/explains in his sermon on the gospel of Luke, "We were cold and dead because of sin and in ignorance of him who is by nature truly God. The gospel ignites all of us on earth to a life of piety, and makes us fervent in spirit, according to the expression of blessed Paul [Rom12: 11] . . . . We have been baptized with the fire of the Holy Spirit."

We are able to interpret the signs of the times; that is, that we are living in the A.D. (Year of the Lord), the age of Christ, the promised Messiah. And we have the opportunity to know him and love him and build a warm spiritual relationship with him through our prayer and devotion. Yet, at the same time, we cannot take the Lord's words in this gospel lightly. There are in our world Christians for whom there is no peace, where they must suffer for their faith in the message of Christ's Kingdom. And there are also those who have neglected or ignored it, who "do not know how to interpret the present time." That is, who are missing out on the gospel of salvation. For these, our church, our community of faithful, must pray ardently. Always mindful of the message in *the exhortation of joy* of Pope Francis . . . which you have in your hands this morning:

[bulletin handout]
The Joy of the Gospel fills the hearts and lives of all who encounter Jesus. Those who accept his offer of salvation are set free from sin, sorrow, inner emptiness and loneliness. With Christ, joy is constantly born anew.

Thanks be to God.

Desire of the Everlasting Hills

TEXT Matthew 15: 10-28

"What was Jesus like? I mean his personality, his temperament, his bearing and composure. Thousands of books have been written about the Lord, dissecting him every which way. Thousands more books have been produced about his teachings by theologians of every stripe. And we Christians who follow him are always searching to understand him and know him better. One of those books -- by Thomas Cahill -- gives this name to Jesus in its title: "Desire of the Everlasting Hills." I like the poetry of that name. It reflects the history of mankind before the Lord's coming, when the Israelites for thousands of years were waiting for a savior God had promised them, listening to the prophets, praying with their holy men.

And the "Desire of the Everlasting Hills" in its imagery also reflects who Jesus is in our time: our desire in every way we turn, whether to search in quest for enlightenment and grace and faith, or, secure in devotion and prayer, to draw nearer to him is our desire. A place to get to know the Lord, to know what Jesus was like is in the gospel writings of Matthew, that we have been reading from all this summer. It was clearly Matthew's intention to portray in a comprehensive and graphic and dramatic way Jesus the Lord, his personality, his character, and precisely his teaching. Mathew wanted in the first place the community of Jesus' followers to understand that, indeed, he is the savior who was promised, that he is the *desire of the everlasting hills.* In fact, at times Matthew's narratives focus on Jesus as coming almost exclusively in fulfillment of the prophesies to the Israelites. In this episode with the woman, whose daughter is sick, we hear Jesus emphasize that he has come for the Jews. He is their savior . . . no mistaking that. *I was sent only to the lost sheep of the house of Israel,* he says to the woman . . . who was not an Israelite but from Cana in a region outside of the country of the Jews. But she knew of his reputation as a preacher and healer. And she picked up on his metaphor. *Even the dogs eat the crumbs that fall from their master's table.* She seemed to have a sense of God's salvation plan . . . that it could include her also. And the Lord confirmed it for her: *Your faith is great!* And he did the healing of her sick daughter.

The commentators say that here was an instance where Jesus indicated that his mission was beyond the borders of the Jews -- as it would be broadcast later in the letters and preaching of St. Paul, whom we have come to know as the "Apostle of the Gentiles"; that is, of the world beyond the Israelites. The divine plan for mankind's salvation through the presence of God in the world in Jesus, the Christ, was to begin with the revelation to one small tribal nation, grow through their desire and faith, and be culminated in the Lord's life, and then spread out to the entire world. To "all nations," he said. And that message and mission continue to this day.

But I want to focus our attention in this reading to the Lord's actions that are a clue to his personality and character. In the instance of the Canaanite woman, when he is petitioned and when he recognizes faith in that petition, he hesitates at first, and then he gives in, he helps her. This same aspect of his personality is apparent in the story of the "persistent widow," that is told in Luke's gospel, where Jesus says to his disciples: *Since she keeps pestering me, I must give this widow her just rights or she will persist in coming and worry me to death.* Also in Luke, Jesus explains God's responsiveness: *One who asks always receives . . . [and] what father among you would hand his son a stone when he asks for bread."* Jesus is soft; he knows mercy. And he wants us to know that.

But let's look at another part of this scriptural reading. While Matthew's narrative was always directed at showing Jesus as the Lord and Messiah, as the *desire of the everlasting hills*, Matthew also points out that some people didn't get the message. Jesus scolds some of his listeners, the teachers, or Pharisees as they were called. They were always focusing on the minutia of the laws, fussing over some dietary rules. So when Jesus said, *Listen and understand: it is not what goes into the mouth that defiles a person, but it is what comes out of the mouth that defiles, they reacted.* Then he carries the metaphor almost to the extreme: *Whatever goes into the mouth enters the stomach and ends up in the sewer.* And now he hits hard: *But what comes out of the mouth comes from the heart, and this is what defiles. For out of the heart comes evil intentions, murder, adultery, fornication, theft, lies, slander. These are what defile a person.* In this Jesus is laying down some clear principles of the morality he taught, and which he commands us to follow. These are the commands he means when he says so often, *If you love me, keep my commandments.*

In the passages appointed for our liturgical reading today, we have the evangelist Matthew presenting two aspects of the Lord's personality. With some of his audience, the Pharisees, he is quite stern, and he describes the nature of sin; namely, it comes from deep within the man who allows himself to be blind to the truth. And he names the sins. But in the second scenario he is gentle and soft hearted; he can't help but to yield to the pleading of the lady whose daughter is troubled. This is the aspect of the Lord's personality that we want to attend to now. Let's assume that we are not blind to his commandments, and we keep them to the best of our graces.

There is a well-known devotion to the kindness and gentle heart of Jesus that was preached by the great French pastor Francis DeSales -- a spiritual mentor by the way, of John Wesley, who read and praised his classic book, *Introduction to a Devout Life*. One of the best sermons I have ever heard – and a short one -- is on this topic of the Sacred Heart. It was given by an Anglican-Use priest who is a pastor in Boston today. Here are some highlights.

> Just as the heart is the seat of human love, the physical human heart of Jesus reveals a fundamental fact of religion: That God loves us. All of the attributes of Almighty God revealed in the Old Testament came into focus when the Word became flesh and dwelt among us. In Christ, God saw with human eyes. When he stretched out his hand to save, it was a human hand he stretched out. And the gospels do not hesitate to describe our Lord's human feelings: When he saw moneychangers in the temple, it filled Jesus with anger: when the seventy returned home from their first successful ministry, Jesus was filled with gladness; and we all know the shortest verse in the Bible – "Jesus wept" . . . at the tomb of his friend Lazarus. In such way, the gospels reveal the anger, joys, sorrows, and disappointments of a human heart.

We might add to that list the Jesus of today's scripture, where he responds with his heart for the woman who begs for his help. This tender Sacred Heart of Jesus is the source of holiness, and our devotion to it bestows a deeper insight into that Divine Love. By devotion we gain a sure confidence in that Love. And as we see something of God's love, we want to respond to it by expressing the love of our own hearts. That's how it works.

Let me close with the closing words of that sermon. "Our hope for the Church, for those outside the church, for the world, for our loved ones, and for our own souls is in the faithfulness of the Heart of Jesus."

Thanks be to God.

Getting to Know Peter

TEXT Matthew 16: 21-28

Who is Peter? You get a pretty good answer to that question in the gospel of Matthew, which we have been reading every Sunday this summer. Go back to Chapter three, where early in his preaching activity in Galilee, Jesus meets Peter and his brother Andrew, fishermen on the lake, near the village of Capernaum. He invites them to follow him. This is the beginning of an adventurous life for Peter, as we shall see. Peter was from Bethsaida, a ways south on the lakeshore -- sometimes called Lake Tiberius or the Sea of Galilee. And while Jesus preached and performed many cures in that vicinity, which Peter surely witnessed, he visited Peter's home where we learn that he cured Peter's month-in-law. *He took her by the hand and the fever left her.* Matthew's account says.

Peter was always the first among the apostles. (By the way, the word *apostle* has the meaning like the word *messenger*, one who is sent out.) In Matthew 10, he is the leader when Jesus sends his disciples out to do some of his work of healing and exorcising bad spirits. The next time we meet Peter, he is attempting to walk with Jesus on the lake. By this time, the disciples were well aware of the power of Jesus and were awed knowing him to be a man with the power of God. Sinking Peter says, *"Lord, save me."* And after they are back in the boat, he says: *"You really are the Son of God,"*

Peter was also one of the three apostles to whom the Lord revealed his divine identity on the Mountain of the Transfiguration. Characteristically, Peter is over-enthusiastic and, in fact, overwhelmed. At first he suggests they set up camp for the Lord and the prophets who appeared. But the evangelist Mark, who was an associate of Peter, writes in his report of the event: *The apostles were so frightened that Peter really did not know what he was talking about.*

But the passage I like most is in Matthew's gospel reading today, that shows the intimate relationship of Peter with the Lord. "When Jesus began to explain to his disciples that he must go to Jerusalem and undergo great suffering . . . and be killed, Peter calls Jesus aside and begins to rebuke him. "*No.* [Peter says.] *This is not going to happen to you.*" What nerve! Only a short while ago Peter had confessed: *"You* are the Messiah, the Son of the Living God." Now he speaks intimately to Jesus of his fear, and says he will protect him. Has he lost sight of the Lord's divinity, or was he so overcome emotionally with his love and respect for Jesus, that all he could see was that he was about to lose this man, his leader, his friend?

We know from the narratives of the rest of the gospels of Peter's contradictory and tense moments after Jesus is apprehended in Jerusalem. He impetuously strikes with a sword one of the officials in the posse that came after Jesus. And a short time later that evening, when the girl in the outer court asks him if he knew Jesus, he says, *"I don't know what you're talking about."* Peter repented for this. And in his long career as an apostle and leader of the Christian movement, yes, even a martyr for the cause, he made up for that cowardly lapse tenfold.

Your kind of want to pray to St. Peter. You feel for him -- at least as you read the details of these tense moments in his life. You may find something of yourself in his personality: at times saying. *"Lord save me!"* or *"Remember, we have left everything to follow you; what are we to have?"* You may even need the assurance Jesus gives Peter when he appears to the disciples after the resurrection, near the lake again, and he says to Peter, *"Simon Peter do you love me more than the others do?"* And Peter answers, *"Lord, you know I do."* May we always have that same fear Peter has of ever losing the Lord, Jesus, our leader, our friend. May we always confess with Peter: "You, Lord, are the Savior, the Son of the Living God."

Peter was a young man when he met Jesus back there on the shores of the Sea of Galilee. He died in his 80s in Rome. In between, his life is chronicled in the Acts of the Apostles, a book by the evangelist Luke, wherein Peter gives one of the greatest speeches of the New Testament. He is convincing. He can speak from personal experience when he addresses a huge crowd in Jerusalem: *"Listen to what I have to say about Jesus from Nazareth. God proved that he sent Jesus to you by having him work miracles, wonders, and signs . . . all of us can tell you that God raised Jesus . . .. Jesus is the one who gave us the Spirit, and that is what you are now seeing and hearing."*

Preaching Salvation through Jesus the Christ, at that time and in that place – the shadow of the Jewish temple – could get you in trouble with the authorities, and Peter and some of the others were arrested and imprisoned. This would not be the last time Peter was arrested and put into prison. He went on in the Asian lands preaching and doing miracle cures -- this commercial fisherman, now filled to the brim with the gifts of the Spirit, wisdom and preaching talent, and an understanding of the scriptures. He founded a community of Christians and a church in Antioch, where he served as bishop for 20 years. Later he went to Rome, and there was arrested with other Christians during the reign of the emperor Nero, and then executed. But not before earning a reputation as the leader among the Christian community, indeed, a bishop, an apostle, an emissary appointed from the very beginning by Jesus -- as we read in Matthew chapter 10: *Jesus called together the twelve apostles and gave them the power . . . and the first among these was Simon, better known as Peter.*

The mission, indeed, the passion of John Wesley, was to teach, and engender Christian holiness in his followers. And in today's scripture readings we have a powerful and explicit and detailed expression of what Christian holiness is. Peter wrote these words in a letter to Christians:

> *Always live as God's holy people should, because God is the one who is holy and he chose you. *** You obeyed the truth, and our souls were made pure. Now you sincerely love each other. And you must keep on loving with all your heart, because God has given you new birth by his message. . .. Be sure, then, that you are never spiteful, or deceitful, or hypocritical, or envious and critical of each other. You are new born . . . and you should be hungry for spiritual honesty which will help you go up to salvation.*

And then we can turn to the Epistle of Paul to the Romans, that we just heard, for further instruction on holiness. How consistent Paul's writing is with the advice and admonitions of Peter's letter:

> *Let your love be genuine; hate what is evil, hold fast to what is good; love one another with mutual affection; outdo one another in showing honour . . . Contribute to the needs of the saints; extend hospitality to strangers. Live in harmony with one another; do not be haughty, but associate with the lowly; do not claim to be wiser than you are. Do not repay anyone evil for evil, but take thought for what is noble in the sight of all. If it is possible, so far as it depends on you, live peaceably with all.*

One final thought about St. Peter, the star of the day. While I was reading about him and his actions and words, I couldn't help but think of who I might cast for him if we were to make a movie of his life. Who would play Peter? My choice: John Wayne.

Peter, the Apostle, pray for us.

Thanks be to God.

490 - Do the Math.

TEXT Matthew 18: 21-35   (9/11 sermon)

How much is 70 times 7? 490. Right. This is the Lord's hyperbole in answering Peter's question about how many times he should forgive his brother who did him wrong. *"Not just 7 times," Jesus says, "but 70 times 7 times."* That's 490. This is not the only time Jesus has used hyperbole to make a point. Recall when he warned of scandal: *"If your right eye causes you to sin, cut it out and throw it away."* Hyperbole. Likewise, here with these numbers, they are not to be taken literally. Rather, the lesson is that God's mercy is inexhaustible, has no limits. It is boundless. And to drive home that point, Jesus goes on to illustrate forgiveness and mercy with the parable of the king who shows mercy to a subject in debt. But then in the second part of the parable, he shows us what happens to one who fails to forgive. [One caution: the Lord's teaching would hold that Christians are expected ordinarily to honor their debt responsibilities. Let's not miss the point and go off on an erroneous tangent here.]

   The topic is mercy. Do we Christians understand the fullness of God's mercy? There is nothing comparable to divine mercy in human experience. While we do see mercy and forgiveness around us at times, our society's inclination seems to be more toward the rules of justice. Which is fine. Divine mercy is on another level -- the reason it may not be easy for us to understand it. It's extreme. Remember, the Lord said, *"Love you enemies, and pray for those who do harm to you."* Extreme. [Matt 5: 43]

   Divine mercy, forgiveness, is a theme that pervades the entire gospel. Let's count the ways.
- Early on, in the Sermon on the Mount, Jesus establishes the principle. The fifth beatitude is *Blessed are the merciful, for they will be shown mercy.*
- Remember the woman at the well, of whom Jesus requests a drink of water? He shows her kindness and consolation, although she is from another community, not of the Jews.

- And in the very next scene in John's gospel, he is approached by a local official whose son is sick. *"Your son will live,"* he assures the man.
- And there's another man, whom he cured, and then he saw later in the temple where he said, *"You are now well; sin no more."* Mercy and forgiveness.
- Likewise the man born blind. Jesus cures him of blindness and later meets him and has this conversation: *"Do you have faith in the Son of Man?" "Sir, if you will tell me who he is, I will have faith in him." "You are seeing him now," Jesus replies.* [John 9: 1-40]
- And of course, the incident of the woman about to be stoned. Jesus sizes up the situation. She is accused by the religious leaders and officials. She is not innocent, but Jesus says, *"I do not accuse you; go on your way, but without sin from now on."* The woman is saved not only in a moral sense by the forgiveness of the Lord, but her life is saved. God's mercy is made available to meet the needs of the situation in every way. [John 7]
- At his life's end, although no mercy has been shown him, his response, his last words, in fact, are of forgiveness: *"Father, forgive them, for they know not what they do."* And for his fellow, who is also condemned – who begs Jesus with his dying breath, "please remember me" -- the Savior has divine forgiveness ready for him: *"This day you will be with me in paradise."*

The list goes on throughout the four gospels. The theme, the very theme of the life of Jesus is mercy and forgiveness. *"I have come to save sinners,"* he said. There is much more in each of these gospel vignettes I've presented, of course; but I have extracted them in such a way as to highlight what takes place in an encounter with Jesus. Whenever someone meets the Lord; whenever he encounters a person in need -- a sinner, but with faith -- Jesus is easy; his first response is to show mercy, to respond with a consoling word, with healing, with forgiveness of sin. It is always an encounter of mercy.

I have said that the meaning of 70 times 7 = 490, rich and boundless divine mercy, is not easy for us to understand. We are more likely to judge mercy in human terms, mixed with what we regard as fairness and balance, something framed by our social conventions and human laws. We may even apply this merely human standard to ourselves. And that's a problem. We think, "How could it be that our sins or failings, our foolishness, could be forgiven? That doesn't compute." We leave it moot. And the shadow of guilt always seems to linger in the recesses of our consciousness.

And the problem is that it inhibits and interferes with our spiritual growth. It can impede our reaching the goal of attaining a holy Christian lifestyle, what we strive for in living out our faith -- John Wesleyan holiness. I subscribe to this formula: Acceptance of divine mercy leads to peace of mind; peace of mind leads the pursuit of Christian virtue; Christian virtue leads to holiness . . . and, I might add, happiness.

To understand the possibility of boundless mercy and forgiveness, we need only to look to its source -- the Lord's redemptive act. The enormity of the sacrificial death of Jesus balances the enormity of divine mercy. Yes, it takes faith. Redemption through the cross of Christ is the central mystery of Christianity. One way to come at it is from the opposite direction. We need redemption; and so if it is out there and offered to us, we are ready to embrace it with our faith. We must reach out and grab it like a life-line, a spiritual life-line that keeps us afloat and secure in the Christian way.

The saints have reached out and embraced God's forgiveness and mercy, and it changed their lives. It's that powerful. St. Peter, after he had denied knowing the Savior in the courtyard on that fateful night. The gospel says he repented. He absorbed a lot of divine mercy, and went on to a great leadership role in the church. St. Paul, once an enemy of the Christian way, is forgiven . . . and with him, the rest is history. Sts. Francis, Ignatius, John Wesley -- all grasped the mystery of God's boundless mercy and forgiveness in an enlightened moment and grounded their holy lives in it. That same mercy is available to us in "an encounter of mercy" -- which is our prayer today. It is here for us . . . to sustain us in our faith. We need only to pray, as in the psalm we sang a few moments ago. "With the Lord there is mercy and the fullness of redemption. Open your ears and hear my voice, and attend to the sound of my plea."

On an occasion like today, when we remember sadly our great loss, and events beyond our control have forced us to acknowledge our human frailty and dependence, this prayer will be evermore fervent.

Thanks be to God.

The Blue Haze: Divine Mercy

TEXT Luke 15:1-10

In the course of his public career as rabbi and preacher, Jesus traveled to Jerusalem, perhaps, three or four times, according to the gospels. Could have been more; but these trips we know of, because of the religious feasts (events) that, as an observant Jew, he attended. The distance was about 70 miles, and would have taken at least four days, three overnights. We know that he had friends along the way, should he need a place to stay overnight. There was the home of Martha and Mary and Lazarus, and there was also the home of Zacchaeus, the man who climbed up a tree to see Jesus over the heads of the crowd. Writes evangelist Luke, When *Jesus reached the spot, he looked up and said to him, "Zacchaeus, come down immediately. I must stay at your house today." So he came down at once and welcomed him gladly.*

All along the way of this journey, Jesus attracted large crowds. And they were a mixed assortment of local people. Writes Luke, Now, *all the tax-collectors and sinners were coming near to listen to him. And the Pharisees and the scribes were grumbling and saying, "This fellow welcomes sinners and eats with them."*

Jesus looks to be at the peak of his popularity in this scripture. The evangelist reports several miracles and many parables, one after another. Two of these parables are in this morning's reading: the shepherd who goes in search of a lost sheep and carries the sheep back on his shoulders, (Don't you love the detail of this account? It was irresistible to artists of every century since.) And the woman who rejoices when she recovers a lost silver coin. Were we to continues reading this chapter of Luke, we would come immediately to the famous parable of the Prodigal Son. All of these three consecutive parables are illustrations of mercy: God the Creator's mercy in the person and teaching of Jesus, the Messiah.

I have preached before on the topic of God's mercy . . . once when the scripture was about the Lord's conversation with the apostle Peter, and Peter asks (Matthew 18:21), *"Lord, how many times shall*

I forgive my brother who sins against me? Up to seven times?" Jesus answered: "Not just seven times, but seventy times seven." I titled the sermon, "490 -- Do the Math." Get it? Anyone remember the sermon? That was exactly five years ago, again on this very Sunday, September 11.

Jesus continued his conversation with Peter on that occasion, with a parable saying, *"This will show you what the kingdom of heaven is like."* It was the parable of the king's official who did not show mercy. The Lord spent a lot of time and effort to get this notion across: *divine mercy*. Is it a hard concept to grasp? Five years ago, I tried to explain that we may have a problem with divine mercy, because we tend to interpret it in the context of our human experience –- but this is *divine* mercy; it's different. I'm quoting from my own sermon:

There is nothing comparable to *divine mercy* in human experience. While we do see mercy and forgiveness around us at times, our society's inclination seems to be more toward the rules of justice. Which is fine. Divine mercy is on another level -- the reason it may not be easy for us to understand it. It's extreme. Remember, the Lord said, "Love you enemies, and pray for those who do harm to you." Extreme. [Mt 5: 43]

Divine mercy, forgiveness, is a theme that pervades the entire New Testament revelation. We read these words in Luke 5:32: Jesus addresses the crowd: *"It is not the healthy who need a doctor, but the sick. I have not come to call the righteous, but sinners."* And I especially like St. Paul's confession in his letter to his partner, Timothy: *"Christ Jesus came into the world to save sinners -- and I am the worst of them all."* And so this purpose is made evident again, as we find in the scripture parables assigned for the service today.

Let us examine the unique aspects of *divine mercy*, as they are illustrated in these parables. (1) The shepherd goes after the one lost sheep: Divine mercy is relentless; it does not give up; it comes after you. (2) The woman who lost and then found a silver coin: Divine mercy is precious, a value to be searched for, to be discovered, and found and embraced. (3) The Prodigal Son: Divine mercy is loving; circumstances of the son's profligate life are brushed aside, irrelevant, and vanish in the embrace of the loving father. You may meditate on these parables and consider the aspect of divine mercy you would have poured out on you. All of them? Not a bad choice.

Now let's see how the pros — I mean the early and great Fathers of the Church — interpret these parables. In his *Exposition on the Gospel of Luke*, Classic Latin Father St. Ambrose sees in the three parables a kind of progression of the elements of divine mercy: (quote) "St. Luke did not idly present three parables in a row.... First mercy comes, then intersession, and third reconciliation. The mercy of the divine act is the same, but the grace differs according to our merits. The weary sheep is recalled by the shepherd (That's me.); the coin which was lost is found (That's Faith.); the son retraces his steps to his father and returns, guilty of error but totally repentant. (That's anyone of us.)." — I interjected the asides here.

In my former sermon on this topic, I made the point that we must act to take advantage of divine mercy, lest we allow our sins to get in the way of our spiritual progress and our pursuit of holiness. Now in this sermon, I want to take another tack. One analyst of the gospels and the life of Jesus (It is Joseph Ratzinger, Pope Benedict 16TH, now retired, in his book *Jesus of Nazareth*.) -- he writes this about divine mercy. "[The follower of Christ] knows that he needs mercy. So he will learn from God's mercy to become merciful himself.... He will always need the gift of goodness, of forgiveness ... and in receiving it, he will learn to pass the gift on to others."

My interpretation of this is that divine mercy is the foundation of all Christian virtues. Once we recognize and ask for and accept Christ's divine mercy in our lives, we are set up to imitate it and to foster compassion and courage and resolve to go along with it; and to spread out of it an array of virtues that comprises our life of personal Christian holiness. Grounded in divine mercy, we become proactive in Christian virtue: the proactive shepherd in the parable who goes after his lost one; the first responders of this day we remember who go into a burning building to find and rescue their neighbors. This is the dynamic power of divine mercy, and it is there for us. It is a catalyst that creates and stabilizes Christian life and readies us for action.

The message of today's gospel parable is to be aware that divine mercy is there for us, and to be prepared and disposed sincerely to receive it. *"This is what the Kingdom of God is like,"* Jesus said to

Peter -- as he went on to tell another parable of mercy. Divine Mercy. It is the *blue haze* that colors the sky of God's kingdom. Don't miss out on it. Extract it from these holy scriptures by your honest and deep prayers, and make it the foundation of your virtuous Christian life going forward.

Thanks be to God.

Pentecost and Ordinary Time

A Big Day [Pentecost Sunday]
The Kingdom Option
'Faith Comes through Hearing'
Jesus and His Friends
The Good Samaritan Story
Social Jesus
'It's a Jungle out There.'
Matthew's Mission
Feast Day of Peter and Paul
A One-on-One with Jesus
'A Hard Rain is Gonna' Fall'
Desire of the Everlasting Hills
Getting to Know Peter
490 -- Do the Math.
The Blue Haze: Divine Mercy
Mark's Gospel: Voice of the Lion
The Lord Plays Favorites.
Back to Basics
Philemon
'If I Were a Rich Man'
Jesus as the 'Boss'
Slogans and Mottos
Corragio
Jesus in a Somber Mood

Mark's Gospel: Voice of the Lion

TEXT Mark 4: 35-41

When you open your Bible (unless it's a Bible in the Hebrew language -- which reads from back to front), you may assume that it is set out in chronological order: Genesis first, the oldest book to be written, and so on. It doesn't work that way exactly. It is true, however, that the Old Testament comes before the New Testament chronically. In the New Testament we find the gospels in this order: Matthew, Mark, Luke, and John. Right? You may be surprised to learn that the first gospel narrative to be written is the Gospel of Mark. After Mark came Matthew and Luke, who relied heavily on Mark for their material. Later John. And the epistles of St. Paul were written before all of the gospels. When the gospel of Mark was written, most likely in Rome, St. Paul had already established a Christian church there. That's what makes Mark so important as an essential and radical source. We are reading passages from Mark every Sunday in this year's liturgical cycle -- Cycle B. Have you noticed?

It makes sense for our Sunday meditation to examine closely the Gospel of Mark. Mark, whose authorship has been attached to this gospel from the 2ND century, was a good writer. With professional literary skill, comparable to that of many classical writers of the Greek language before and after him: Homer (Iliad/Odyssey) for example, or John Chrysostom. The Gospel of Mark was written in Greek, the common language in that region. Some scholars believe Mark may have been a companion of the apostle Peter; and therefore, he would have had firsthand knowledge of Jesus and his activities. He was writing for the new Christians in Rome, who had heard the preaching of the apostles, but not heard the story of the Jesus' life. Mark writes in a realistic style. We describe some of our American writers, the novelists, as realists. They give you a sense of immediacy, being right there, on the scene. Ernest Hemingway, the novelist, is a realist; and I have always felt that Mark's gospel has that same feeling of realism. The descriptions are detailed and direct, in short phrases and sentences. Jesus had spent the day preaching to large crowds in Capharnum, near the Sea of Galilee. Mark writes:

> *They left the crowd, and his disciples started across the lake with him in the boat. Some other boats followed along. Suddenly a wind storm struck the lake. Waves started splashing into the boat, and it was about to sink. Jesus was in the back of the boat, and he was asleep with his head on a pillow.*

Is that a realistic scene or what! As a result, in Mark's writing we get a close look at Jesus in his humanity. In today's reading we hear that he was tired, exhausted, had to get away from the crowds for a while. He was sound asleep, the dangerously rough water notwithstanding, and his disciples had to wake him up. A human, like any one of us at the end of the day.

The Sea of Galilee, also called Lake Tiberius after the Roman emperor of that time, was in the region where Jesus grew up. It was where he first met Peter and Andrew and invited them to accompany him on his ministry. They belonged to a fishing family there. It's a fresh-water lake, about 12 miles long north to south, and 8 miles at its widest. In the 17TH century, the artist Rembrandt created a painting of that gospel scene, the boat under sail in the storm -- probably a sudden squall, which we all have experience of. In modern times, every year, swimmers compete in crossing Lake Tiberius on a 5000-meter race. That's about three miles.

Did I mention that the symbol of Mark is a winged lion? I use that reference in the title of this sermon. The origin of the symbol is complicated, with links to both the Old and New Testaments; but it has been a part of Christian tradition from the earliest centuries.

In addition to giving us a sense of the Lord's humanness, Mark also shows the divine power of Jesus. The passage we read today is a perfect example. Jesus the man, like us, is tired and resting; Jesus the Son of God, orders the winds to cease. Mark's gospel is characterized by many miracle accounts. There is more narrative content of signs and wonders (miracles) in Mark than in any of the other gospels.

Mark set out from the very beginning to teach his listeners what the life of Jesus was all about. It's very first lines are: "This is the Good News about Jesus Christ, the Son of God." Only Mark, of the four evangelists, uses the phrase Good News as the title of his narrative; that is, the Greek word *euaggelion* [yu-ahn-ge-le-on], meaning literally, *God's good news.* It comes down to us through the Anglo-Saxon translation as "God's spell" or God's story, and eventually *gospel.*

Then to clarify as a kind of sub-title to his work, Mark takes a verse from the prophet Isaiah: *. . . as God has said through the prophet, "I am sending my messenger to get my way ready for you."* In recent years -- the past 200 -- scholars have developed great insights into the gospel of Mark. They show how Mark, the writer, made use of the writings of the Old Testament prophets -- Isaiah, as in the verse I just quoted, but others as well. He was well-versed in the sacred scriptures. In this blend of his narrative with material from the prophets, he advances his thesis that Jesus is truly the Messiah, but -- and here is Mark's point -- not the kind of Messiah you might have been expecting. Mark understands, as one who was a follower of Jesus and heard him preach and observed his works, that this Messiah will redeem through his sacrificial death -- as in the sacrifices his people knew. So he lets us know as early as his 3RD chapter that Jesus has opposition to this teaching. And in his account of the Lord's passion and death on the cross, he shows us what this opposition leads to.

The Jesus who rises up from the pages of Mark is a young man in a hurry. He speaks directly and confronts the power of evil, sickness, and death. He moves quickly from place to place, yet stops to heal a woman who for over a decade suffers a debilitating and humiliating illness; and he returns to her grieving parents a 12-year-old girl who died. He shows compassion for the hungry crowd. In the overview, Mark's Jesus is a man of action, who summons people to a radical faith and says that those who want to follow him must take up their cross.

When we hear the gospel, God's good news/God's story in the Sunday service, we must find in it a message that draws us closer to Jesus; and the more we understand it and understand how it has been handed down to us over hundreds/thousands of years, the closer it brings us to knowing Jesus and loving God as we are commanded. The first generation of Christians must have been excited at hearing Mark tell his story, his experience with the Lord . . . so thrilled that they have preserved it for us. [In hundreds of manuscripts.]

Let me close with the words of one of those early Christians who made a career of studying the gospels and writing about them. His name is Origin, from Alexandria in North Africa in the 3ʳᴰ century, and he wrote this about the passage of Mark we read today:

> *For as many as are in the little ship of faith and are sailing with the Lord; as many as are in the bark of holy church and will voyage with the Lord across this wave-tossed life . . . although the Lord himself may sleep in holy quiet, he is but watching your patience and endurance, looking forward to the repentance, and to the conversion of those who have sinned. Come then to him eagerly, instant in prayer.*

Thanks be to God.

The Lord Plays Favorites.

TEXT Luke 18: 1-8

All the experts -- the Fathers of the early church, the Doctors and theologians down through the centuries -- comment that the message of this parable is "persistence in prayer." And why shouldn't they? The evangelist tells us the meaning of the parable in the very first sentence: *Then Jesus* told them a parable about their need to pray always and not to lose heart.* That's not a bad idea, and a good theme for a sermon on Laity Sunday. After all, us laity do a lot of praying, and it's good to hear the Lord tell us how to be effective in our prayers.

Among the "experts" who reinforce this message with their expert commentary is Cyril of Alexandria, 5TH century bishop, who writes that, "The present parable assures us God will bend his ear to those who offer him their prayers, not carelessly or negligently, but with earnestness and constancy." Augustine in a sermon says that, "By this, the Lord wishes us to infer how much care God bestows on those who beseech him; for God is both just and good." Here is Martyius, an 8TH century holy Christian Monk in Syria who left us a classic spiritual book, the *Book of Perfection:* "It is quite clear that God does not neglect us. Even if he makes us wait, he will nonetheless answer us and see to our case all of a sudden. When we pray all the time, we should not grow weary. We should eagerly cry out to him day and night, begging him with a broken heart and a humble spirit."

That should lift/buoy up our confidence in prayer, assure us that we are doing the right thing, knowing that Christ's followers have from the very beginning and onward through the centuries taken to heart his command to pray and the very words he taught: *When you pray, say: 'Father, hallowed be they name.'* You know the rest.

But we can go further in interpreting and understanding the teaching of Jesus in that parable. I was struck by the phrase, *God will grant justice to his chosen ones*-- the *elect,* as it is often translated. Who are the *elect,* his chosen ones? A great deal has been made of this term in the course of theological history. It has a deep technical meaning for theologians, the gospel interpreters. The apostle Peter addressed his first epistle to *the elect who are gathered like foreigners* in the towns of

Asia Minor. And further on in the next chapter, Peter: *you are a chosen people, a royal priesthood, a consecrated nation, a people set apart.* Paul in Romans 8 refers to the *elect, those God has chosen;* and he writes warmly in 2 Thessalonians: *We must be continually thanking God for you, brothers, whom the Lord loves, because God chose you from the beginning. You are God's chosen race, his saints, he loves you, and you should be clothed in sincere compassion, kindness and humility, gentleness and patience.* (Col. 3:12.) There are many many more, clear and definitive expressions in the gospels, and epistles of the apostles, of the chosen, the *elect*.

And so out of these expressions in the scriptures there grew certain strains of theological thought that have heavily impacted the path of Christianity. It was John Calvin, trained in Paris but later moved to Geneva, a lawyer, who took the lead in the Theology of the Elect. He is regarded as one of the world's greatest theologians ever -- right up there, they say, with Augustine and Thomas Aquinas. His three volume work, *Institutes of Christian Religion,* is the bedrock of Protestant theology, although even in its own time it was widely criticized and modified by others. In this *magnum opus,* Calvin exposed the doctrine of the Elect, drawn from the scriptural passages we've heard this morning. But he severely interpreted them so as to mean that Christians, the Elect, were predestined as chosen by God, and there was nothing you could do about it. There are the Elect, those chosen by God for salvation, and then there is everybody else.

But most of the reformers who followed after John Calvin -- with the notable exception of our own Massachusetts Pilgrims and Congregationalists, who were strict Calvinists -- many reformers revised the doctrine of the predestined elect to allow for man's free will, so that he might freely chose his path to salvation . . . with the help of God's grace, of course. John Wesley was among the latter, he who passionately believed man is called to live "by his free efforts" a life in pursuit of holiness.

This leads us to the theology of the doctrine of Grace, another topic of great study and profound theologizing. But we're not going there. A holy quagmire, I call it.

It is sufficient for our pastoral purpose here to point out that any controversies about grace finally came to an end in 1997, with the Joint Declaration on the Doctrine of Justification, a document that stated: "[we] are now able to articulate a common understanding of our justification by God's grace through faith in Christ." . . . to which Catholic, Lutherans, and Methodists formally subscribed, thus ending a theological controversy that was a major cause of the split in Western churches in the 16TH century. In my view, the war is over.

Let us now go back to the parable's message, *persistence in prayer*. And my thesis: the Elect, God's favorites. First, on God's favorites, the Elect. We all know from our bible reading that God did play favorites -- so to speak -- by choosing or *electing* an obscure nomadic tribe in the Mediterranean Sea region as the people he would reveal himself to. Up to that time, the people of the earth could only conjecture about god, about their world, what it meant, and what its origin is. They imagined many gods, one or two for each phenomenon they experienced. They had gods for the sea, the sky, the earth, and so forth. St. Paul, when he traveled through Athens, said to the philosophers and thinkers there, *"I see you have many gods; you are a religious people."* And then he continued on to explain to them the One God, the true God who was their creator and who visited the world in the form of a man, his Son.

This God had revealed himself to one nomadic tribe of people -- Abraham and his offspring. He chose them for this Revelation, and they were called henceforward the *chosen people,* the Elect, God's favorites. When God's Son, the Messiah, came, Jesus, he expanded the world of his chosen people, the Elect, his favorites, to all who would be his followers, who kept his commandments. From John's gospel: *"If you abide in my word, you are truly my disciples. If you keep my commands, you will remain in my love, just as I have kept my Father's commands and remain in his love."*

Which bring us back to that point where, in the passage from Luke we read this morning, Jesus calls his followers who keep his commandments, the *elect:* whose prayers, if they are persistent, he assures us, God the Father will surely answer. John Calvin wrote a treatise on prayer in which he counsels persistence -- if in a florid style of language: "So true it is that prayer digs up those treasures which the Gospel of our Lord discovers to the eye of faith. The necessity and utility of this exercise of prayer no words can sufficiently express. Assuredly, it is not without cause our heavenly Father declares that our only safety is in calling upon his name, since by it we invoke the presence of his providence to watch over our interests."

And of persistent praying, our mentor, John Wesley, said in a sermon: "God's command to pray without ceasing is founded on the necessity we have of his grace to preserve the life of God in the soul, which," insists Wesley, "can no more subsist one moment without it, than the body can without air."

As you pray "without ceasing," and are *persistent* in your prayer, do not fail to consider that you are among God's favorites. That's the point Jesus makes, when he explains the meaning of his parable. *"God grants justice to his chosen ones."* He plays favorites. We can believe that is us. We are the faithful. We are here. We know what it means to have a favorite -- a favorite team, a favorite meal, a favorite song, a favorite friend. We know what it means to be a favorite. How consoling to be the Lord's favorite, to be among his chosen. What power, what assurance that gives to our prayers!

Thanks be to God.

Back to Basics

Matthew 22: 34-46

"Which commandment in the law is greatest?" The question was asked by a lawyer, and according to the way the evangelist Matthew recounts it, the questioner was somewhat disingenuous: ". . . a question to test him." But Jesus answered without hesitation: "*You shall love your God with all your heart, and with all your soul, and with all your mind. This is the greatest and first commandment. And the second is like it: You shall love your neighbor as yourself.*" Any further questions, counselor? No further questions.

Well, I have one: Why is it that nobody gets it? I shouldn't say *nobody;* you are all here in good faith. But much of the world seems oblivious to what is most basic in human existence, the importance, yes, the duty (Jesus calls it a "commandment.") of acknowledging God, our Creator. Men have always known God, in every age. St. Paul in his famous address to the men of Athens, philosophers they were, recognized their devotions: "I see you are religious," he says referring to the many shrines to gods he had seen as he walked through the city.

But then he explains to them that their piety was misdirected and they were in error in their seeking of many gods. He goes on to teach them: *"I want to tell you about the God who made the world and everything in it . . . . he gives life and everything else to all people . . . . he is not far from any of us, and he gives us the power to live and to move and to be who we are. We are his children."* And then Paul goes on to tell the story of Jesus and God's plan of redemption. That story seems to be lost in today's world, although we need it. And that basic act of acknowledgement is missing or feeble. We have forgotten "the first and greatest commandment: You shall love the Lord your God with all your heart, and with all your soul, and all your mind." From the lips of Jesus, this is not an option.

Perhaps, what is most astounding and what could put off some in attending to God's message in revelation, is this idea of love. "You shall *love* the Lord your God." The world, before the revelations of the Old Testament and the Gospels, had not a clue, not an inkling of a God whose relationship with his creation was one of love. Oh, they had their sacrifices. That was always instinctive -- to placate the gods, they would say. But for the ancients, worship of the gods was a one way street. Their world could not have imagined that God would send them love and care, until it was revealed to his beloved people of Israel. And then fulfilled in the ultimate expression of divine love . . . the coming of Jesus, his life and sacrifice, the Son of God. This was the fulfillment and the crowning glory of God's love for mankind. The Creator's affection for his creatures came in the person of his Son, and the redemptive act of his death and resurrection.

Who could have thunk it? And it is the primordinal sacred mystery of our existence to this very day. At the core of the mystery is love. We must understand that mankind's relationship to the Creator will always involve love. God is in fact the source of love, the model of love, the essence of love, the ideal of love. Writes the evangelist John, who was an intimate of Jesus, "God is love." (*Deus charitas est.*) And the perfection of love is in the coming into history of Jesus. Today we understand that the Christian way, following Jesus, is the way of love. What love is is difficult to grasp completely. But it is found in the lives of great Christians. And it is the life blood of holiness.

There are dissertations upon dissertations upon dissertations treating the notion of love and all its forms and complexities. Not to mention poetry and literature and music and every kind of art men produce. But just because love is complex and the notion may be vague and confusing in the abstract, it is not difficult, not impossible for us to grasp the meaning of love . . . because we have experience of it, we have experiences of loving and being loved in many circumstances, in relationships with family and friends and even other objects. From experience we are able to recognize the many mixed elements of love: affection, attraction, trust, loyalty, generosity, sacrifice, pleasure. And we can add to these St. Paul's litany: *Love is patient, love is kind, love is not envious or boastful or arrogant or rude* . . . and more. The list goes on, and it is a magnificent list. So when we are commanded to love God, we know what our duty is and how to do it: to direct this love with all its components to God our Creator, and to let overflow love of our neighbor. As Christians, this is our life and we do it with confidence. Bottom line: love the Lord with all your heart and soul and mind, and love of neighbor derives from this. For love of neighbor apart from God leads nowhere; while love of neighbor through the love of God leads to satisfaction and peace and ultimately to God's reward for us.

Let us now take this to the next level, for which I introduce you to Francis DeSales, (I should say St. Francis DeSales.) also a lawyer, by the way, trained at one of the great European universities before choosing the priesthood as his career. Later he took the office of Bishop of Geneva in Switzerland in the late 16TH century, around the time Calvinism was flourishing there. Francis DeSales taught and wrote of Christian love, the stuff of which holiness is made. And he insisted that holiness was the calling of and was attainable by every Christian. Holiness is not the exclusive franchise of the hierarchy or religious leaders, priests and bishops and monks in monasteries. It is to be the lifestyle of Christians of every level of life and every occupation, whether farmer or tradesman, or lawyer or merchant or shopkeeper or homemaker. Do you see where this is going? Personal holiness. Yes. As you might have guessed. John Wesley, coming along about 75 years later, was a fan of DeSales. We know that he read his book on the "Introduction to the Devout Life." I like to think that John Wesley also read "Treatise on the Love of God," the book that earned DeSales saintly recognition.

Let us assume that both Francis DeSales and John Wesley knew that it was incumbent upon every Christian to commit to a life of holiness and that to quote DeSales, "there is a natural inclination in a man's heart -- 'though a sinner -- to love God above all things." And in another place he writes that "human beings have planted in their innermost depth the longing for God; and in him alone can they find true fulfillment and complete joy."

With leaders like this to inspire and support us, it should not be difficult for us to follow to that commandment: *Love your God with all your heart, and with all your soul, and with all your mind. . . . and you shall love your neighbor as yourself. This is the greatest and first commandment, Jesus teaches.* We accomplish it when we worship, like today, this morning, and whenever we pray. These are the basics. We could pray also for our brethren *in absentia* -- those who for some reason have not responded to that innermost longing of the human heart, to love God our Creator . . . and who are still searching for peace.

Thanks be to God.

Philemon

TEXT Philemon 1-21 / Luke 14:25-33

My dear friends in the Lord -- or as Paul says in addressing his letter to Philemon, "My dear friends and co-workers" . . . referring to his mission of spreading the Gospel, and in which Philemon and his family had helped him.

There is so much to talk about in these two readings that it could take a month of sermons to fully do justice to them. Here are a couple of themes. In Paul's letter, we are given a glimpse of life in an early Christian community, the church of the 1ST century. Christians are a small group, separated, conducting their calling in closely bonded groups. The Eucharist of Christ Jesus was likely held in the home of Philemon, with Apphia, probably the wife of Philemon, and Archippus, whom Paul calls "our fellow soldier" in the group. But they are at peace, and Paul wishes he could return to them eventually in Christ's community of Colossia, and stay with them for a while. He however, is being detained in Rome. That's another situation the early followers of Jesus had to face. The civil authorities were suspicious of them, and, as in Paul's' case, detained them. This time the charges against Paul were found to be groundless. Eventually, they got him and he died at the hands of Roman authorities, not only a prisoner for Christ, but a martyr for Christ. I trust from the sentiments that come through in this letter that he would welcome that outcome.

We also can glean from the letter the closeness in love of the first Christians. There is a kind of pop hymn I recall hearing young people sing: "They will know we are Christians by our love." That's another theme and message we can take away from the letter to Philemon. Let me go over that passage again, as it is filled with affection toward Philemon and his family.

> *When I remember you in my prayers, I always thank my God because I hear of your love for all the saints and your faith towards the Lord Jesus. I pray that the sharing of your faith may become effective when you perceive all the good that we may do for Christ. I have indeed received much joy*

> *and encouragement from your love, because the hearts of the saints have been refreshed through you, my brother.*

Indeed, as the song says "They will know we are Christians by our love."

The passage we read from Luke doesn't seem at first much related to Paul's letter to Philemon. And you might be asking, Why did the liturgists put these two readings together? Paul's letter gives off a warm feeling of camaraderie, and what Luke (who, by the way, was with Paul in Rome) wrote presents a rather stern Jesus telling it like it is to be his follower. This chapter 14 of Luke is filled with scenarios of Jesus as a teacher, laying out his message is a variety of settings: at the dinner of a friend, where a crippled man approached him and he healed the man; out in the open where crowds could gather around him. And Luke records one parable after another. This one that includes the man who built a tower; after that the "salt of the earth" metaphor; then the women with a silver coin; and climaxing with the longer story of the two sons -- the famous "Prodigal Son" parable. The people who heard him on this occasion received the full course of his teachings. And in the middle of the stories, seeing them insistent in following and listening to him speak, he tells them what it's going to cost if they really want to be disciples -- to *hate father and mother, wife and children, brothers and sisters.* (In the Greek, the language of Luke's Gospel, the sense would have been to *prefer* the Lord over father and mother, etc.) All the commentators regard the words of Jesus here as hyperbolic, exaggerated to make a point. Throughout history some followers have taken him quite literally. The great Russian novelist (and Gospel commentator) Tolstoy, for example, is said to have considered literally the Lord's admonition *"to cut off your hand if it leads you to sin, because it is better to lose one part of your body than have your whole body thrown into hell."*

But we could get distracted if we were to focus only on the harshness and literalness of the Lord's words. We know from so much else of his teachings; we know of his tenderness in so many other scenes in the Gospel, that he is not a harsh man. Following Jesus is not easy, it is a burden, but recall these familiar words: *"Take the yoke I give you. Put it on your shoulders and learn from me. I am gentle and humble and you will find rest. This yoke is easy to bear and the burden is light."*

His words here in the passage from Luke, which he spoke to the crowd who followed him, should convince us of the seriousness of living the Christian life. We should not be surprised if it is inconvenient (to say the least) at times; if it goes against the grain of those living all around us. There is a notion we hear of when people are called upon to correct and discipline persons they are responsible for: "Tough love." I'm sure you have heard the phrase. Following Christ requires *tough love*. Not tough love in the sense of the context I just described. But tough love in the sense that our love must be hardened, not vulnerable to temping circumstances we might encounter, tough and insistent when we are called upon to help others and required to give something of ourselves. Yes, as tough, that is, as deep and firm as the love we have for our father and mother, wife and children, brothers and sisters. We know what that love is. It is in our blood . . . literally. It is often demanding. It challenges us. That's the love Jesus says he requires of us. But, and here is the bonus: when that hard love bonds us to Jesus, the reward, the satisfaction is immense. We know how satisfying human love can be . . . husband and wife, mother and father, brother and sister. How much greater -- beyond our imagination -- must be the reward and satisfaction of the love of Christ. *"What can separate us from Christ's love?"* St. Paul says. He has already pledged his love to us *"laying down his life."* What he demands of us as he speaks in this passage from Luke, he will match . . . on the Cross, his sacrifice to the Father.

So that is what Christian life is all about -- the close bond with our brethren when we come together in worship like this, as demonstrated by Paul's relationship with Philemon and the Christians of Colosse in the 1ST century. And the internal toughness of love in our hearts as we bond spiritually with Jesus. These are the graces we build on.

Thanks be to God.

'If I Were a Rich Man'

TEXT Luke 16: 19-31

Introductory Note. To begin with, I want to thank Rev. Beverly for inviting me to preach today: and I also wish to thank you all for welcoming me into this congregation.

I like to develop my sermons from the text of the scriptures, and the scriptures read today are filled with good messages that seem to come at us in a very direct way. For example, the Pauline letters to Bishop Timothy. 1 Timothy and 2 Timothy and the letter to Titus are called the Pastoral Epistles, because they were sent to the pastors of the young church communities in the first century of Christianity, to advise them on how to conduct and manage their communities. We are now, centuries later, one of those communities of Christ's followers. Up front in 1 Timothy (the passage from last week), we're instructed in how to pray:

> *I urge that supplications, prayers, intercessions, and thanksgivings should be made for everyone, for kings and all who are in high positions, so that we may lead a quiet and peaceable life in all godliness and dignity. This is right and is acceptable in the sight of God our Savior, who desires everyone to be saved and to come to the knowledge of the truth.*

Then in the section from 1 Timothy read today we hear Paul's advice to certain members of the Church:

> *As for those who in the present age are rich, I command them not to be haughty, or to set their hopes on the uncertainty of riches, but rather on God who richly provides us with everything for our enjoyment. They are to do good, to be rich in good works, generous, and ready to share, thus storing up for themselves the treasure of a good foundation for the future, so that they may take hold of the life that really is.*

This is the passage that connects us with today's Gospel reading from Luke: The parable of the rich man who to goes to Hades. We say *hell*. (Some wise guy has said that the lesson of this parable was intended for Episcopalians, not for us poor Methodists . . . a little clergy joke.)

But we have to look seriously at what Jesus is saying about riches. This is a hard-hitting parable, what with the rich man punished and crying out to poor Lazarus for relief. And this is not the first time Jesus speaks of the rich man. In Matthew's gospel, we read: *"Again I tell you, it is easier for a camel to go through the eye of a needle than for someone who is rich to enter the kingdom of God."* That's Matthew 19: 24.

We have to talk about riches and the Christian life. Consider how one becomes a rich man. There are three ways. You are born rich, you work to acquire riches, or you're lucky. And it could be any combination of these. That happens to be the same three ways a person becomes poor: born poor, no work, bad luck. What should be evident is that being rich or poor is in itself irrelevant to living the Christian life. Being a follower of Jesus, living the Christian life is not a factor in rich or poor, wealth, or poverty. There were, in fact, some pretty saintly rich persons among our Christian ancestry. At least I can presume that Louis IX, the saintly king of France in the 13TH century, was wealthy. So also was Elizabeth of Hungry, a princess; and even our local modern saint, Elizabeth Seaton, was from a wealthy New York family.

On the other hand, we have some famous poor Christians. Francis of Assisi comes to mind first. He was knick-named "il Poverello," or *the little poor man*. (Although Francis came from a middle-class family.) It happens that there are many holy persons who became poor for Christ, following the directive of Jesus who said to a young man who was upright and honest, *"If you really want to be my disciple, you must give up your riches to the poor."*

It all adds up to this: in the pursuit of holiness and happiness in the Christian life, being rich or poor doesn't have anything to do with it. But there are some considerations. There is plenty of evidence in the gospels, and in the letters of Paul, warning that riches can interfere in the spiritual life, and urging those who are wealthy to help out with charity toward the poor. *"Be generous and share,"* Paul writes in the letter to Timothy. On the other hand, being poor can also present some obstacles to one's pursuit of Christian life. It's a distraction. There is less time for doing good works and prayer. But we are talking here about the Christian community, and here is where rich and poor come together, each helping the other along the way. In this life, there is not a great "chasm" between rich and poor.

But lest you think following Jesus, living the Christian life, being a part of a Christian community is always going to be the drudgery of having to be poor, or having the stresses of trying to work out your salvation with your wealth . . . . Not at all. The Christian life is the pursuit of happiness now and, of course, in the next life. How many times did Jesus say, "*I am the way and the life . . . I have come to give you life*"? Remember that among the Lord's parting words to his disciples he said , "*If you keep my commandments, you will remain in my love . . . I tell you this so that my happiness may be in you and your happiness may be complete."* And in 1 Timothy again, it says that the Lord *richly provides us with everything for our enjoyment,* so that we might *live a quiet and peaceful life in all godliness and dignity.* That should be all anyone needs to be happy and content in the Christian life. But, of course, if you wish, you can always sing the prayer of Tevye, the milkman, in that famous musical: "If I were a rich man . . .

> *Dear God, you made many, many poor people.*
> *I realize, of course, that it's no shame to be poor.*
> *But it's no great honor either!*
> *Lord who made the lion and the lamb,*
> *You decreed I should be what I am.*
> *Would it spoil some vast eternal plan*
> *If I were a rich man?*

Thanks be to God.

Jesus as the "Boss"

TEXT Mark 10: 35-45

Please don't misunderstand that title. It is meant to refer to the task the Lord has in managing his disciples; and I take from this morning's scripture that the job has its challenges. The sons of Zebedee, James and John have a question. They want a favor from Jesus, a special place in their relationship with him, favorable treatment. In Matthew's version of this event, they have their mother intervene for them with this request.

According to Mark's narrative, Jesus had a kind of knick-name for these two -- James and John: the "Sons of Thunder." They were fishermen like the others, who worked with their father Zebedee, who owned a boat and the business. There was another occasion, when the "Sons of Thunder" urged Jesus to retaliate forcefully against a community which did not welcome his presence. *"Let us call down fire from heaven to destroy them,"* they urged Jesus. That's probably how they got their nickname. Of course, Jesus told them to calm down. And then there was the time when they came to him reporting that some other disciple, not of those in the close band with Jesus, was performing exorcisms, attempting to cure people of illness . . . interfering. They told Jesus that they would put a stop to that.

Jesus had his handful with these two. But they were special to him, in this, that they were present at that marvelous event recorded in all three synoptic gospels, the Lord's Transfiguration, when the Lord's divine character was displayed in one spectacular moment on Mount Tabor in Galilee. Peter was with them there. And Peter was another apostle with whom Jesus seems to have some management problems. He once asked a rather bold and impertinent question: *"What about us? We have left everything and followed you. What are we to have, then?"*

And there was the time he argued with Jesus about his going up to Jerusalem and facing the danger that had built up against him because of his preaching. *"Get behind me Satan,"* Jesus says, as if Peter's idea will prevent his mission. Later, Peter, impetuous, violent, would pull out his sword and wound one of the posse, the arresting force, that came after

Jesus. And again Jesus had to rebuke him: *"Put your sword back into its place; for all those who take up the sword shall perish by the sword."* It wasn't long after that Peter, in his human weakness, said he didn't know Jesus when he was questioned.

One more. Add to this list Thomas, the stubborn disciple to whom Jesus had to physically demonstrate/prove the fact of his resurrection from the dead. In all of these instances, Jesus was in control . . . OK . . . the boss. These were his charges, the men he deliberately chose. There were 12 of them. We call them the "apostles," which is a word for messenger, more precisely a messenger who represents the sender, like an ambassador. These are the men Jesus supervised, and I contend he was a good manager/boss. He would often call them friends; they called him *master,* and they called him *teacher.* In the end, every one of them proved his love and loyalty to the Lord by suffering a martyr's death in defense of his teachings.

Jesus was a good boss, a good manager. Let him manage your life as he did theirs. He knows how to handle human idiosyncrasies: pride, vanity, self-centeredness, negative skepticisms, unbelief. He's gentle about it. He will help you in your pursuit of holiness -- though he may challenge you. To the Sons of Thunder who requested a prominent place among his followers, he had an answer for them, which he presents in simple metaphorical terms: To *drink the cup* that he will drink. That is, accept suffering as the way to glory. It is the cup of which Jesus says praying to his Father on the night before his death: *"My Father! If it is possible, let this cup of suffering pass from me. Yet, not my will but thy will be done."*

Jesus often spoke of his redemptive mission. It is an underlying theme of Mark's gospel. Just before this little episode with James and John, he had explained to his disciples, who were "confused" that (and I quote) *"We are on our way to Jerusalem where the Son of Man will be handed over . . . and they will sentence him to death . . . and they will beat him and kill him. But three days later he will rise to life."*

James and John would have heard him say this, but I think they wanted a shortcut to the glory of the risen life. Comments St. Augustine on this passage, "These disciples who wanted to sit, one on his right hand, the other on his left, were looking to glory, but they did not see the way to get there." That is, to, as Augustine calls it, "the homeland." And "the homeland is life in Christ; the way is dying with

Christ; the way is suffering with Christ [and] the goal is abiding with him eternally." Or stated another way, the way to glory, the Christian way of life, must always entail suffering.

We may not know how or to what extent Christian suffering may enter our lives. Or do we? But we know that, from our understanding of the words of Jesus, it is inevitable. Somehow. Jesus spoke of it in this way: And he said to [them] all, *"If any [man] will come after me, let him deny himself, and take up his cross daily, and follow me."* And in another place: *"For whosoever will save his life shall lose it; but whosoever shall lose his life for my sake and the gospel's, the same shall save it."*

We do not need to understand these words literally. Although the many saints and martyrs of Christianity may indicate otherwise. Jesus always spoke in parables to allow broad interpretations of his words.

> *Very truly I tell you, unless a kernel of wheat falls to the ground and dies, it remains only a single seed. But if it dies, it produces many seeds. Anyone who loves this life will lose it, while anyone who hates his life in this world will keep it for eternal life.*

This message should not be interpreted as to present an overly grim aspect of Christian living, but rather to put into context the ordinary (can we say ordinary?) trials and vicissitudes of our daily existence. Life is not perfect. But if our life is under the management of Christ, and we are living these trials with him, we are drinking that cup. And we're ready for glory. As St. Paul would say in his letter to the Galatians: (Galatians 2: 20*)* *" I am crucified with Christ: nevertheless I live; yet not I, but Christ lives in me, and the life which I now live in the flesh I live by the faith of the Son of God, who loved me, and gave himself for me."*

Living the Christian life under the management of Jesus, we are participating in our own redemption, which affords us a sense of peace and contentment, and leads inevitably to that final joy and happiness. To get there, may I suggest we use this prayer, composed by Ignatius of Loyola; St. Ignatius that is, who was the founder of the Society of Jesus, the Jesuits.

Take, Lord, and receive all my liberty,
my memory, my understanding
and my entire will,
All I have and call my own.
You have given all to me.
To you, Lord, I return it.
Everything is yours; do with it what you will.
Give me only your love and your grace.
That is enough for me.

Thanks be to God.

Slogans and Mottos

TEXT Mark 13: 28-44

She put everything she had into the treasury of the temple. Everything she had. And Jesus took note. This incident gives us a foundation for a slogan or motto for the Christian way of life: To put everything we have into it.

We have slogans and mottos in all our activities. There was once this slogan used in Navy recruitment advertising: "Be all that you can be." That comes close to what we hear in the gospel today. There is the Marine Corp motto, *Semper Fi*, a Latin phrase meaning to be *faithful always*. We like mottos and slogans; they are succinct little reminders that keep us focused. One that I really favor is one that Bill Belichick uses in training his team. He's the football coach of the New England Patriots. It's simple. He has one rule for his players; it's posted on the wall in the clubhouse: "Do your job." I like this one, because it tell us that we're part of a team with a specific role to play, and that we're supported by our team members.

Now let's go back to that scene in the temple. The writer, Mark, who was undoubtedly there, an eye witness at the time, since he was an associate of the apostle Peter, and we know that Peter followed Jesus closely. Mark gives us some detail: "Jesus sat down." We don't often pay much attention to the -- call them -- "stage directions" in the gospels -- details like this one. "Jesus sat down." What does it tell us? That he was tired? Probably. That he was comfortable and at ease in the temple? Yes. He was teaching. He is always teaching. Several passages in this chapter begin this way: "Jesus was teaching in the temple," or "As Jesus was teaching . . . ." On this occasion, he was teaching in a relaxed and casual way, sitting down, as he did frequently. Mark says a large crowd was listening to him, among them some other scripture teachers of whom Jesus was critical, because they were not exemplary, and he says that they cheated widows out of their homes.

We will now follow the interpretation of this scene in the commentaries of the early Church Fathers, and we'll see that Jesus lays down several principles of his Way, of what has become the Christian way of life for his followers. But first, who are the Fathers of the Church?

Like the "Fathers of our country," they are those persons in the earliest days who by their writings or teachings, by their lives, influenced the growth and development of our country, or in this case, our church. Their wisdom flows through, even up to the present time -- in the case of the Fathers of our country -- 200 years, and we often hear their words quoted; in the case of the Fathers of the Church, about 1500 years, and we have many of their writings and sermons to study. (Online too.) There was Washington, Jefferson, and Hamilton and so forth. And there was John Chrysostom a Greek bishop, Augustine, a Latin bishop in North Africa. And Venerable Bede an English monk. And many others, of course.

Teaching us about today's Gospel scene, Chrysostom says that having wealth or many resources or advantage has no bearing on one's readiness for belonging to the kingdom of heaven. All one needs, in his words, is "a Christian disposition." The widow made her gift with eagerness and she gave of herself everything. Jerome, another of the Fathers, a priest in the 4TH century, who was the translator of the bible into the Greek language, writes that the widow offered all the substance that she had -- referring to the two coins (pennies), she offered two testaments of her faith, he says.

Bede says that Jesus teaches us in this scene that it is "the treasure in one's heart" that counts most in earning the rewards of God's kingdom. Paulinus, the Latin poet, a Roman citizen of southern France, and a convert to Christianity, praises the widow for her concern for the poor. She thought not of her own poverty, but of the needs of others, willingly sharing of what God had given her. There you have four principles that Christians live by. (1) that all are welcome to share God's graces; (2) that your faith is a total commitment . . . (3) made deep in your heart; (4) and that you look out for and help others. There is a long, long tradition of teaching like this in our church. It begins with the Lord, himself. He was a teacher. They called him "teacher', or rabbi, which means teacher of the sacred writings. The Fathers of the Church are a part of that long tradition. They are the earliest practitioners -- after Paul, who was the greatest, except for Jesus himself.

Our faith and the way of Jesus, Christian life, is delivered through this tradition of teaching. We learned about faith from our teachers -- our parents, or our priest or minister. "Faith comes through hearing," Paul wrote to the Romans. That is, from someone teaching us. It does not come from instinct, or imagination, or osmosis, or even inspiration, but through teaching directed at our minds. Jesus is our teacher in this scene in the temple that Mark describes; he sits down and begins teaching.

Veterans Day is the day we celebrate today. Once called "Armistice Day," marking the cessation of hostilities in World War I, it has evolved to be the day on which we honor all who have served in the armed forces in defense of our country -- Veterans who have come and gone and those who are with us today. If you are a veteran, or if you will be a veteran someday . . . and everyone has veterans close to them . . . you know that serving is a job. One is trained for it. One is taught how to perform it, and one is called upon to execute it according to that training (teaching). So with our Christian life. The way of life that Jesus taught us in the gospel, and that his followers and the great teachers have taught us over the centuries, in our religious schools and in our Sunday liturgies down to this very day. Take account of your faith and how well you have learned it. Continue to listen and learn at every opportunity. We are Christians. We have been taught, trained in our faith and the way of life laid out for us in the gospel, modeled in the person of Jesus our teacher and articulated in his words to us.

For empowerment, we call upon our mottos and slogans: *give your all* as Christians, like the widow in the gospel; *be all that you can be* as a follower of Christ. God gives us the strength through grace to achieve our full spiritual potential. Be *faithful always* to the gospel -- to the promises made in your Baptism and Confirmation or in the Sacrament of Marriage. You know what you've been called upon to do; you know what you have been trained for. In your Christian life, attend to that simple and powerful slogan of the coach: *Do your job.*
And remember you have a calling and are part of the broad Christian community, the church, which you can count on for the support of God's grace. Do your job.

Thanks be to God.

'Corragio'

TEXT Matthew 13: 25-30

Corragio. Are you familiar with the word? I like the sound of it. It is the Italian word for *courage* . . . often used as an exhortation to be courageous. I recall a TV newscaster once used it as his sign-off: "Good night and *corragio."* It is akin to the Lord's counsel to his disciples: "Be not afraid." Also the slogan of the late Pope John Paul. Let us use it here as the key to our commentary on today's gospel.

Any questions about the meaning or the message of the gospel parable we just read? I'm certain there are many. I have a few. So let's clear them up. As you are well aware, through the past several months, evangelist Matthew in his narrative of the life and actions of Jesus is intending to give us a careful portrait of the Lord and his teachings, in particular as his teachings refer him as the Savior promised in the history of the Israelites, so presented in the books of the prophets. The Old Testament, we call them. The Lord's personality comes through in these stories. If you read the gospel of Matthew from the beginning (the Lord's birth) to the end (the Lord's crucifixion and the resurrection), you will have a complete picture of the unfolding of God's plan of redemption through Jesus. You will also, if you look closely, get a glimpse of the personality of the Lord.

In the 11TH chapter of Matthew, Jesus says of himself: *"Come to me, for I am meek and humble of heart."* In another place, Jesus describes himself as the good shepherd who looks after his sheep and who goes in search of a lost sheep. *"I am the good shepherd; I know mine and mine know me."* In one famous parable, he identifies himself as a good and forgiving father who welcomes, even celebrates, the homecoming of one of his sons who had gotten into trouble out on his own. The "prodigal son." You cannot help but be attracted to the person of Jesus in the parables. In these roles, he is easy to love. His teaching also presents us with a picture of "the kingdom of God"; that is, the community which his followers are invited to join; and he teaches us how to be his followers. And so, from the gospel of Matthew we learn the Christian way of living.

Now let's get to this parable. A wealthy man goes away and leaves some of his wealth in the hands of his servants to manage. First, understand that the term *talents*, used in the parable, is not exactly the same as we mean it in today's vernacular, as in "Hollywood has Talent." Or "Jason is a talented musician." The word has correctly evolved to have this meaning -- a skill or special ability. But as it was used by Jesus in his time and place, it had the meaning of a value, a measure, a way of evaluating precious coins; so that in the context of this parable it is rightly understood as a sum of money -- the amount of ten talents or five talents or one talent that could be invested for profit. According to the parable, some of the servants are successful and increase their holdings. One is not, and this angers the wealthy man when he returns. The interpretations of the meaning of this parable of Jesus vary widely. Some commentators have said the parable is an endorsement of the capitalist investment system; others have said it is simply a warning against laziness.

I haven't found any commentary that I entirely agree with, except maybe that of Gregory the Great, the pope whom John Calvin, (of all people) called "the last great pope." He, Pope Gregory, said of his time -- the late 6TH century, that "many people in the church resemble that unprofitable servant. They are afraid to attempt a better way of life, but not afraid of resting in idleness." Most commentaries I have not found helpful. This parable is admittedly a quandary. Is the Lord really presenting himself as the wealthy man? Could Jesus be as stern as the wealthy man is, with that pusillanimous servant who is too afraid to invest his one talent, and whom he sends to punishment . . . "into the dark where there is the weeping and gnashing of teeth"? No more Mr. Nice guy here. This doesn't sound to me like that gentle forgiving good shepherd we learned of in earlier parables, and who once said, "Let the little children to come to me."

So I offer my hand at an interpretation that will help us understand the Lord's lesson here, and give us direction on how to live a Christian life as a committed follower of Jesus. This is a parable about courage and daring. There is no question that courage must be among the Christian virtues. How could there be so many Christians who have died for the faith, otherwise? Not to mention, obviously, the courage of Jesus himself who went to Jerusalem and faced torture and accepted death as a part of God's redemption plan, and its mystery for our salvation.

In this parable, the point is made where two of the servants were successful in increasing their monies, because of their courage and enterprise; the other was fearful and did nothing with his one talent. To live the gospel requires some daring, some courage to make progress in Christian holiness. In Christian marriage, for example; it requires some daring to make a big commitment, not knowing what the future will bring. Of course the Christian couple can depend on God's grace to sustain them in a blessed marriage. But choosing a Christian marriage is an act of the virtue of courage . . . that, sadly, not everyone these days is willing to make. Other callings of Christian life: the single life, the dedicated religious life will always demand courage in their pursuit. And so many of one's day-to-day choices will demand courage, if you are to stay within the bounds of Christian virtue. Courage is the choice to do a good thing and the right thing. To use all our gifts given to us in our life calls for daring and sustained courage. In this, we have the example of the good servants to whom the master says, "Well done." And as you have seen also in this parable, the Lord does not look kindly on the servant who is afraid to act boldly. In the Christian life, you cannot stand pat. Christian living is "pro-active." After all, at one point the Lord said to his followers, *"You are the salt of the earth. . ... You are the light of the world. . . . . So let your light shine before men, that they may see your good works, and glorify your Father who is in heaven."* To follow this command calls for an output of daring and courage.

You may think that in facing life's challenges you are all alone. But for those with faith, the grace of God always comes into play. It is here to support you. You supply the daring, you muster up the courage, and God's help is with you. A favorite saying of mine . . . or rather of the great St. John Chrysostom, puts these situations in terms of God's love: "Even if we are unable to unravel the details of our personal and collective history, we know that God's plan for us is always inspired by his love."

This week we celebrate the nation's military veterans. In them we recognize a model of courage. In the military, it is a special and conspicuous courage that they must always have at the ready to be called upon, because theirs is a business of mortal high stakes. The Lord Jesus goes before them in showing courage in his life, from whom they may draw strength. The military model is not unknown to Christians. Some of our great saints were soldiers -- Francis and Ignatius -- and so the military metaphor is valid, because Christians have been called "soldiers of Christ," and all of us must cultivate that steely virtue. In all things have courage . . . we say, corragio!

Thanks be to God.

Jesus in a Somber Mood

TEXT Mark 13: 1-8

Eschatology. There's a big word. Five syllables. Make a note of it, because you will hear it a few times in this sermon. It's derived from the Greek language, like many of our words. It means *pertaining to the last things. Escato* in Greek means "last" or "final." Eschatology is in Christian theology a study of the last things: death, the end of the world, resurrection. The passage from Mark that we read in today's assigned scripture is referred to as the Lord's Eschatological Discourse. It is found in Matthew's and in Luke's Gospels as well. It should be obvious to you that the passage presents some difficulties of understanding for us. Difficulties in the sense that we have to give some penetrating thought to it to discover the meaning of the Lord's message. Let us look at two aspects of the Lord's words. One, they are puzzling. What does he mean? And second, his mood is somber.

The 2ND Temple

For meaning we consider that Christians have for 2000 or more years heard these words; and so there have been dozens, hundreds -- more --- of interpretations and opinions as to their meaning. Consider first that Jesus was a prophet, out of the tradition of the great prophets of the Israelites. Of course, he is the greatest one. From time to time he spoke as a prophet to his friends, and to the audiences who heard him preach.

Just a couple of examples: When Jesus made a dramatic entry into Jerusalem on a donkey, the crowd shouted, *"This is Jesus the prophet from Nazareth in Galilee."* And the Samaritan woman from whom Jesus requests a drink of water . . . after he admonishes her gently about her husband (or husbands), says: *"Sir, I see that you are a prophet."* It is not unusual for Jesus' disciples to hear him speak this way, here prophesying the destruction of the temple in Jerusalem.

As for its meaning, there are myriad opinions and analyses, all sensible. For example, one modern scholar sees this passage as Jesus explaining symbolically that his Kingdom, the Kingdom of God, which was the theme of much of his preaching, does not come to fulfillment on this earth in our time, but only after some sentinel/dramatic conclusion. Like his own life: his mission, the redemption of mankind, was only completed by his death, his life ending, when he said at the end, *"It is finished."* This interpretation is in harmony with another prediction the Lord once made: when he said in answer to a challenge by some Jewish leaders after he had made a scene, castigating them for allowing commercialism in the temple area: *"Destroy this temple, and I will rebuild it in three days."* The evangelist John, who reported on this scene, explains that *he was talking about his body as a temple. And when he was raised from the dead, his disciples recalled what he had told them.* (John 2: 19-21)

Another aspect of this scene is the reality of his prophesy. The temple was destroyed about 40 years later, when the Romans invaded Jerusalem. Although this prophecy is rendered in symbolic terms, and has its prophetic purpose, the thought of the actual fact of the destruction of the temple would have saddened Jesus. He loved the temple. As every Jew did. It had been there more than 400 years. Currently, it was being renovated and expanded by their Roman ruler. (Like NYC) It was the place Jesus knew from his childhood, and he preached there many times. But this was the last time he would enter the temple, the last lengthy oration recorded of him in the gospel accounts. He is at the end of his public ministry. A sad moment, as he looks down from nearby Mount Olivet. In Luke's description of the scene, it says Jesus wept at the thought of how the city of Jerusalem had failed him, by rejecting his teachings. There was the temple, a place holy to the Jews for eons, the center of their lives in every way, the focus of their very existence as the host nation of the one God's true revelation. And as we have just mentioned, how solicitous Jesus was of its sacred character, as on that day when he shouted with a just anger: *"Get those merchants out of here; don't make my Father's house a marketplace."* And at that moment, (records evangelist John) *the disciples remembered a prophesy* from (Psalm 69) scriptures: *"My love for your house, O God, burns in me like a fire."*

Jesus says his farewell to the temple in prophetic fashion. About 40 years after this his death, the temple was indeed destroyed, "not a stone left upon a stone," in the invasion of Jerusalem by Roman armies.

"Nothing lasts forever." That is, nothing in this life, nothing of earthly existence. And I think by his prophesy Jesus meant to impress this upon his disciples. And before each one of them would reach the heavenly kingdom, their lives would go down too, like his, brutally, martyrs in testimony to the gospel and the truth of divine revelation.

It is a valuable lesson for us to grasp as well. This reality of the Christian life's purpose is defined by its end. When we consider the last things, life's *eschatological* -- if you will -- character, we have a platform from which to understand why we pray; we are prompted to be attentive to every word of the promises of Jesus; we are moved to seek his graces and his peace. These eschatological scriptures come at Sundays at or near the end of the Church year, just before we begin the new Church year in Advent. The Church calls on us by these scriptures, to review our lives, in our minds, prayerfully, from the vantage point that it is ended/completed or up to now, or near completion. Not to be grim or depressed about it. Not at all. But realistic. Be proud of living the Christian life. This is a healthy exercise for our souls. Whatever its circumstances may have been: some good things, some not so good, some successes, some things left undone, some sorrows, some tedium, some joys, some sadness. No matter. It's all on the record.

When we have done this, our next move ought to be to turn, to reach out for God's mercy and love -- so evident throughout the life of Jesus. *"Come to me, all you who are weary and burdened, and I will give you rest. Take my yoke upon you and learn from me, for I am gentle and humble of heart."* If it's mercy you crave, consider the woman who showed Jesus hospitality in Peter's house: He says to her, *Your sins are forgiven; your faith has saved you; go in peace.* Or when he turns to the thief on the cross: *"This day you will be with me in paradise."* And as if his actions are not convincing enough, he says explicitly to a group of teachers of the mosaic law: *"I desire mercy . . . for I have not come to call the righteous, but sinners."*

It may seem a lonely task looking back; but the Lord has always promised to be with us, with just the embrace we may need. Here are his words near the end of his life, when he was with his friends:

> *Stay joined with me, and let my teachings become a part of you . . . and be assured that I will keep loving you if you obey me; just as my Father keeps loving me because I have obeyed him.* In a somber mood, no longer, he continues: *I have told you this to make you as completely happy as I am. Now love each other, as I have loved you.*

And here is my favorite part going forward:
> *Then my Father will give you whatever you ask for in my name.* (John 15: 9 etc.)

Thanks be to God.

Part II

Past Sermons

New York 222
Boston 247
Buffalo 253
Other Pulpits . . .258

New York

Sermonettes

The next three sermons were given as "Sermonettes" (6 minutes) at NBC-TV sometime in the mid- 60s -- a part of the network's public affairs programming in engaging clergy from Catholic, Protestant, and Jewish congregations in New York. The sermons were pre-recorded and broadcast (including a photo for TV) at various times in the station's radio and television early morning and late night schedule. I was given the assignment by my Superior at St. Francis Church, 31st Street.

The Poverty Mystique

It usually happens about twice a year that a priest from St. Francis of Assisi Church in Manhattan comes to NBC to give the week's sermonettes. And I suppose it is inevitable that he will take one day out to speak about his patron. Not that St. Francis of Assisi is an obscure religious figure who needs the promotion. On the contrary. It is safe to say that nearly everyone around the world, East or West, who has had any acquaintance with religion has at least heard his name.

Here is an issue we might use to begin a discussion about Francis of Assisi: his unusual popularity. How is it he is so well known? He lived, after all, only the brief span of 45 years, and in a small town in a distant country 700 years ago. He never left any monuments, neither art nor voluminous writings. It is true there are certain superficial details of his life, which have come down to us almost in the manner of fables by word of mouth. His taming of a wolf, for example, or his love for birds and animals. But these are far from adequate for explaining the sustained impact his life has had on human history. Must there not be, we have to ask, some excellent principle of wisdom upon which he had a steady hold, some vision which directed him and lifted him above the stature of ordinary men? Otherwise how could he have lived that life of simplicity and beauty to which men of every age and nation have been overwhelmingly attracted? There was a principle. A single one. It is not so plain and obvious that the mere mention of it makes us understand

St. Francis immediately. If that were so, we could all be St. Francises instead of his humble admirers and feeble imitators.

As a young man, John Bernadino (his real name) decided -- as no doubt every young man since has decided -- that there was something wrong with the world and things were getting worse instead of better. He did not sit down and concoct a plan of reform. Being a Christian he knew that the message of salvation had already been given men in the Gospel. The trouble was that as the centuries passed, the impact of the Gospel message lessened, and the word of God was being allowed to die out. So he set out humbly, with no intention of attracting even a single follower, to live the Gospel life plainly and honestly. He bypassed all the scholarly philosophies of life, whether religious or secular, and went directly to the words of the Lord that had been recorded by the evangelists and handed down in the Church. He there discovered, with an intuition which was his special grace, that the simplest, most telling, and most imitable and practical fact about the life of Jesus was his poverty. Jesus was born a poor man, lived as a poor man, and died without even the means of burial.

Francis had great faith, and it struck him that to live the Christian life was to live as Jesus had lived -- poor. He had reduced Christianity to its ultimate practicable principle. This was his secret. Whether he was right or not, would remain to be seen in the conduct of his life. The world now looks upon that life with wonder and admiration.

It may seem a bit daring in these latter days to try to pass poverty off as an ideal to be striven after. There is a *war* on against poverty. We are accustomed to think of poverty as an ugly and totally undesirable condition. This is admittedly true of the poverty which rampages out of control and infects like a disease. But it is no less true of wealth, which rampages out of control and harms and destroys. What we are looking for is some intermediary condition wherein the things we possess and strive for can be controlled in good order. Such a condition can be maintained by the practice of *the virtue of poverty,* that is, by doing without things and making a way of life of it. This is to make a mystique of poverty, to make being poor an ideal, to be without for the love of God and in imitation of Jesus.

There is an inevitable objection: You have to have money. Otherwise you will starve and your children will go naked. True enough. And I might further add that you spend most of your adult life working to get money and things, and once you gather momentum in this necessary pursuit it is difficult to slow down much less reverse direction. Yet to be poor voluntarily is a proven virtue, and each person can determine the extent to which it must enter into his/her life. It is an enormous challenge, but at least we have one thing to encourage us in meeting it: the life of Francis of Assisi. Poverty worked for him.

Taking over the Sex Revolution

Among of revolutions that our age is invited to analyze, is the one called the "sex revolution." And without doubt, the most fascinating analysis offered go far is that of Russell Baker writing in the *New York Times*. Mr. Baker maintains, though facetiously, that despite the multitude of magazine, newspaper, and Sunday supplement articles -- some against, some neutral, none for -- that have appeared on the subject of this revolution, only a minute portion of our population is really getting any benefit from it. If Baker is right, his analysis is reassuring. Then we're really not going the way of all empires; we just like to think we are in some particulars. But the whole sensational discussion, whether it is based on fact or wishful thinking or mere marketability, may indicate some kind of restlessness in our moral thinking.

The human body is implicated in all of these discussions. There is the underlying question of its manageability, which is crucial because a person's body (trite as it may sound) is with him/her wherever he/she goes. It is even a bit inaccurate to speak of the body as if it were something in any way distinct from the person. The body is the human person engaging *things*; just as the mind is the human person engaging *ideas*. By the body's operation a person works, plays, achieves, builds, conquers, leads, and so on through a long list of human activities and enterprises. The body takes part in a man's joys when he sings and dances, in his sorrows when he bows his head and weeps. There is no barring it from any human activity.

But what is more important, the body has a special capacity for and insists upon being involved in the ultimate things to which human life tends: love, the production of new life, death, and final salvation. For this reason, in the traditions of our religion, the human body has always been held in highest esteem, considered sacred. It is, moreover, the medium through which divine life comes to us; it is the outward receptor of the Sacraments. At this point the revolutionaries are toying with the idea of denying the body its rightful concern with ultimates. As if by a mere revision of one's thinking, the body could be made to direct its full powers toward trivialities: kicks, experiments, unsubstantial pleasures. The revolutionaries are assuming some kind of a casual distinction between body and mind, and making the one indiscriminately subservient to the other. It is as if an adult, because he holds a position of leadership over a child, were to turn the child into a beast of burden. The old Pinocchio story. Whereas the child was never meant to live in such a manner, but to have fulfillment in accordance with his whole natural capabilities.

Or, the revolutionaries, aware of the awesome potency of the body's particular sexual potency which is ever present and alive, proclaim that it is unmanageable. But since the body is identical with life, this is to say that life is unmanageable. And to follow such a conclusion is deadly. For one who gives up all hope of managing his body gives up as well all hope of managing his total life.

Life is manageable and the body is meant to engage in all the ultimate hopes and aspirations of life. It is no wonder then that as Russell Baker implies, the "sex revolution" is barely getting off the ground. But there is no sense in stifling the energies of a good lively revolution. Perhaps It can be taken over. All the ultimate goals of the human body could be specified and reaffirmed. They are revolutionary enough given the high purpose for which divine revelation has destined mankind. There is marital love: the body avails it of a means of expression and directs it to fruitfulness. There is virginity: the body guards its own integrity in order to give substance to a person's dedication to God or to a charitable human cause. There is chastity: the body under discipline fortifies human love whether in or out of the marriage state, or it becomes a sign of religious dedication.

Someone will say, "It's too difficult; I'd rather not." Agreed. To manage one's body and to engage it in ultimate concerns is to live. And to live has never been found easy. But almost everyone is willing to give it a try.

G.F. Proud

The Church Around Us

Sometime you may have the occasion, as I had recently, of sitting up late at night before the television and watching David Suskind, surrounded by scholars and clergymen and cigarette smoke, discuss the passing of institutionalized religion. I was intrigued for the hour. And then afterwards, a few days later, it occurred to me that you simply cannot talk about religion or the church as an institution the way you talk about General Motors and wonder whether it's going to fold or not in the face of progress. The church is not in that sense an institution, does not aspire to be one, and hopes it does not pass itself off as one. What exactly the church is is a large question, and until recently the answer has not been entirely clear. What I mean is that, perhaps, the most significant document turned out at the current Vatican Council is the one published one year ago Sunday, in which the Church is described thoroughly and definitively. It may sound strange that the Church which grows out of a twenty-century old tradition should at long last sit down to explain what it is all about. Yet this is what has happened. In all the Councils which have occurred up to now, matters other than the nature of the Church have been discussed. It is no wonder that people are not sure what the word church means. Some few think of it as a building. Others as a body of bishops with the pope. Then there are those who consider the church an institution, or identify the church with the city of Rome. I suppose it is legitimate to use the word church in each of these contexts. But what the Vatican Council says in its "Constitution on the Church" is something else again.

The Church is a manifestation of divine power rising out of the Judeo-Christian tradition and operating in the world in such a way as to return mankind to the Creator. This power affects men by inspiring in them faith, hope, and love. By it men are bound together and made to recognize their dependence upon one another and upon the Creator for the achieving of their common final salvation. Under its influence, men observe the law of love of God and neighbor, and serve God by giving him praise in everything they do.

The spiritual force which the Church is is strong enough and extensive enough to embrace all men and to draw them together in a unity which regards neither racial or national boundaries. It grows slowly and steadily toward this purpose. Yet despite the absolute transcendental character of the Church it will always find among its membership persons who are inspired to be its spokesmen, to direct its purely temporal course, and to present its visible image. It is the greatest of mistakes, made by so many people whether adherents or not, to identify the Church with its visible image alone. For this divinely driven force which is the Church --

although it needs human resources to carry out its mission, is not set up to seek earthly glory, but to proclaim, even by its own example, humility and self-sacrifice. Christ was sent by the Father to bring good news to the poor, to heal the contrite of heart, to seek and to save what was lost. Similarly, the Church encompasses with love all who are afflicted with human suffering; and in the poor and afflicted, sees the image of its poor and suffering Founder. It does all it can to relieve their need; and in them it strives to serve Christ. While Christ, holy, innocent and undefiled, knew nothing of sin, but came to expiate only the sins of the people, the Church embracing in its bosom sinners, at the same time holy and always in need of being purified, always follows the way of penance and renewal." [Constitution on the Church, Vatican II]

This is perhaps high-sounding theological language. It comes directly from the Vatican Council's description of the Church. But it sets out unmistakably the compassionate character of the Church. It portrays the Church as a living and moving force which is all around us, and which can draw together all men for good.

Institutions and organizations fold up in the course of time. Men die and others take their place on earth. But the spiritual, divinely driven force in this world which the Church is, and which all men can adhere to by faith, hope, and love, will not pass away.

†

St. Francis Church, New York
(Composed on a Washington Square bench, Holy Saturday 1965.)

Easter 1965

TEXT Mark 16:17

He is going to galilee ahead of you, where you will see him, just as he told you.

On at least two occasions that we know of before his death, Jesus announced publicly, if in cryptic language, that once he was buried he would rise again from the tomb. There was the time very near the beginning of his preaching career when the Pharisees challenged his divine authority, and he told them, no doubt gesturing toward his body, "If you destroy this temple, in three days I will raise it up again." Then there was the time toward the end, when they asked him for a sign proving his right to speak for God; and he used a story from the scriptures to make a prophecy:

> *Jonas was three days and three nights in belly of the sea-beast, and the son of man will be three days and three nights in the heart of the earth.*

And might we not also infer that he had even planned a rendezvous afterwards with his disciples, for the angel at the tomb says, "He is going to Galilee ahead of you, where you will see him, just as he told you."

Yet we read here that the women went to the tomb to anoint the body of Jesus, just as they might any ordinary person who had passed away. They are acting as if they had not an inkling of Christ's promise to rise again. And these women were known followers of Jesus for the past two or three years, who had listened to his words, and who professed deep love for him. How do you explain it? Had they paid no attention to his prophecy? Had they failed to understand this most crucial part of his message?

These women, my dear friends, and the Apostles too, are like you and I -- poor human creatures with timid minds, who have difficulty absorbing the meaning of words, who seldom dare to think the unthinkable. Although they had heard the resurrection foretold in his words, only when they experience it as an event do they begin to understand. The event of discovering the empty tomb at last strikes into their consciousness the whole meaning of his life and message: mankind is redeemed, death is no longer final, there is a new life, a new existence available to men.

We arrive at the Church today in the same frame of mind as these women. We are moved more by events than by words. We may have read in the newspaper that spring is here, that skies are clearing, that temperatures are warming, but we did not feel the exhilaration, the new life of spring, until we walked this morning in the bright air and felt the warm breezes on our hands and face. When we experience the event of spring, then we know.

And often too, we who are his known followers, who profess love to him and have read his words, but have not grasped the meaning of his promises, have not felt the imperative of his commands . . . we must experience the event. Today the event of Christ's resurrection is present to us. It is contained in sacramental mystery; but it is no less effective, if we open up our experience to it. It is in the Eucharist, in the gift offered, transformed, and shared at the communion table. It is declared in these sacred readings. The Mass of Easter today is the liturgical event in which we can come to understand the whole meaning of Christ's life and message. Let it then, and the prayers with which we all perform it, strike deep into our consciousness the meaning of Easter: There is life available to us, a life which has come forth from the tomb with the risen Savior, and which -- if we follow earnestly and loyally -- will bear us over and through death and into the realm of his glorious reign.

†

St. Francis Church, New York, 1968

The Assumption

One anachronistic term which, curiously, the great renewal of Vatican II has not gotten around to weeding out is "Holy Day of Obligation." I submit we should replace it with "Holy Day of Celebration." You say I am just playing with words -- inanely. But attend to the theory of poetry which dominates the advertising industry, namely that *words make things,* and you will see the significance of this. For example, if we are told enough times that cigarette smoking refreshes your taste, pretty soon every time we think of cigarettes, we think of refreshment. Whereas, I think the last thing a cigarette will do to your taste is refresh it. Similarly, if we are told long enough that today is a holy day of obligation, every time we think of the feast of the Assumption, we will think of an obligation; whereas, what it truly means, and whether it is worth an extra effort at worship eludes us.

But the feast of the Assumption is truly an occasion for a Christian celebration when its real meaning is considered. It is not merely, or even primarily, a day for giving honor to Mary, the Mother of Jesus. It is rather a day for remembering deeply and seriously that the Christian way leads to victory. We are reminded by the fathers of the Council to view Mary not so much as a special being whose prerogatives and achievements under God's favor are impossible to comprehend, but rather as a member, like us, of the Christian community . . . except the foremost member, the follower of Christ *par excellence.* Essentially, what befalls her befalls every faithful believer. As the way of following of Jesus led to victory for her, it will lead so for each of us.

There seem to be currently two philosophies about where life leads: on the one hand, some say that a worthy life will lead to a gradual improvement of our earth, a state in which things will be better for everyone. Countering are those who say that a life worthily or unworthily or whatever doesn't lead anywhere or leads nowhere, and doesn't make any kind of sense no matter how you go about it. A Christian subscribes to neither of these notions. Instead he/she believes that his way of life leads to the final victory of sharing the company of the Lord.

We acknowledge this belief explicitly today, on the feast of Our Lady's Assumption. Because in her certain entrance into the company of Jesus, her son, we see what is in store for us if, as St. Paul puts it, "we are not found wanting." And I say our day -- this liturgical day-- is more than a day of acknowledgement (and let's get rid of the word *obligation*), it is a day of celebration. We celebrate joyfully here and now, for these few moments, the one thing that makes all the trouble and sweat and anxiety of pursuing the way of the Gospel add up -- final victory: peace and rest in the company of the Lord.

†

St. Francis Church, October 2, 1966
18th Sunday after Pentecost

The Paralytic

Sacred Scripture is so rich and filled with meaning that besides the simple and clear illustration of the Lord's power to forgive sin, we can discover another beautiful doctrine in today's Gospel. St. Matthew says that, "He went down into a small boat, and crossing over the sea, came to his own city." This means that God, in the person of his Son Jesus, came down from heaven and crossed over the immeasurable ocean that separates divinity from humanity, and came into this, his own, because he made it. He came on a mission to heal mankind of a paralytic condition -- sin. So, like the poor sick man of the gospel, all men can lift themselves up and go home to the heavenly home.

It is St. Peter Crysologus, a Greek Father of the early Church, who commenting on this passage over ten centuries ago, draws out this analogy and lesson. Peter goes on to point out that like a good physician, Jesus walks among the sick. That is, God walks among men, in order to avail them of spiritual healing. But it is not only for bringing us ultimate salvation that God walks among us, continues Peter, "Jesus meant by his love to invite us, by his kindness to attract us, by his affection to conquer us, and by his humanity to convince us. This is his way; rather than frighten us or drive us away by domination or show of power."

The Lord came over to our city, in order to take upon himself our weakness and give us his strength, to be human that we might be divine, to accept injury in order to bestow dignity, to suffer weariness in order to restore vitality. In the face of this doctrine, what should our response be? The answer is also contained in the gospel story. "At seeing these things, the crowds were filled with awe and they gave glory to God." We are here this morning to make response, and to give glory to God, to worship. And we so respond, not only because we are in the crowd and have observed his gentleness, but because we are also paralytics and Jesus has singled out each one of us for healing. Now he commands us to rise from the pallet of our sinfulness, and start on our way to the heavenly home.

†

St. Francis Church, New York, March 14, 1965

On Selma, Alabama

We have received a letter from our servant in the lord, the Cardinal Archbishop. He calls our attention to the tragic condition of Selma, Alabama, and he urges us to pray that "the evil which has been let loose there, by the failings of poor, weak men who are prone to sin like you and I, be swiftly quelled by God's almighty power and gifts, so that justice and peace might prevail." The Cardinal need hardly remind us of what has been going on in Selma; we have learned only too well from the daily news media. He need hardly urge us to pray; for who can sit before his television set at home, who can read his newspaper on the subway and not be aware of a mounting catastrophe, and not utter some kind of a prayer in his heart that it be averted.

But the Cardinal asks us today to sense the evil of Selma and to pray for its extinction not as separated individuals but as connected members of the Church, as God's people gathered for worship in New York. The Church in New York is called upon to muster all its strength and spiritual power and bring them to bear for the cause of peace and justice in Selma. It is fitting, therefore, that before we pray we consider the case of Selma. Let us examine its meaning in the light of that truth which radiates from divine revelation, and which the Catholic Church, conscious of its sacred mission, must illumine every human problem.

On the front page of the Brooklyn Tablet this week, there is quoted statement of Archbishop Paul J. Hallinan of Atlanta: "The trouble in Selma is not caused by Negroes or by outsiders. It is caused by state and local officials, who do not believe in either American law or Christian morality, and by a population which lets them get away with it." The trouble to which the Archbishop here refers is discrimination against Negroes in the matter of their right to vote. Selma, Alabama, is a city the size of Rockville Center or Newburgh, with nearly 30,000 citizens. The majority of its citizens are Negroes; that is, over 15,000. Yet only 350 Negroes are registered to vote. The extreme imbalance of these figures can only be accounted for by the presence of racial discrimination. It is discrimination disguised under voter registration laws that circumvent the 15TH Amendment of the United States Constitution. The details of these laws are not important. They may have been revised from time to time under the pressure of federal courts; but the ingenuity, the unscrupulosity, the desperation of the lawmakers has preserved their original purpose. It is no secret. In 1902, when the movement among Southern legislations to disenfranchise Negroes was enjoying unchallenged success, a Virginia lawmaker admitted boldly: "Discriminate! Why that is precisely what we propose. That exactly, is what this convention was elected for -- to discriminate to the very extremity of permissible action under the limitations of the Federal Constitution, with the view to the elimination of every Negro voter who can be gotten rid of legally, without materially impairing the numerical strength of the white electorate."

Nothing has happened to alter this purpose and its implementation in the South for the past half century. And no American citizen, whether he live in the North or South or East or West, need be told that it violates all our national beliefs and ideals. But to what extent is it also a violation of human rights and dignity and therefore the grave concern of the Church? In the encyclical Peace on Earth, Pope John 23RD wrote: "The dignity of the human person involves the right to take an active part in public affairs and to contribute one's part to the common good of the citizens." And in the same solemn teaching he has warned that, "if any government does not acknowledge the rights of man, or violates them, it not only fails in its duty, but its orders completely lack juridical force." The least and minimal exercise of the right to take an active part in public affairs consists in voting for public officials. Wherever this is denied, the Pope argues, whether by force or by legal prescription, it is clearly wrong and such legal prescriptions are meaningless.

And wherever a human right is denied, human dignity is under attack. It is the sacred mission of the Church to proclaim and defend the dignity of the human person, no less when it is attacked by advocates of discrimination, as when it is attacked by advocates of abortion or euthanasia or radical contraception. For Christians believe and acknowledge, before the rest of the world, that every human person, no matter what his race of age or economic condition is of such dignity and value that the Son of God died to make salvation available to him.

Then there is this consideration: what about the demonstrations, and our priests and nuns joining in? Pope John further teaches that "he who possesses certain rights has likewise the duty to claim those rights as marks of his dignity, while all others have the obligation to acknowledge those rights and respect them; and men have the right to associate and assemble in order to achieve just aims." It is certain that Pope John means that men must claim their rights peacefully and without violence or wrongfully inciting others to violence. The demonstration which our priests and nuns were involved in falls within the bounds of these principles. Such a demonstration (and mind you, I am not talking about a sit-in . . . that is something different) is nothing more than a parade that attracts attention and advertises an issue. In this same instance, the issue was injustice in Selma, Alabama. The St. Patrick's Day parade on 5TH Avenue is a demonstration in the very same sense, except the issue is different and the historical setting happens now to be amiable.

Such is the case of Selma, Alabama. And today our Cardinal Archbishop urges us to respond together as God's people and pray that this evil will be destroyed. We seek no revenge. We sponsor no hate. We are Christians. If we single out an enemy, it is to love him. Everyone in Selma needs the help that our prayers together can provide.

There will come a moment shortly in the canon of the Mass when the priest pauses -- you will notice it -- to mention the special needs of the day. Let us use that moment silently and intensely to pray for the people of Selma . . . and indeed, for all people into whose lives the power of evil has been let loose.

†

New York comments, October 1965

Pope Paul at Yankee Stadium

It is over a month now since Pope Paul VI visited the United Nations and set foot for the first time on American soil. Undoubtedly, historians will need wider perspective than a month to review and measure the significance of his visit. The whole spectacular event kind of floored New York, and I don't think I'm engaging in hyperbole to imagine the city or the nation just now coming to its senses and taking a calm dispassionate look at what happened last October 4TH.

I happened to be in Yankee Stadium that night. I heard the Pope's sermon on peace. It was not the best conditions for listening to a sermon, what with the sound system in the stadium ringing echoes and feed-back through the stands. A transistor radio helped. There were lucid paragraphs here and there which impressed. And the whole sermon, whether audible or not, was reinforced by the splendor of the scene. I got the impression at the time, although vague and unsubstantial, that something was happening to the country, that it was undergoing some kind of maturation ceremony, that the religious spirit of the nation had come of age and was being officially recognized by the great potentate of religion of the Western hemisphere. Since that night, I have read over Pope Paul's sermon several times, and I think I can substantiate my impression.

We are a young country. "A young and glorious continent," the Pope called us. And scholars will go further and tell us that we have been a naïve country as well. Despite our strength, our courage, our new wealth, we've stumbled awkwardly at times like an adolescent, in foreign, in social, in economic affairs, they are forced to conclude. It is not unlikely, therefore, that religiously we have also been naive and awkward at times. But somehow, we have survived, reached maturity. And here is the representative of Judeo-Christian civilization, the man who is spokesman for that tradition which has touched upon, approved or disapproved, every single empire that has grown up in the West, at last bestowing his approval upon us. We made it.

And then Pope Paul VI placed upon our shoulders the responsibility of a mature civilization: the task of building peace. They are moving words he speaks about peace. Nothing new or especially original, but in the context of this ceremony, moving. Like the young man who at confirmation or bar mitzvah hears all that advice about growing up that he has heard every day for the past several years, but on the ceremonious occasion the advice seems to hit harder, to take.

He said, "you must love peace," meditate on its real meaning until it lives in your minds and hearts. Children must be taught to understand peace. He says you must serve the cause of peace honestly, not making use of it for selfish aims. Not using it as a cover for cowardice, which refuses to make sacrifices for the common good; not using it to evade the call of duty or to seek one's own interest and pleasure.

"Peace is not a state which can be acquired and made permanent. Peace must be built. It must be built up every day by works of peace.

These works of peace are first of all social order; then aid to the poor who still make up an immense multitude of the world population, aid to the needy, the weak, the sick, the ignorant."

The whole sermon is a big order for any single individual. I love peace. I want it. Where can I begin? The answer I find in Pope Paul's definition of peace. He says it is "Order in relation to God and to men." It is wisdom; it is justice; it is civilization. Whoever loves peace loves mankind, without distinction of race or of color.

People always have problems about what peace is. They will say, OK, but supposing such and such happens. Then what do I do? I don't understand peace. Could the reason that we don't understand peace be that we are not used to the idea. We've never meditated upon it. We've only absorbed slogans that contain the word. The one easy thing to discover about the revolutionary kind of peace that the Pope urges is that it is the opposite of war and contention in every conceivable way. It takes two to make a fight. It only takes one to make peace -- his own peace, which alone matters . . . because peace is the ordered relationship of a man with God and with his neighbor, who is his equal in the sight of God and who is equally at the mercy of the Creator.

For over two and a half centuries, the people of this continent have been growing up spiritually. Perhaps we have now officially come of age. And just as our growth and acquisition of strength and wealth presented a challenge, which was met by every individual American of our past; so now the adjustment to peace in maturity presents a challenge to every man of us.

†

St. Francis Church, New York, January 10, 1965

Holy Family Sunday
(Birth Control)

Celebrating a feast in honor of the Holy Family is relatively new in the Church. Some of you here may remember its beginning. Pope Benedict XV introduced it into the Church year in 1921. His purpose was to promote devotion and honor toward Jesus, Mary and Joseph under the title of the Holy Family, and also to stress the meaning of family life, in the light of Christian Revelation. Today's celebration then directs our attention to the fact that the three persons most intimately involved in God's Redemptive Plan based themselves, acquired holiness, achieved love, as members of a human family. The subject, therefore is Christian holiness.

And the message is that Christian holiness is learned first and foremost by the exercise of virtue in working out the relationships which arise naturally in a family. That is, a Christian will never love, will never be honest, will never be chaste in his dealings with the all men, unless he first achieves these virtues in dealing with the members of his own family. For the Christian way is love. And love is the perfection of relationships. And the most immediate, sensible conscious relationships of life are those which arise from the very nature of the family.

Having made this brief preface to a discussion of family relationships, I would now like to jump very quickly to a specific family relationship – that of husband and wife. And to a very specific aspect of that relationship. The subject of parenthood -- particularly as it is affected by methods of family limitation (Birth Control is the popular term, though it always strikes me as contradictory.) has been prominent in the news this past week. A priest spokesman for the NCWC (National Catholic Welfare Conference -- which is a kind of pentagon for the American Catholic bishops) made it clear that the Church's opposition to unnatural methods of birth prevention has not diminished one bit, and that therefore any federal program of distributing information concerning unnatural methods of family limitation will not be supported by Catholics. And this all happened just about at the time when we were thinking that the teaching of the Church with regard to "birth control" was liberalizing. Are people confused? They have every reason to be? My purpose here is to dissipate that confusion and to place before you one or two principles on which this current theological thinking with regard to birth control is based. I would have you understand that there is no contradiction in the Catholic attitude on birth control, and that however scientists and theologians conclude their ever-deepening investigations of human reproduction, it will always be in the interest of love, the Christian perfection of the husband-wife relationship in the family.

In the first place, what is normal and natural in the process of human life and behavior is at once the object of investigation and the guiding principle for both scientists and theologians. To a certain degree, what is normal and natural in human life and behavior can be discovered by anyone. You don't need to a scientist to tell you that love sexually expressed between a man and a woman tends to produce new life. You don't need a theologian to tell you that parents ought to love and care for the new life and that their mutual affection produces. These truths are most obvious in nature. Anyone can perceive them. But when it comes to refining and analyzing these truths, then we call upon the specialists. The scientist must show us precisely how the human body functions and how its functions can be perfected, improved. The theologian must show us how to act so that our deliberate, intelligent behavior is in accord with nature and does not oppose or frustrate normal human processes.

Common, crude, and mechanical methods and devices for preventing human conception are soundly opposed by Catholic teaching, because they seem to be contrary to the natural and normal tendency of the human reproductive process. They have no scientific respect for human life and behavior. They are mere expedients which all normal thinking human beings must ultimately regard as repulsive. Therefore, Catholic teaching authority is and will ever be opposed to their use and promotion. On the other hand, certain drugs called *progesterones,* -- commonly misnamed as the birth control pill -- have been found by scientists to influence the female reproductive process. How these drugs may be used so as to assist and regulate that process rather than frustrate and destroy it is the common concern today of both scientists and theologians.

They attend to the fact that the female fertility cycle follows a regular monthly pattern. This is normal and natural. Progesterone drugs are prescribed by a physician to promote and perfect this cycle, so that its phases can be accurately predicted. As such their use is morally permissible, and perhaps even desirable. Scientists and theologians also observe that childbirth is normally and naturally followed by a long period of infertility -- called the lactation period -- which allows a woman to regain her strength before conceiving again. This period, whether breast nursing is done or not, should normally and naturally last as long as a year. Therefore, progesterone drugs might (always under the direction of a physician) be used for that length of time -- 10-12 months – in order to guarantee the natural lactation period.

At the present time, scientists and theologians are acutely aware that their knowledge of human process and human behavior is far from comprehensive. There is always more to be discovered and proven. Their conclusions must be carefully studied, not jumped upon as some final panacea-cure-all. Therefore, Catholics should approach this popular subject thoughtfully and confident that Church teachers will help them to understand. We might also pray today to the Holy Family, petitioning Jesus, Mary, and Joseph to bless Christian family life, to protect us from error, and to give us the strength and enlightenment to achieve the perfection of Christian love in our families that will help us solve the problems and tensions of the 20TH century.

†

Description of the Mass

For the nuns on E. 44TH St. – 1965

Since there is a whole week ahead of us together, I thought it might be useful if I gave the daily homily time over to a description of the Mass, as it is currently undergoing revision. To begin with, the whole purpose of the revision is not to streamline or modernize the Mass, but to make its intrinsic nature and purpose more clearly manifest. For "there are many elements in the Mass," says the Sacred Decree, "which, with the passage of time, came to be duplicated, or were added with but little advantage, or have suffered injury through accidents of history."

The intrinsic nature of the Mass is that of a ritual and sacrificial meal in the tradition of the ancient Jewish Paschal meal --indeed, it was while partaking of the Paschal meal that Jesus gave us the Mass. It consists therefore of a preparation, the *Offertory,* wherein the gifts of bread and wine are brought to the altar and ritually offered to God by several prayers. Then there is the great Eucharist Prayer, extending from the Sanctus to the *Pater Noster,* during which God changes our gifts into the Body and Blood of Christ. Next follows the Communion, in which all partake of the sacred meal. Finally, and most obviously, there is a time of Thanksgiving. This entire rite is the central action of the Mass. It is called, sometimes, the Eucharistic Service.

Now preceding the Eucharistic Service, and somewhat distinct from it, there is a broad preparation or orientation which may be called the Service of the Word, for the key element of this service is not the Eucharistic Gift, but the Word of God or the Bible. It consists of at least two readings from the Bible and an explanation or commentary by the priest. Interspersed between and around the sacred readings there are prayers of preparation and praise.

Now we are almost to the beginning of the Mass. The beginning, the psalms, the hymns, the antiphons that are arranged there make up an elaborate Entrance rite. For the time being then, let us think of the Mass as made up of these three segments: The Eucharistic Service, the Service of the Word, and the Entrance Rite. As this week progresses, we shall take each of these segments and show how the current revision aims to make them more clearly perceptible and more meaningful, so that -- again in the words of the decree, "devout and active participation by the faithful may be more easily achieved."

The first segment of the Mass, the Entrance Rite, is at present made up of the prayers at the foot altar, the *Introit*, the *Kyrie*, the *Gloria*, and the *Collect*. If we examine it closely, we note a duplication. Consider this common sequence: hymn, expression of contrition, prayer of petition. The Prayers at the foot of the Altar contain this same sequence of prayers.

The hymn is psalm 42; the *Confiteor* is the expression of contrition; the two prayers which follow the word *Oremus* are the petitions. Then comes the *Introit*. It is a hymn also, consisting of a psalm and its antiphons. However, only a remnant verse of the psalm remains, so much has it been abbreviated. The *Kyrie* is an expression of contrition, and the *Collect* is a solemn prayer of petition. Originally the Introit was the hymn (with the psalm intact) which the people sang as the priest entered the sanctuary. It is a processional song. When in the course of time it was reduce and no longer sung by the people, another entrance hymn was added and given to the priest to recite by himself as he approached to the altar -- psalm 42. In accordance with the customary sequence, the two prayers were added to it. The elements of contrition were even later additions.

When the liturgy is restored to some extent this Lent, the psalm 42 will be eliminated entirely, because it is a duplication. On certain occasions, when the Mass is preceded by another ceremony, such as the Sunday *Asperges,* the prayers at the foot of the altar will be eliminated as well, and the Mass proper will commence absolutely with the Introit. Our practice here has been to assign the prayers at the foot of the altar to the priest and the server quietly, because of this character that these prayers have. And It is most fitting that the first words the congregation hears of the Mass are those of the Introit.

As for the Introit itself, I've described it as an entrance song sung by the community while the priest enters. Consequently, it does not really belong to the priest to say. Beginning in Lent, a choir or the entire congregation will chant or recite or sing the Introit where it is possible, and the rest of the psalm verses will be added to make it lengthier and more meaningful. The priest, where this is done, will not recite the Introit at all.

Next comes the *Kyrie,* which as the language (Greek) testifies, is the introduction into the Latin liturgy of an Oriental exchange alternating antiphon-response chant. One side announces a verse, the other side responds or repeats. This is a kind of prayer very common even today in Oriental rites. We have a sample of it in the Kyrie, and it will remain thus in the Mass. The priest beginning and alternating the prayer with the congregation.

The Gloria is a great hymn of praise which brings the Entrance Rite toward its climax. It is a hymn which belongs to neither the priest nor a choir to sing alone. But it is the moment in the fore-Mass when the entire gathering of Christians join together for song. Henceforth the entire congregation will be encouraged to sing it, and the priest who as leader introduces it, may even join in himself.

After the Entrance Rite reaches a peak of intensity in the Gloria, it suddenly and solemnly rushes to conclusion in the Collect or Prayer of the Assembly. This prayer is uttered by the priest alone, who now functions clearly as the mediator, and who brings the particular petitions of the community before God. The Congregation answers "Amen." The Entrance Rite is over. The Priest may then sit down to listen to the first reading of the Service of the Word.

†

G.F. Proud

Confirmation

If you had ever wondered what theologians do, or how the teaching Church arrives at what we call dogmas, there is a good illustration in the readings today. Confirmation. A sacrament. We believe in it as an article of our faith. By article of faith, I mean what followers of Jesus, Christians, have always believed going back to the very days which are the setting for these scriptural readings. We have no other way of knowing about this sacrament, except what Christians before us have always known and have passed on to us. And from passages like this in the Acts of the Apostles written by St. Luke

Of course the rank and file Christians, the people like those St. Luke was addressing, or like ourselves, might not have reflected on Conformation or given it a formal name as "Sacrament." You and I received Confirmation, most likely, as young teenagers. And we had to learn that it was a special gift or grace of the Holy Spirit. But we probably never gave much thought as to how we knew that or why the teaching Church told us that.

Well here it is now -- here is why we are taught about Confirmation and believe: It happened in the town of Samaria, a region north of Israel in what is now Lebanon. Philip, one of the apostles, was going forth as Jesus had ordered and was baptizing in His name. The people in Samaria became believers and followers of Jesus because of Philip's preaching. They were baptized. In fact, as Luke tells it, there were some marvelous events associated with the coming of the Gospel to this community -- healings of cripples and paralytics and more. So they were baptized.

And then it says Peter and John came along and prayed that they might receive the Holy Spirit. (quote) "They put their hands on them and they received the Holy Spirit." (end quote) Now couldn't theologians draw conclusions from that about Conformation? It was a gift or grace different from Baptism, and it was given after these Christians were already baptized.

And then in the next reading in the liturgy today, the gospel, St. John's most beautiful passage recounts Jesus telling his friends, the disciples, the apostles we call them now: "If you love me and obey the commands I give you, I will ask the Father and he will give you another Paraclete . . . to be with you always, the Spirit of truth." The gift Jesus promises, rendered in the Greek language *Paraclete* means advocate, protector, counselor. It is a notion the gospel writer may have had difficulty in conveying fully. This is always happening in translating a language. There just doesn't seem to be one word which says exactly what the writer intends. Perhaps our contemporary word "Ombudsman" might be appropriate here -- the person who can take care of everything for us.

What all of this adds up to is the certainty of the presence of a person, a power, a force, apart from, distinct from Jesus and the Father that is available to strengthen us. Or as Jesus says . . . who will remain with us always and be watching over us. It's all right here as clear as light in these readings. Don't you agree? And by our experience, the Holy Spirit we refer to comes to us by the laying on of hands of the Bishop in what we have named *Conformation,* a sacrament.

But I have not pointed this out to you merely as a lesson in theology to prove something or to demonstrate how theology is presented. I think we now have to consider how this reading touches us. It is God, though Jesus, through his chosen apostles, through his Church, assuring us that -- my favorite phrase -- "everything's gonna be all right." Have you ever said that to someone? "Everything's gonna be all right." To a loved one in distress, to a child who is hurt or frightened. Has anyone ever said it to you? Doesn't it penetrate deeply and relieve your fears and insecurities, perhaps only for a moment? . . . especially when it comes with a hug . . . And from a strong person you know loves you. "Everything going to be all right. I'll take care of you." And isn't this what is happening when we are touched, a hand is laid on our head or shoulder in the coming of the Holy Spirit in the sacrament?

And isn't it capable, together with our faith, of bringing us deep down inside *peace* . . . as Jesus promised on this same occasion to his disciples?

We may not often reflect upon all the good things, these graces, this assurance we have by reason of our true faith as followers of Jesus. But we have it. These readings this morning should remind of the security we possess as Christians. Maybe it lies dormant because of all the distractions which surround us. But should you need it, today's liturgy reminds you that you can call upon it. "If you love me and obey the command I give you, I will ask the Father and he will give another Advocate to be with you always, the Spirit of Truth, who will remain with you and will be within you." I like that. That makes me feel good.

†

G.F. Proud

On the Closing of Vatican II

St. Francis Church, New York, December 5, 1965
2ND Sunday of Advent

On December 8^{TH,} next Wednesday, the great engine of the Second Vatican Council will grind to a halt. Pope Paul VI will declare it officially closed, although the many reforms which it has set in motion will continue to affect us for years, for decades to come. At this point in its history, our beloved Archbishop and Cardinal has asked the priests of his diocese to address you today on the subject of the Council and to attempt to give it perspective and to access its achievements.

Seen in broad perspective, Vatican II is but one of a continuing series of Ecumenical -- that is, world-wide Church Councils. There have been twenty in all, and the business of each without exception has been to proclaim to the world the belief of Christians. But in each Council, the proclamation of a single great mystery of our faith has been outstanding. At Nicaea, the first Ecumenical Council, in the 4TH century, the issue was the divinity of Christ; and that ancient body of Church teachers proclaimed it revealed that Jesus is the Second Person of the Trinity, the Son of God. At Ephesus in Asia Minor in the 5TH century, the mystery of God's Incarnation was proclaimed: that is, Christ is fully man as well as God and the Son of a woman, Mary.

At Trent in Italy in the 16TH century, the mystery of God's dealings with men through grace and the seven sacraments was made clear and beyond any doubt. At Vatican I in the 19TH century, the mystery of the supreme and unerring teaching capacity of the bishop of Rome, the Pope, was confirmed universally. In Vatican II now, what has happened? What mystery has unfolded to us in exact and unambiguous declarations? It is the mystery of the people of God, the mystery of the Church itself.

When Vatican II is reviewed centuries from today, it will be seen to have announced to the world what is the nature of that community of believers held together over centuries by faith in the revelation of Jesus. The "Constitution on the Church" made public one year ago last November 21, is the key to Vatican II. It is what Vatican II was all about. I am not saying that up to now no one has known what the Church is. That would be foolish. We have known that the community of believers is a divine enterprise and does not depend for its presence or continuance upon mere men. We have by grace found ourselves living in and receiving the blessings of this fellowship. But only gradually have we grown conscious of what a great mystery it is, of who we are in it, and of how it moves toward its goal. It is a fact that only in the past 100 years have theologians concentrated on and given scientific (that is, theological) definitions to the community of believers in Christ. The fruits of their labors are now apparent in the proclamations of Vatican II. New facets of the Church's splendor have been exposed and its mystery has become a grand object of faith and awe and edification.

The "Constitution on the Church" has in the first place explained that the Church is not an organization in the ordinary sense. It is a society of those who follow Christ. It is Christ's kingdom. And it is bound together by a power from above, by the power of the Divine Trinity. Its life and progress through the ages of the world are a mystery as real and as great as any other in Revelation.

The Council has gone on to describe in its several decrees the separate and special roles of each member in the Church -- of the bishops, of the priests, and of the laymen. The Council has issued a statement on the place of Religious Life in the Church. It has declared what the proper work of the Church is in the Decree on the Liturgy. The relationship of the Church to those outside its membership has been outlined in two decrees: the one on Ecumenism, the other on Religious Liberty. Finally, in the schema to receive approval tomorrow, Vatican II has taken up all the problems with which the present age confronts the Church: war, poverty, population growth and so forth.

Unlike other preceding Councils, Vatican II was not forced into session be reason of a particular heretical attack. Yet it is no less urgent. It has, perhaps, headed off an attack. I like to think of an old pastor I once knew, who the bishop had only to call on the telephone and make a mind suggestion and he promptly executed the Bishop's least wish. Here we have twenty- seven hundred bishops* who have crossed oceans and continents and to put their commands in writing and deliver them to us with ceremony and display. Should we then receive their words calmly with the blasé attitude of wait and see what happens.

Everyone must hear this Council, and perform his/her role in carrying its commands out, in adopting its studied words, and adopt its views intelligently without any respect for past customs or prejudices or ways of doing things or manners, even if for you this means pressuring your leaders to inform you and lead you. For it is proposed beyond a doubt now who the Church is, and upon whom it will depend, and whether the Church advances and is on the move again in order to meet the crying needs of the 20th century world – you and I.

Historian John O'Malley SJ has calls Vatical II the largest meeting in the history of the world.

†

Boston

St. Anthony's Shrine, Arch St., Boston, December, 8, 1963

Immaculate Conception

Something slightly unusual has happened to you today. You came to a Franciscan church on the feast of the Immaculate Conception. And I hope to make it a small occasion in your spiritual life that you will not soon forget. For as wonderful and joyous as this holy day is in every church in the Catholic world, it is especially wonderful and joyous in a Franciscan church... because Mary, under the title of the Immaculate Conception, is the heavenly patron of the followers of St. Francis. Just as it is the Carmelite tradition to honor Mary as patroness under the title of Our Lady of Mount Carmel; and just as it is the Dominican tradition to honor Mary as patroness under the title of the Lady of the Rosary, it is the Franciscan tradition to honor Mary as patroness under the title of the Immaculate Conception.

The Franciscan tradition of Marian devotion begins with St. Francis. The first chapel given to his little band was named in her honor. He composed prayers honoring her. This is one of them:

> *Hail holy Lady, most holy Queen, Mary, mother of God, yet a virgin forever, chosen by the most high Father in heaven and consecrated by him with his most holy beloved Son and the Spirit, the Paraclete. You in whom there was and there is all the fullness of grace and everything good: hail his Palace, hail his Tabernacle, hail his Home, hail his Vesture, hail the Handmaiden, hail his Mother!*

No wonder the followers of St. Francis have always considered true devotion to Mary an essential characteristic of their way of life. They were always inventing new ways to express this devotion.
(1) Shortly after the death of Francis, his Order adopted the custom of singing a hymn to Mary at the end of their daily prayers. Today, this hymn is a part of the prescribed prayers of every priest.

(2) St. Bonaventure, an outstanding General of the Order of St. Francis, promoted the Catholic custom of reciting the Angelus in honor of Our Lady three times each day.

(3) Jacapone di Todi, a Franciscan brother, composed a hymn to Mary that we sing during the Stations of the Cross in Lent – the *Stabat Mater*.

(4) But undoubtedly, the greatest Franciscan achievement in the area of devotion to Mary is the defense and propagation of the doctrine of the Immaculate Conception. John Duns Scotus, an English friar, who lived at the end of the 13TH century, explained that since it is entirely possible for God to create a soul shielded from the stain of Original Sin, and since such a privilege is befitting the Mother of Christ, God must have done so.

Strengthened by arguments of Franciscan theologians, and fostered by the zeal of Franciscan preachers through the next several centuries, this ancient belief of Christian Catholics was judged by Pope Pius IX to be an essential part of Catholic Faith. And in 1849 he proclaimed the Dogma of the Immaculate Conception. Only nine years later, in 1858, Mary appeared to St. Bernadette at Lourdes and called herself the "Immaculate Conception."

So, briefly I have outlined the gradual process by which the Church became conscious of the devotion to the Immaculate Conception, Mary Immaculate, and the part the followers of St. Francis played in this process. The Order is proud of its Marian tradition and it invites you -- if you have any partiality to the ideas of St. Francis -- to attach yourself to it. You are in a Franciscan church. Rejoice with us today. And make a prayer to Mary Immaculate a part of every day.

†

Sermon given on Holy Thursday at Cushing Convent, Boston.

Holy Thursday

May the Lord inkindle in us the fire of his love and the flame of everlasting charity. This short prayer, which I have chosen for my text, belongs to the incensing rubrics of the solemn liturgy. It is whispered by the celebrant to the deacon, as he hands over to him the smoking thurible.

Dear sisters in Christ, today is the first time since my ordination to the priesthood five years ago, that I shall enjoy the privilege of celebrating the Mass of Holy Thursday. And of course, in order to prepare for these ceremonies, especially as they have been redesigned in recent years, I had to plunge into the ceremonial books. There I found, strikingly enough, that the first sentence of Father McManus' *The Rites of Holy Week*, is this: "Sanctity is the purpose of the new Holy Week."

Perhaps up to this time I had been thinking only on a surface level about Holy Week. Mostly I had considered how the restored ritual made the services more convenient for the laity, or more appealing -- they could see more of what was going on. Or I assumed that the Holy Week ritual had been adjusted to give others (beside the clergy) a feeling of sharing in the worship of these sacred actions. But ultimately, it is what Fr. McManus says: "Sanctity is the purpose of Holy Week." To us religious, sanctity is the commanding purpose of life. We should then make our meditations this week on the liturgical services and learn what they can teach about becoming saints.

The theme of today's liturgy is threefold: the institution of the Holy Eucharist, the establishment of the priesthood, and fraternal charity among Christians. So much do religious cherish the Holy Eucharist, that they begin the schedule of their day with its celebration. So necessary do they consider it for the growth of holiness in their community that they go to great lengths – and the Superior is even anxious – to secure its celebration every day. No inconvenience is so great that it cannot be bypassed to have Mass in the convent every day, or to have other Eucharistic services when they are called for. If such difficulties came between the religious and other lesser devotions, those devotions would easily be given up. But it is a fact that religious cannot live without the food of sanctity, which is the Eucharist.

Today at this service, we commemorate the occasion on which Jesus gave us the gift of his Body and Blood. We should then make it a day of thanksgiving. And resolution. Our thanksgiving should be a return of love to Jesus. Our resolution should be to eliminate routine and slothfulness in the reception of this sacrament. The second theme of today's liturgy is the priesthood. Because on the Thursday before he died, Jesus instituted this order when he said, "Do this in commemoration of me." Religious are so absolutely dependent upon priests for the sacred things which bring sanctity that they must cultivate a greater love and respect for the priesthood and for priests than any others. And this basic love and respect in no way should depend upon whether the priest is pleasant, unpleasant, well-mannered or boorish, holy or unholy, prompt or late. A priest does not want love and respect, or the opposite, for any of these reasons, unless there is love and respect toward him for the reason that he brings the sacraments of Christ. St. Francis made a very penetrating remark about the nature of the priesthood. Recall that he was not himself a priest, nor did he live in an age of particularly holy priests. It was this:

> And it is my will to love and honor priests; and I will not regard sin in them, because I discern the Son of God in them, and they are my masters. And I do this for the reason that in this world I see nothing bodily of the most high Son of God himself but his most holy Body and Blood, in which they have charge and they alone administer to others.

The third theme is fraternal charity among Christians. It is included because there is no separating the Holy Eucharist from brotherly love, either in its institution or in its daily celebration anywhere in the world today. Jesus gave us the sacrament of his Body and Blood on an occasion on which he performed an outward physical unmistakable act of love toward the apostles. He washed their feet. We should not dare to take this gift each day unless we can follow his example. There must be outward unmistakable gestures in our life regularly -- because we come to take the Eucharist regularly.

And while I must end quickly now because I have gone on so long, it is perhaps this theme – fraternal charity -- which is the overall theme of the Mass today. The Eucharistic was given out of love. The priest must carry it to every age out of love; and those who receive it must let it transform their lives and spread around them like fire. This is our Eucharistic prayer today: "May the Lord inkindle in us the fire of his love and the flame of everlasting charity."

†

Sermon given on the 1ST Sunday of Advent, December 1, 1963, at the Cardinal Cushing Convent, Boston.

Paradoxes

Our faith is filled with paradoxes; so it should not perplex us to find an enormous one presented in the Mass today. The paradox is this: that while the first Sunday of Advent is the beginning of the Church Year, the theme of the Mass is the end of the world and the Judgement. Yet, when the Church employs paradox in the liturgy to teach us, it should not confuse us. Paradox is not a confusion of the truth, but rather a compression of the truth. So, by examining thoughtfully the Mass of today, we may come to be more fully enlightened.

There are three meanings of the paradox. The first may be expressed by the line "In my beginning is my end." Advent is a time of beginning, because it celebrates the beginning of the fullness of revelation. The feast for which it prepares us celebrates the beginning of our Savior's life on earth. The Mass instructs us that our spiritual preparation for meeting our Infant Savior should be intermingled with our spiritual preparation for meeting our Triumphal Judge. As we pray with the prophets of the Old Testament that the Savior come, we should be mindful of the words of John's gospel of the New Testament: "Come, Lord Jesus." As we kneel at the manger cradle of our beginning, we should consider the judgement seat of our end.

The second meaning of the paradox may be expressed in the line "In my end is my beginning." That is, it is out of consideration of our final destiny, coming face to face with God in heaven, that we begin to live a meritorious life on earth. The life of Jesus on earth, beginning with the poverty and humility of his birth, is the example we follow. By this beginning, I do not mean only the conversion of a lifetime or the answering of a religious vocation, or even the recovery from a fall. In a life aimed at Christian perfection, every day must be a new beginning. So it was said of St. Francis by his biographers that anywhere, anytime along the road, we might hear him say what he was wont to say in cheer: *Brothers, let us begin to serve God our Lord, for up till now we have made little or no progress.*

Third, and finally, the liturgical year begins with the announcement of the end and Judgement, because throughout the liturgical year we celebrate in a hidden way the same sacred mysteries which will be revealed to us in heaven. The holy year that begins on the first Sunday of Advent is a vestige, a foretaste of the blessed eternity which begins at the Judgement.

Our prayer for every day might be expressed in the wonderful ambiguity of the Mass Collect: *Bestir, O Lord, thy might, we pray and come, that defended by thee, we may deserve rescue from approaching dangers brought on by our sins, and being set free by Thee, obtain our salvation.*

†

Buffalo

St. Patrick's Friary
102 Seymour Street, Buffalo, New York 14210

Last Sunday after Pentecost

Buffalo, November 24, 1968

You may be well-aware of the fact that the calendar year that we keep in our cycle of worship does not coincide exactly with the ordinary calendar year. In other words, the yearly series of Sunday Masses ends today, and the new series will begin on next Sunday, the first Sunday of Advent. Whereas, in our business or secular calendar December is the last month and January the first.

Appropriately enough, since today is the end of the year of worship, the passage selected for reading from the gospel contains the Lord's prophecy of the end of this earthly life, when, as we have read, "they will see the Son of Man coming upon the clouds of heaven, power and glory." I might note, incidentally, that a similar passage from St. Luke will be read next week -- the first Sunday of the year of Worship; because it is felt, that even at the beginning, we do well to be reminded of our end.

As for today's reading, you will readily admit that it is mysterious and difficult to understand. This is true but not unusual. Jesus was a prophet, and his words of prophecy, like the words of every biblical prophet, are clouded with mystery. Rather than attempt to interpret them directly, let us instead pay attention to the reaction of the early Christians to this prophecy. For this, we can turn to Paul's letter to the Christian community at Colossae -- the passage we read from the Epistle. Paul was writing this time to people he did not know personally, because they had received the message of Christ from another missionary. However, he clearly felt a closeness to them, and wished to encouraged them in the way of life of their common faith. He says that he prays that their knowledge of God will slowly increase by "spiritual insights" and grow in goodness; that they will wait patiently on the Lord's pleasure; that they will endure joyfully while continually giving thanks to God. And he reminds them that once and for all they have been set free of their sins by the redemption of the Son of God.

This is an excellent description of the way of life of Christians. Christians live in a state of awaiting patiently and enduring until they meet the Lord in the Second Coming, which his prophecy mysteriously foretold. There is no more anxiety trying to figure out what life is all about; there need not be any special tension wondering how it's all going to end. There is no purpose to being troubled by human weakness and sin -- our own or others. That's all over. All the answers are in. We are a redeemed and free people, waiting only for that day when we shall meet our Lord and Redeemer face to face . . . if in this faith, we persevere.

But the way of life of awaiting the Lord's coming is not passive. We do not simply sit around on our front porches. Our tasks are clearly outlined by St. Paul. We are to increase our knowledge of God by prayer and reading the Bible. We are to grow in goodness, expand our charity, multiply our virtues not our sins. Endure in our faith, despite hardships and pain. And we are to give thanks to God for "making us fit to share the light which his saints inherit." This means by worshiping as we do today when we pray together, and share the Lord's gift of his body and blood at this table.

There is one other note in Paul's description of the Christian life that we should not overlook. He says, "joyfully." I fear that many Christians whom we know fail to look upon their faith with joy and happiness. Or they fail to show or express it. They do not even speak to one another when they come to Church, as if Church-going were some kind of a distasteful burden that is not talked about. Such a misunderstanding of our common faith is all wrong. Come this new year of worship, let us dispel it, shake off the gloom. We await the Lord. That is our life. Let us do it with joy together. And let us encourage each other.

†

The Lord's Persistence

20TH Sunday after Pentecost

It may sound irreverent to say it, but by reading only the parts of the New Testament that are presented in the Mass each Sunday, we may tend to get a distorted picture of Jesus. Only a small percentage of the Gospel accounts are included in the assigned reading for the Mass, and for the most part, these inclusions usual have to do with miracles. We might have the impression, therefore, that the evangelists wanted to create the image of Jesus as a super miracle worker. This is not so at all.

And if you were in the habit of reading the whole text of each of the gospels of the New Testament, you would soon discover much more about the Lord than the miracles which are recorded of him. We may even look more closely at the brief liturgical (i.e., Mass) text that we have here today, and learn more than the miracle alone indicates. It tells us that Jesus was in Galilee again: "He came once more to Cana of Galilee," says the verse of introduction. And Galilee was his home district, the place 60 or so miles north of Jerusalem where he had been raised. Nazareth is in the district of Galilee.

On another occasion, when Jesus came back to his home country -- after he had begun his teaching career in the city of Jerusalem -- he was not well-received. He was, in fact, mocked and denounced. That is why at this point in his account, John is quoting the Old Testament [that is, the prophets] about Jesus, when he writes that "a prophet goes without honor in his own country."

This may explain also the hint of sarcasm in the Lord's remark to the royal official: "Unless you people [the country people of Galilee] see signs and miracles, you won't listen to me." But in the end, as we see, Jesus wins the trust of the official and his whole household, and no doubt of the people present.

It is possible to notice in this incident and its background, something more than the miracle; namely, the persistence of Jesus in his mission to bring truth and salvation to men. Even though he was belittled and not listened to, he came back to Galilee to win those people over. The Lord is also persistent in his mission to convert each of us by his grace. If we did not respond totally and find faith when we first heard his word and teaching, we can be assured that he will come back, and that he will keep coming back, until he has turned us around and away from our sins to follow him whole heartedly. He will persist. But let us not persist in stubbornness. Rather let us open ourselves to his power, let it begin to work on us effectively, so that our whole household finds faith -- that is, so that our whole interior being with all talents and feelings responds to his saving word.

June 14, 1969

Confidence

If you listen to or read St. Paul's letters long enough, pretty soon you begin to discover that whenever he is encouraging others, he is also encouraging himself. He is like a leader taking his men on a dangerous mission, urging them to be brave all along the way . . . and his knees are shaking too. So Paul's first words to us this morning are, "We continue to be confident"; that is, . . . in God's power to bring us through life with strength, and honor, and spiritual success. And Paul says this not as one speaking from the other side who has already made it, but as a sharer and a worker of the faith.

The other readings also press the theme of confidence in the all-caring power of God. If God wishes a tree to grow, announces the prophet Ezekiel in a kind of poetic passage, it will grow. The tree can be understood to mean the community of true worshipers, the Church, the Christian community. Its roots are in the revelations to the people of the Old Testament. Its budding appearance is Jesus. His followers are its branches and its fruit. This is God's work and it will succeed.

The same kinds of examples or parables are given in the gospel, and there the Lord stresses how little we know about the growth of things: "Through it all, the seed sprouts without his [the famer] knowing how it happens."

Do you know that there has always been an extreme tendency in the history of Christianity of persons who feel that they are completely and totally capable and responsible themselves for their own salvation -- and when they stretch -- for everyone else's salvation? I think we exhibit some of this anxiety when we fret about matters -- especially when we think we are doing good works -- which do not go exactly as we would plan them.

It is good to remember once in a while that the person most interested in the world's salvation and in our own is God. Because as St. John wrote, "He loved us first." Not that we are to sit back and do nothing. We are called to work at it, but with confidence rather than anxiety. And often our work will be nothing more than worshiping. That is, giving thanks to God for his care for us. As we have done just a moment ago, when we said, "It is good, Lord, to give you thanks," And as we will say again many times through the Mass.

†

Other Pulpits

Maryland Sermons

Mother's Day 1965

Text John 16: 21

A woman, when she is in labor, has sorrow because her hour has come; but as soon as she has given birth to the child, she no longer remembers the anguish, for joy that a human being has been born into the world.

It is really only a coincidence that we should read these words in the Mass today – Mother's Day. Here Jesus happens to have employed an image of motherhood in order to announce and explain a truth about our Christian way of life. We should understand in the first place that Jesus is recorded to have spoken these words a few hours before his death. In a very true sense, they are a part of his farewell address to his apostles. Yet they are addressed not only to the apostles, but to his followers of every age in history. And, in fact, the words reveal a principle by which Christians must interpret the meaning of history.

When St. Augustine in the 5TH century commented on the phrase "a little while," he explained that the "little while" Jesus refers to, the little while he will be absent, is not the little while between his death and resurrection -- for he adds, "I go to the Father." The "little while" is therefore the time after Jesus goes to the Father by his Ascension. The "little while" is that span of history -- in which we now live -- between Christ's disappearance from the earth and his second coming at the world's end -- or if before that time -- when each of us meets him in death. What is that span of history like? It is not an endless succession of moments and hours and years. It is brief, and compared to God's life a mere "little while." It is not a purposeless evolution of nature. It is a path which leads to a rendezvous with the Savior, for he says, "a little while and you shall see me." Nor is the "little while" a dull and eventless aftermath, as if the Savior had once and for all extracted himself (by his Ascension) from human history. Rather, for Christians, the flow of history is a time of vigilance and expectation, preparing for that event in which Christ the King, either in our individual lives or in the universe, will culminate his salvific victory.

And what shall our experience of the "little while" time be like? "You shall lament and weep," he says; "you shall be made sorrowful." Then, lest the apostles -- or you and I -- be too much frightened, he delivers that beautiful image: It will be like child-bearing, that unique human phenomenon in which sorrow ends in joy, in which the agony points not to death but to life. In our experience of the "little while," there will be duration and crisis, and tension and anxiety; but all these feelings are controlled and made significant in the expectation which Jesus gives rise to by his words, "I will see you again."

It is our custom in America, for one reason or another, to honor and respect motherhood one day a year. As Christians, we should be reminded of the special meaning the Lord, by his words, has attached to motherhood. It is an ever-present sign to us of the heavenly fulfillment toward which time and history and our lives are tending. Perhaps only mothers, who have the experience of carrying and giving birth to a new life, can fully understand what Jesus here teaches about life. And perhaps too that is why it is their sacred charge is to teach men how to live.

†

Christmas, 1967

The birth of the Lord Jesus, with all its attendant wonders, with all its warm and endearing detail, which we commemorate today in these readings signifies this: It is the unique and astonishing intervention of God's power into the steady, relentless, truculent march of human history. It is the once when the course of human events is not left to the whims and determinations of men.

But this is not to say that the nativity of Christ, as it occurred on that obscure day 20 centuries in the past, was a sudden and unexpected phenomenon. On the contrary -- the scriptures of the Old Testament, particularly the prophesies of Isaiah, which we read throughout Advent and in our Mass, attest to the enormous and far-reaching preparation for Bethlehem. And it is not only the prophets whose lives were spectacularly disturbed by God's long-range purpose. Consider Zachery and Elizabeth, devout and retiring Israelites, the tranquility of whose lives was imposed upon because God determined that their son, John, would be deeply involved in his redemptive plan.

Friends, the impact of Christ's nativity upon human history has not diminished. The imposition of God's providence upon our lives has not subsided. Just as the event of Christmas was grand enough to have stirred generations in anticipation, so it can now stir generations in retrospect: if not by prophesy and special mission, by faith and the universal presence of grace.

Therefore, when at times you are bewildered to observed the irresistible press and flow of human history -- with its social accomplishments, its scientific achievements, its continuing wars, its reversals of fortune, be assured by the event our liturgy renews and reinforces today, that God still intervenes. That is, provided we are his agents, communicating with his grace, doing his work in charity. And so as long as there exists in the world alive and believing Christians, history can never ride its course by mere human whim, uncontrollably, at random.

†

Septuagesima Sunday 1967 and 1968, sermon delivered respectfully in Somersworth NH and Galeton PA

Christian Community

Suddenly, with the bells of Christmas still ringing in our ears, and perhaps some holiday bills still unpaid, we find ourselves on the threshold of Lent. The violet vestments are the most evident sign. These three Sundays --- Septuagesima, Sexagesima, and Quinquagesima, meaning roughly the 70TH, 60TH, and 50TH day -- were assigned in the 6TH century as an extension of the more ancient 40 days of Lent. Today's Mass, Septuagesima, was also meant to rally together the Christians of Rome against the danger of barbarian invasion in the 7TH century. Accordingly, its deep and permanent theme concerns the fellowship of the Christian community under the protective covenant of God.

By covenant we should understand a kind of contract or bargain in which men agree to show their faith in return for God's favor. So, by

Christian baptism, we have joined the covenant as a new redeemed people of God, a united community, like the chosen people of the Old Testament who joined God's covenant when they attached themselves to Moses. St. Paul even refers to them as if they were "baptized into Moses." This all may sound like too much subtle and complicated theological talk. Nonetheless, it is fact: As Christians, we are truly a formed community, much like the people of the Exodus moving through the desert. We also are on a perilous journey, and we are united by our common faith in God's promises and by our common hope in Christ's salvation.

The signs of our unity include the pledge of baptism which we all have received. And (here to follow St. Paul again) we eat the same spiritual food, that is, the Eucharistic Body and Blood of Jesus. It is not unusual either that the Mass of this day presents the parable of the laborers in the vineyard, as a way of emphasizing the theme of Christian community. Although Jesus used this example to show that those who come late, as well as those who come early, share full membership in his community of followers, the parable of the laborers also suggests the way by which we may sense belonging to this community; namely, by working together. Everyone will agree that working together is the best way for making people feel a sense of belonging.
(1) Workers on a job get to know each other and become aware of their fellowship precisely because of the work they are doing together.
(2) A whole town will experience itself as a real unit when it pitches in on a community project.
(3) Players on a team (The St. Bonaventure Bonnies, for example) especially sense their unity because their success depends so much on working together. We even have a special word which combines the idea of work with the idea of unity – *teamwork.*

The message is clearly this: We are a community of Christians. If we want to experience our fellowship together, we must work together. Our work is worship, so we are gathered and pray together this morning. Our work is love and kindness toward one another, so we check anger and gossip. Our work is helping the needy among us, so we are generous with our goods and with our time. And our work is believing and hoping, so we encourage and console each other.

There is one more thing about the Christian community and its work. Its work must be excellent. There is to be no mediocrity, no job half done. As St. Paul puts it: (I paraphrase) if you enter a race you run to win, not to come in second. Or as an old saying goes, a job worth doing is worth doing well. So must we regard our work in Christ's community of followers as a job eminently worth doing well. Then we shall sense the joy of Christian fellowship, working together under God's new covenant . . . and no danger on the way can ever disturb us.

†

New Year's Day 1967, Portsmouth NH

The Response

As you might know, our meeting here this morning is not so much a celebration of the New Year, nor even, strictly speaking, of the feast of the Circumcision, but rather of the octave of Christmas. That is, the liturgy considers Christmas such an enormous event that it wishes to commemorate it not simply one day but a whole week. Today is the last day of the week of Christmas, the eighth day or the octave.

The gospel account we read relates the incident of the Lord's parents bringing him to the Temple in Jerusalem for the performance of the traditional Jewish rite of circumcision. But we must look for the meaning of this incident in the context of Christmas. The liturgy means to teach us that the feast of Christ's Nativity commemorates that divine event by which God reached out to the world of humanity in giving his son Jesus to us to lead us to salvation. Or, as St. John the Evangelist, has written: *God so loved the world, that he gave up his only-begotten Son, so that those who believe in him may not perish, but have eternal life.* (John 3: 16)

And the feast of the octave of the Nativity means to teach us that the world of humanity must make a response to God's act. In every love relationship between persons there is the action of giving on the part of one person, and the response to the gift on the part of the other. A young man gives a lady a ring. It is a gift which is a sign of his love. The young lady must not only receive his gift graciously but she must respond; that is, return a sign of her love. The response may be a word or a gesture, a kiss. The sign she makes says not only, "I accept," but also, "I am joined with you in this endeavor of our love."

In the Old Testament, when God revealed his concern for the human race to the Jewish people, and promised them a plan of redemption, they in turn determined upon a ritual by which they would, though each generation, make a sign of their response and of their involvement with God in the great redemptive endeavor. So it is that the parents of Jesus bring him to the temple to make the sign of circumcision.

In the new age, wherein God has fully revealed his plan, and has enacted the redemption of mankind through the sending of his Son, all the world and each individual must make a sign of his/her involvement with God. As full-fledged followers of Christ, the major sign of our involvement with him is the pouring of the water of Baptism. Baptism is then a parallel of the rite of circumcision. But it is more. For as circumcision was a sign of human response to the promise of salvation, Baptism is a sign of human response to the fulfillment of that promise, to the enactment of salvation.

What we must measure then today is the extent to which we are genuinely conscious of our response to God's salvation . . . which has been signed by our baptism. Our entire life as committed Christians must be the extension of our baptism; that is, our entire life and our behavior ought to be a sign of our response to God's gifts. Thus, by the manner in which he/she lives under the sign of baptism, the Christian says to God, "Not only do I accept, but I return myself to you "and so join with you in this holy endeavor of love."

†

Rye Beach, New Hampshire
(Sermon at student Mass – Wednesday, 2nd Sunday after Easter)

Cool Prayer

Text 1 Peter 4: 7-11

Let me return to the reading which Michael gave for my commentary. We have been listening to this epistle of St. Peter ever since Low Sunday. In the present selection, Peter seems to be counselling the brethren against "blowing their cool." For as the Jerusalem Bible has it, he writes: "Brethren, everything will soon come to an end; so to pray better keep a calm and sober mind."

Biblical scholars think that Peter was writing to console Christians undergoing a persecution, and he means here that the persecution will soon be over, and they should not let it break up their community. It is fair, I trust to bring a broader interpretation to these words and think of Peter making a philosophical comment on the passage of time and the transience of all things. This is a clamorous truth about existence that we only occasionally assent to, even though it unceasingly affects our living. Everything will soon come to an end. Things change. Friends depart. Institutions crumble. Teeth decay. Hair falls out. St. Peter advises: Keep a calm and sober mind so you can pray.

St. Francis once stressed the very same point in these words. "Let everything be subservient to the spirit of prayer and devotion." This principle may contain the meaning of that word *detachment.* You are not to be so hung up on things which encase your daily existence, that their inevitable and persistent changing disturbs the steady balance of your relationship to God. Nothing which happens to you should ever give cause for your saying, "I can't pray." This is not easy advice to follow . . . but it is basic. Our only hold on permanence is prayer, and the condition of prayer is cool.

†

Vespers for Ellen

 At her burial in St. Mary's cemetery, Shelter Island NY, July 26, 1014

I'll call this a sermonette; that's an abbreviated sermon. The kind you may remember hearing way back when TV stations would sign off at midnight. With "Today's Sermonette." The topic is God's tender mercy, and my scriptural text is Evangelist Mark's account of the Lord's raising the daughter of Jairus. Jairus was the leader, an administrator, of the Synagogue where Jesus often preached. Here's the passage:

Mark 5:21-43 New King James Version (NKJV)

A Girl Restored to Life and a Woman Healed

Now when Jesus had crossed over again by boat to the other side, a great multitude gathered to Him; and He was by the sea. And behold, one of the rulers of the synagogue came, Jairus by name. And when he saw Him, he fell at His feet 23 and begged Him earnestly, saying, "My little daughter lies at the point of death. Come and lay Your hands on her, that she may be healed, and she will live." So Jesus went with him, and a great multitude followed Him and thronged Him.

Now a certain woman had a flow of blood for twelve years, and had suffered many things from many physicians. She had spent all that she had and was no better, but rather grew worse. When she heard about Jesus, she came behind Him in the crowd and touched His garment. For she said, "If only I may touch His clothes, I shall be made well."

Immediately the fountain of her blood was dried up, and she felt in her body that she was healed of the affliction. And Jesus, immediately knowing in Himself that power had gone out of Him, turned around in the crowd and said, "Who touched My clothes?"

But His disciples said to Him, "You see the multitude thronging You, and You say, 'Who touched Me?'" And He looked around to see her who had done this thing. But the woman, fearing and trembling, knowing what had happened to her, came and fell down before Him and told Him the whole truth. And He said to her, "Daughter, your faith has made you well. Go in peace, and be healed of your affliction."

While He was still speaking, some came from the ruler of the synagogue's house who said, "Your daughter is dead. Why trouble the Teacher any further?" As soon as Jesus heard the word that was spoken, He said to the ruler of the synagogue, "Do not be afraid; only believe." And He permitted no one to follow Him except Peter, James, and John the brother of James. Then He came to the house of the ruler of the synagogue, and saw a tumult and those who wept and wailed loudly. When He came in, He said to them, "Why make this commotion and weep? The child is not dead, but sleeping." And they ridiculed Him. But when He had put them all outside, He took the father and the mother of the child, and those who were with Him, and entered where the child was lying. Then He took the child by the hand, and said to her, Talitha, cumi, which is translated, "Little girl, I say to you, arise." Immediately the girl arose and walked, for she was twelve years of age. And they were overcome with great amazement. But He commanded them strictly that no one should know it, and said that something should be given her to eat.

What struck me when I heard this passage read in church recently was this line: *He went into where the girl was with three of his disciples. He took the daughter of Jairus* -- (Mark says she was 12 years old.) -- *He took her by the hand and said in his language "little girl, stand up." She rose immediately. Every one was greatly surprised, and then a few minutes later Jesus said. "Give her something to eat."*

The Lord Jesus' magnificent divine power of healing and mercy is not displayed with flare. Not dramatic. Not with broad gestures or proclamations. He had been followed by crowds when Jairus approached him, but he sent them away and allowed only the family and three of his disciples into the house and into the room where the girl lay. In the end he said, don't tell anyone. His mercy is not always openly displayed, but it is there and effective. He took the little girl by the hand: "Little girl, he said: stand up. . . . Now give her something to eat."

I think we miss the tenderness and compassion of Jesus when we don't look closely at the gospel. Mark, the Hemingway-like stylist of the evangelists, doesn't miss a small detail. "He took the little girl by the hand," And Mark goes right to dialogue to tell the story: "Little girl, stand up." The mercy of Jesus toward us, his people, is all over the gospels, and it is intimate and tender, often accompanied by a gesture, something tactile. The woman at the well: to whom he said, "Give me a drink." And then carried on a conversation about himself and *living water:* that is, God's grace, God's favor. The man born blind: he touches his eyes. The old woman in the crowd who touches his cloak. Ellen would have been one of these to whom the Lord showed his tactile love, his tender mercy. [Jesus took the little girl by hand.] Ellen was not a secular, although she lived and moved in that secular city we love (and hate) so much. She would visit the church across the street from her apartment on E. 55TH Street. The pastor there knew her and gave her the sacraments. She often spoke of attending vespers, solemn vespers, at the church of St. Thomas on 5TH Avenue. And so we offer here these vespers, the liturgical prayer at day's end.

LEADER: Light and peace, in Jesus Christ our Lord.
PEOPLE: Thanks, be to God.
LEADER; Bless the Lord who forgives all our sins.
PEOPLE: His mercy endures forever.
LEADER: O gracious Light, pure brightness of the ever-living Father in heaven.
PEOPLE: O Jesus Christ, holy and blessed!
LEADER: Now as we come to the setting of the sun, and our eyes behold the vesper light . . .
PEOPLE: We sing your praises, O God, Father Son, and Holy Spirit.
LEADER: You are worthy at all times to be praised by happy voices, O Son of God, O giver of light.
PEOPLE: Be praised and glorified through all the worlds.

Vespers Evening Prayer: Be present, O merciful God, and protect us through the hours of this night, so that we who are wearied by the changes and chances of this life may rest in your eternal changelessness; through Jesus Christ, our Lord. Amen.

Thanks be to God.

Memorial Day Parade Orient NY 2017

Prayer at the Monument

As we prepare to pray, I look out at the waters of this island and call to mind Herman Melville's great novel of whaling, *Moby Dick*, and of this very sea that surrounds us. There is a chapter in the book entitled "The Sermon." The preacher, a Methodist minister, tells the bible story of Jonah. Jonah resisted God's call, but in the end was saved by God's unrelenting mercy. That message, delivered to the seamen of Melville's New Bedford 165 years ago, may have appeal for us.

We are here to remember those whose lives have yielded to the sea's perils: 46 souls of the Andrea Doria by Nantucket, Margaret Fuller among the dead off Fire Island in the 19th century, friends, those we have known, many whom we have not known, neighbors, those who served our country as our guardians with honor. The historians count over 300 tragedies at sea here in these surrounding waters.

For all of these, we survivors pray. May they, through the mercy of God, rest in peace. And we pray for ourselves. We know that our human existence, on what poets and preachers have named "the sea of life," is temporal and can be just as unsteady.

We might also take this occasion to note in the gospels that the Lord, Jesus, himself, had his encounters with the sea, the Sea of Tiberius or Galilee, near where he lived and where his friends lived and worked. Four of the men he chose to accompany him, as his close associates, on his mission of preaching God's kingdom, were fisherman. He spoke often with nautical images. "I will make you fishers of men," he commissioned them. On one occasion, Peter their leader, attempts to come to him across the water's surface without the proper faith, and (quote) *When he (Peter) saw the wind, he was afraid and, beginning to sink he cried out, "Lord, save me." Jesus offers him a hand saying: "Take courage! It is I. Don't be afraid." Immediately Jesus reached out his hand and caught him.*

These stories are told for us. We can be Jonah; or we can be Peter. And today we have the occasion and the moment to reflect on them. They demonstrate/exhibit the persistent and solicitous mercy of God, of which we must avail ourselves and be ever grateful, and give him glory. Let us now pray with the prayer that is the last verse of the navy hymn:

> O Trinity of love and power!
> Our brethren shield in danger's hour;
> From rock and tempest, fire and foe,
> Protect them wheresoe'er they go;
> Thus evermore shall rise to Thee
> Glad hymns of praise from land and sea.

Thanks be to God.

Appendix

Great Preachers

> Chrysostom . . . 273
> Augustine 275
> Wesley 277
> Emerson 279

John Chrysostom (347-407)

An Easter Sermon

Let all pious men and all lovers of God rejoice in the splendor of this feast; let the wise servants blissfully enter into the joy of their Lord; let those who have borne the burden of Lent now receive their pay, and those who have toiled since the first hour, let them now receive their due reward; let any who came after the third hour be grateful to join in the feast, and those who may have come after the sixth, let them not be afraid of being too late; for the Lord is gracious and He receives the last even as the first. He gives rest to him who comes on the eleventh hour as well as to him who has toiled since the first: yes, He has pity on the last and He serves the first; He rewards the one and praises the effort.

Come you all: enter into the joy of your Lord. You the first and you the last, receive alike your reward; you rich and you poor, dance together; you sober and you weaklings, celebrate the day; you who have kept the fast and you who have not, rejoice today. The table is richly loaded: enjoy its royal banquet. The calf is a fatted one: let no one go away hungry. All of you enjoy the banquet of faith; all of you receive the riches of his goodness. Let no one grieve over his poverty, for the universal kingdom has been revealed; let no one weep over his sins, for pardon has shone from the grave; let no one fear death, for the death of our Saviour has set us free: He has destroyed it by enduring it, He has despoiled Hades by going down into its kingdom. He has angered it by allowing it to taste of his flesh.

When Isaias foresaw all this, he cried out: "O Hades, you have been angered by encountering Him in the nether world." Hades is angered because frustrated, it is angered because it has been mocked, it is angered because it has been destroyed, it is angered because it has been reduced to naught, it is angered because it is now captive. It seized a body, and, lo! it encountered heaven; it seized the visible, and was overcome by the invisible. O death, where is your sting? O Hades, where is your victory? Christ is risen and you are abolished. Christ is risen and the demons are cast down. Christ is risen and the angels rejoice. Christ is risen and life is freed. Christ is risen and the tomb is emptied of the dead: for Christ, being risen from the dead, has become the Leader and Reviver of those who had fallen asleep. To Him be glory and power for ever and ever. Amen.

This is a condensed sermon of Chrysostom. Typically, his sermons would be more than 3,000 words.

Augustine of Hippo (354-430)

Sacrament of the Eucharist - # 272

What you see on God's altar, you've already observed during the night that has now ended. But you've heard nothing about just what it might be, or what it might mean, or what great thing it might be said to symbolize. For what you see is simply bread and a cup -- this is the information your eyes report. But your faith demands far subtler insight: the bread is Christ's body, the cup is Christ's blood. Faith can grasp the fundamentals quickly, succinctly, yet it hungers for a fuller account of the matter. As the prophet says, "Unless you believe, you will not understand." [Is. 7: 9] So you can say to me, "You urged us to believe; now explain, so we can understand." Inside each of you, thoughts like these are rising:

Our Lord Jesus Christ, we know the source of his flesh; he took it from the virgin Mary. Like any infant, he was nursed and nourished; he grew; became a youngster; suffered persecution from his own people. To the wood he was nailed; on the wood he died; from the wood, his body was taken down and buried. On the third day (as he willed) he rose; he ascended bodily into heaven whence he will come to judge the living and the dead. There he dwells even now, seated at God's right. So how can bread be his body? And what about the cup? How can it (or what it contains) be his blood?" My friends, these realities are called sacraments because in them one thing is seen, while another is grasped. What is seen is a mere physical likeness; what is grasped bears spiritual fruit. So now, if you want to understand the body of Christ, listen to the Apostle Paul speaking to the faithful: "You are the body of Christ, member for member." [1 Cor. 12: 27] If you, therefore, are Christ's body and members, it is your own mystery that is placed on the Lord's table! It is your own mystery that you are receiving! You are saying "Amen" to what you are: your response is a personal signature, affirming your faith. When you hear "The body of Christ", you reply "Amen." Be a member of Christ's body, then, so that your "Amen" may ring true! But what role does the bread play? We have no theory of our own to propose here; listen, instead, to what Paul says about this sacrament: "The bread is one, and we, though many, are one body." [1 Cor. 10:17] Understand and rejoice: unity, truth, faithfulness, love. "One bread," he says. What is this one bread? Is it not the "one body," formed from many? Remember: bread doesn't come from a single grain, but from many. When you were baptized, you were *leavened*. When you received the fire of the Holy Spirit, you were *baked*. Be what you see; receive what you are. This is what Paul is saying about the bread. In the visible object of bread, many grains are gathered into one, just as the faithful (so Scripture says) form "a single heart and mind in God" [Acts 4: 32].

So let us give God our sincere and deepest gratitude, and, as far as human weakness will permit, let us turn to the Lord with pure hearts. With all our strength, let us seek God's singular mercy, for then the Divine Goodness will surely hear our prayers; it will deepen our faith, govern our minds, grant us holy thoughts, and lead us, finally, to share the divine happiness through God's own son Jesus Christ. Amen!

This is an edited version of an Augustine sermon of 1,600 words.

John Wesley (1703 – 1791)
(Preached at St. Mary's, Oxford, before the university, July 25, 1741.)

The Almost Christian

TEXT: Almost thou persuadest me to be a Christian.
- Acts 26: 28.

AND many there are who go thus far: ever since the Christian religion was in the world, there have been many in every age and nation who were almost persuaded to be Christians. But seeing it avails nothing before God to go only thus far, it highly imports us to consider,

First. What is implied in being almost;

Secondly. What in being altogether a Christian.

Now, in the being almost a Christian is implied, First, heathen honesty. By the rules of this they were taught that they ought not to be unjust; not to take away their neighbour's goods, either by robbery or theft; not to oppress the poor, neither to use extortion toward any; not to cheat or overreach either the poor or rich, in whatsoever commerce they had with them; to defraud no man of his right; and, if it were possible, to owe no man anything.

Again: the common heathens allowed, that some regard was to be paid to truth, as well as to justice. Yet again: they expected whatever assistance any one could give another, without prejudice to himself. And this they extended not only to those little offices of humanity which are performed without any expense or labour, but likewise to the feeding the hungry, if they had food to spare; the clothing the naked with their own superfluous raiment; and, in general. the giving, to any that needed, such things as they needed not themselves. Thus far, in the lowest account of it, heathen honesty went; the first thing implied in the being almost a Christian.

If it be inquired, "What more than this is implied in the being altogether a Christian" I answer: First. The love of God. For thus saith his word, "Thou shalt love the Lord thy God with all thy heart, and with all thy soul, and with all thy mind, and with all thy strength." Such a love is this, as engrosses the whole heart, as rakes up all the affections, as fills the entire capacity of the soul and employs the utmost extent of all its faculties. He that thus loves the Lord his God, his spirit continually "rejoiceth in God his Saviour. All his desire is unto God, and to the remembrance of his name. His heart is ever crying out, "Whom have I in heaven but Thee and there is none upon earth that I desire beside Thee." Indeed, what can he desire beside God? Not the world, or the things of the world: for he is "crucified to the world, and the world crucified to him." He is crucified to "the desire of the flesh, the desire of the eye, and the pride of life." Yea, he is dead to pride of every kind: for "love is not puffed up," but "he that dwelling in love, dwelleth in God, and God in him."

May we all thus experience what it is to be, not almost only; but altogether Christians; being justified freely by his grace, through the redemption that is in Jesus; knowing we have peace with God through Jesus Christ; rejoicing in hope of the glory of God; and having the love of God shed abroad in our hearts, by the Holy Ghost given unto us!

This sermon has been edited. Wesley's sermons are typically over 3,000 words.

Ralph Waldo Emerson (1803-1882)

Pray Without Ceasing

It ought to be distinctly felt by us that we stand in the midst of two worlds, the world of matter and the world of spirit. Our bodies belong to one; our thoughts to the other. It has been one of the best uses of the Christian religion to teach that the world of spirits is more certain and stable than the material universe. It is time greater force should be given to the statement of this doctrine; it is time men should be instructed that their inward is more valuable than their outward estate; that thoughts and passions, even those to which no language is ever given, are not fugitive undefined shadows, born in a moment, and in a moment blotted from the soul, but are so many parts of the imperishable universe of morals; they should be taught that they do not think *alone*; that when they retreat from the public eye, and hide themselves to conceal in solitude guilty recollections or guilty wishes, the great congregation of moral natures, the spirits of just men made perfect; angels and archangels; the Son of God, and the Father everlasting, open their eyes upon them and speculate on these clandestine meditations.

The necessary inference from these reflections is the fact which gives them all their importance, and is the doctrine I am chiefly anxious to inculcate. It is not only when we audibly and in form, address our petitions to the Deity that we pray. We pray without ceasing; every secret wish is a prayer. Every house is a church; the corner of every street is a closet of devotion. Do you not know that the knowledge of God is perfect and immense; that it breaks down the fences of presumption and the arts of hypocrisy; that night, and artifice, and time, and the grave, are naked before it; that the deep gives up its dead, that the guts of Chaos are disemboweled before him; that the minds of men are not so much independent existences, as they are ideas present to the mind of God; that he is not so much the power of your actions, as he is the potent principle by which they are bound together; not so much the reader of your thoughts as the active Creator by whom they are aided into being; and casting away the deceptive subterfuges of language, and speaking with strict philosophical truth, that every faculty is but a mode of his action; that your reason is God, your virtue is God, and nothing but your liberty can you call securely your own?

Since, then, we are thus, by the inevitable law of our being surrendered unreservedly to the unsleeping observation of the Deity, We cannot shut our eyes to the conclusion that every desire of the human of the mind is a prayer uttered to God and registered to heaven.

Emerson's sermons are typically 2,000 words. This is an edited version.

Acknowledgements

Photos/Images

The Good Shepherd, p. 46 image from Pinterest, Greek icon, author unknown, used under Creative Common license. (cc)

Lamb of God photo p. 46 Romanesque *Agnus Dei*, Santiago de Compostela, Galicia. Source Own work Author Froaringus. Creative Common usage. (cc)

Agnus Dei photo, p. 184 stained glass window in the Rights Chapel at Trinity Moravian Church, Winston-Salem, NC. Author J. Jackman. Creative Common Usage. (cc) Permission is granted under the terms of the GNU Free Documentation License.

Sermon excerpts.

Chrysostom. Used with permission of *EWTN (Eternal Word Television Network)*, www.ewtn.com

Augustine. Source, *earlychurchtexts.com*. Permission granted per K. Knight, www.theology.nd.edu

Wesley. Excerpts from John Wesley's sermon are included here with the permission of the General Board of Global Ministries, United Methodist Church. www.umcmission.org

Emerson. Source: *Complete Sermons of R.W. Emerson*, University of Missouri Press. Permission granted.

Books by Geoff Proud

With Dr. Frederic J. Vagnini

Contact: gfproud@gmail.com   www.advabcethecause.net

CPSIA information can be obtained
at www.ICGtesting.com
Printed in the USA
BVOW04*0222070617
486097BV00004B/14/P